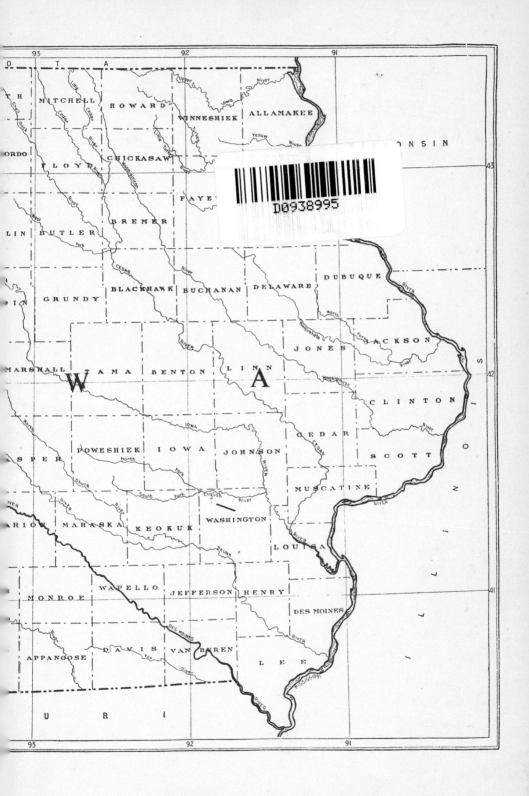

IOWA ON THE EVE OF THE CIVIL WAR
A Decade of Frontier Politics

UNIVERSITY OF OKLAHOMA PRESS : NORMAN

Morton M. Rosenberg

⊠ ⊠ ⊠ ⊠ ⊠ ⊠ ⊠ ⊠ ⊠ ⊠ ⊠ ⊠ ⊠ ⊠ ⊠

IOWA ON THE EVE OF THE CIVIL WAR

⊠ ⊠ ⊠ ⊠ ⊠ ⊠ ⊠ ⊠ ⊠ ⊠ ⊠ ⊠ ⊠ ⊠ ⊠

A Decade of Frontier Politics

International Standard Book Number: 0–8061–0989–0

Library of Congress Catalog Card Number: 77–177343

Copyright 1972 by the University of Oklahoma Press, Publishing Division of the University. Composed and printed at Norman, Oklahoma, U.S.A., by the University of Oklahoma Press. First edition.

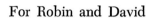

For Robin and David

Preface

THE EVENTS which formed the background for, and ultimately precipitated, the Civil War have long intrigued students of United States history, as their many scholarly publications readily attest. Historians have studied the period from the broad panorama of national developments, as well as from the narrower, though no less significant, confines of state and local perspective. State-level investigations, published and unpublished, have usually focused on a central theme, such as the formation of the Republican party in the several states of the North or the secession movement of the various states of the South. This book seeks to examine and describe the broad spectrum of political activities in Iowa, a raw frontier state, the first free state admitted to the Union from the trans-Mississippi West, during the exciting years of the last antebellum decade.

I wish to express my sincere gratitude to many persons who rendered invaluable aid during various stages in the writing of this book. The staffs of the Iowa State Department of History and Archives, the State Historical Society of Iowa, and the Ball State University Library were extremely generous with their time and assistance. My colleagues Robert Evans and Raymond White read the manuscript, made many useful comments and suggestions, and offered excellent advice on matters of form, style, and content.

Additional thanks are due the following committees and officers of Ball State University: the Research Committee, for awarding me a faculty research grant which aided the completion of this book; Richard W. Burkhardt, Vice-President and Dean of Faculties, for his unqualified support; and the Publications Committee and the University Foundation for providing grants-in-aid which helped make possible the publication of this book.

Dr. Everett Ferrill, Chairman of the Department of History of Ball State University, merits special mention as an unfailing source of encouragement and inspiration. His assistance in many practical ways cannot be adequately acknowledged.

I also wish to express my appreciation to William Peterson, Superintendent of the State Historical Society of Iowa and editor of the *Iowa Journal of History*, for permission to incorporate as substantial portions of Chapters II and IX two of my articles which originally appeared in the *Journal* under the titles "Iowa Politics and the Compromise of 1850" and "The Election of 1859 in Iowa," in 1958 and 1959, respectively.

Finally, a number of competent typists deserve commendation for their diligent labors in preparing the manuscript for publication: Toni Ave, Carol Cooper, Kathy Davis, Jan Foust, Barbara Hickner, Jana Jackson, Sue Morthland, and Donna Sitler. Rhonda Jackson ably assisted in reading proof.

Needless to add, any errors of fact or interpretation which may appear are solely my responsibility.

Muncie, Indiana
January 16, 1972   MORTON M. ROSENBERG

Contents

IOWA ON THE EVE OF THE CIVIL WAR
A Decade of Frontier Politics

The People of Iowa on the Eve of the Civil War

THE STORY of Iowa during the turbulent decade of the 1850's is the narrative of an energetic, vibrant frontier state. Bounded on the east by the Mississippi and on the west by the Missouri, Iowa prided itself on being the first free state admitted to the Union from the Louisiana Purchase. As a self-conscious western frontier state, Iowa entered the arena of national politics only four years before the opening of the final antebellum decade.

In the 1850's, Iowa was primarily a land of farms and farmers. Although there existed the usual community artisans, shopkeepers, and professional men, the overwhelming source of Iowa's income, and hence the chief support for its nonfarming residents, was the soil. The federal census statistics for 1850 and 1860, as well as the state census for 1856, disclose name after name with "farmer" listed as the occupation. Scattered through the lists other occupations appear, here a lawyer or a doctor, there

3

a blacksmith, now a merchant, occasionally a miller, sometimes a minister or a miner, but all are outnumbered by the farmers.[1]

Figures for the value of farms and farm implements testify to the prominence of agriculture in Iowa. In 1850 there were 14,805 separate farm holdings in the state. A decade later the figure stood at 61,163. The value of these farms in 1850 was $16,657,567; this placed Iowa in twenty-seventh position among the states. Ten years later Iowa moved up to twenty-first place with a total farm value of $119,899,547. In the value of machinery and farm implements the gains made during the decade kept pace. In 1850 the value of farm implements and machinery was $1,172,869, giving Iowa twenty-seventh place in the nation. In 1860 the state climbed to twentieth place, the value of machinery and farm implements increasing to $5,327,033. Perhaps the best indication of the importance of farming is provided by the figures for improved land. In 1850, Iowa ranked twenty-fifth among the states with an improved acreage of merely 824,682, but in 1860 it rose to fifteenth place, boasting of 3,792,792 acres of improved land.[2]

Livestock and grain production figures similarly demonstrate the emphasis on agriculture in Iowa. In 1850 there were 38,536 horses on Iowa farms; a decade later the number increased to 175,088. During the same period the number of mules increased from 754 to 5,734; oxen from 21,892 to 56,964; milch cows from 45,704 to 189,802; other types of cows from 69,025 to 293,322; sheep from 149,960 to 259,041; and hogs from 323,247 to 934,820. The total value of all livestock on Iowa farms soared from a meager $3,689,275 in 1850, good enough only for twenty-seventh ranking, to a respectable $22,476,293, or nineteenth place, in 1860.[3]

[1] The Seventh Census of the United States: 1850, and The Eighth Census of the United States: 1860, manuscript census reports for Iowa located at the Iowa State Department of History and Archives in Des Moines; The Census Returns of the Different Counties of the State of Iowa for 1856.

[2] John A. T. Hull (comp.), Iowa Historical and Comparative Census, 1836–1880, 141, 179–80.

4

The statistics for grain and other crop production likewise reveal the importance of agriculture in Iowa's economy. In 1850, Iowa ranked eighteenth among the states in total grain production with an output of 11,809,250 bushels. Ten years later the state had advanced to tenth place, with an output of 57,613,564 bushels of grain. The biggest single crop was corn, followed by wheat, oats, buckwheat, barley, and rye. In 1860, Iowa ranked seventh in the nation in corn production, with 42,410,686 bushels, a fivefold increase over the figures for 1850. In wheat production Iowa moved from fifteenth place in 1850, with an output of 1,530,581 bushels, to eighth place in 1860, with a production of 8,447,403 bushels. The picture is similar for other grains: the volume of oats jumped in a decade from 1,524,345 bushels to 5,887,645; barley increased from 25,093 bushels to 467,103; buckwheat and rye also followed this trend of greatly increased harvests.[4]

In addition to its grains Iowa produced other crops which solidified its position among the farming states of the nation. In 1850, Iowans harvested 276,120 bushels of Irish potatoes, as well as 6,243 bushels of sweet potatoes. A decade later the volume climbed to 2,806,720 bushels of Irish potatoes and 51,362 bushels of sweet potatoes. Iowa ranked thirteenth in the country in potato production. Gains of like proportions were made by such other commodities as wool, butter, cheese, and hops.[5]

Further illustrating the preponderant position of agriculture in Iowa are the contrasting statistics for manufacturing in the state during the same period. In 1850 there were 1,707 persons working in manufacturing establishments of all kinds, the total numbers of which are not available. A decade later 1,939 manufacturing concerns employed only 6,307 workers. The value of all

---

[3] *Ibid.,* 88–92, 143, 179–81.
[4] *Ibid.,* 64–74, 76, 179–81.
[5] *Ibid.,* 134, 136–37, 179–81, 187–88.

manufactured products in 1850 was $3,773,075. In 1860 the figure stood at $14,289,015. When these totals are contrasted with the totals for the value of farms and farm production, the differences are even more striking.[6]

The leading manufacturing firms in 1850 quite naturally were those producing farm equipment. Five such plants, employing fifteen persons, existed that year. No statistics are available for lumber- and sawmills or for meat-packing or slaughtering plants for the same year, but they could not have been numerous since there were only 1,707 factory workers in the state. In the next ten years the number of sawmills increased markedly as the demand for wood products soared with the rapidly growing population. These mills, however, had a capital value of but $1,606,210, produced goods valued at $2,124,502, and employed only 1,680 workers. In 1860, Iowans also boasted one paper mill, twelve woolen mills, and fifteen meat-packing firms, with a total productive value of merely $901,926.[7]

The only other industry of any importance in Iowa during the early period of its history was the lead-mining industry centered at Dubuque, opposite the Galena fields of Illinois. Yet even mining was but a small factor in the economy of the state.[8] In fine, agriculture was Iowa's major form of business enterprise during the 1850's.

The pattern of settlement in Iowa during the antebellum period dramatically underscored the state's frontier condition. The early pioneers, who had crossed into Iowa from the larger states and territories nearby, as well as from more distant areas, settled mainly along the Mississippi River and inland from that waterway in the southeastern portion of the state. Except for a cluster of five counties in the extreme northeastern corner of the state, the entire northern half of Iowa was still uninhabited in

[6] *Ibid.*, 189.
[7] *Ibid.*
[8] See L. H. Langworthy, "Dubuque: Its History, Mines, Indian Legends, etc.," *Iowa Journal of History and Politics*, Vol. VIII (1910), 366–422.

1850. In the southwestern part of the state only three counties—Pottawattamie, Fremont, and Page—contained settlements of any size.[9] The remainder of the land in this area, as in the north, was largely unsettled.

These boundaries of settlement remained appreciably unchanged until well into the 1850's. Even by 1854, aside from the northeastern tip, the entire northern half of Iowa lay untamed. Though people had begun to move into the southwestern portion, the bulk of Iowa's population, growing numerically from 191,000 in 1850 to about 326,000 in 1854, continued to cling to the original areas of settlement—that is, in the southeast and along the Mississippi. Other portions of the state remained unpopulated until the closing years of the 1850's, and even then settlement there continued to be sparse.[10]

When the last antebellum decade opened, the state of Iowa was a way station on a well-traveled route to the Far West. The discovery of gold in California two years earlier still continued to lure thousands away from their farms and offices.[11] One newspaper of the day lamented that California would in no way benefit Iowa, since the population of the former was increasing at the expense of the latter. But this was a pessimistic view of events. Nevertheless, the migration from Iowa to the gold diggings in California in the spring of 1850 approximated ten thousand people.[12]

Still, even while thousands abandoned their plows, forsook their tools, or deserted their offices in the quest for quick wealth, many more thousands of strong-bodied men, women, and children poured into Iowa from the South, from the North and

---

[9] Cardinal Goodwin, "The American Occupation of Iowa, 1833 to 1860," ibid., Vol. XVII (1919), 96; Hull, Iowa Census, 196–99.

[10] Hull, Iowa Census, 196–99; Census of Iowa by Counties as Returned to the Secretary of State for the Year 1854.

[11] Louis Pelzer, "The History and Principles of the Democratic Party of Iowa, 1846–1857," Iowa Journal of History and Politics, Vol. VI (1908), 189–90.

[12] The Iowa Weekly Republican (Iowa City), April 3 and May 1, 1850.

Northeast, and from abroad in ever-increasing numbers. Only this migration into the state can account for the increase in the population during the first half of the 1850's, which more than offset the departure of other thousands to seek homes in the Pacific coastal regions and in the Mormon paradise of Deseret. The natural increase in the population during this period totaled 54,125 persons.[13]

Several factors tended to encourage heavy immigration into the state. The most compelling factor, perhaps, was hunger for land. The construction of railroad lines to the Mississippi was a great improvement in the facilities for overland travel. No less than three railroads reached the Mississippi from the East in the mid-1850's. These were the Rock Island, the Northwestern, and the Burlington, which came to the great river in 1854, 1855, and 1856, respectively. In addition, guides for immigrants were published in newspapers throughout the East and South describing in glowing terms the wonderful opportunities to be found in Iowa. Iowa became a common household term in the eastern states. Speculators in land, land-investment companies, and railroad companies encouraged thousands to migrate to the new areas west of the Mississippi.[14]

An almost insatiable land hunger was a major characteristic of the American pioneer. He constantly sought to acquire new and better land holdings. In New England the farmer had to work a soil which was of a poorer quality than that held by his counterpart of the Middle West. In the South the small landholder could not compete with the larger plantation owners, who devoured the best croplands. Iowa appealed to all those who wished to toil for their daily bread on more favorable terms. Not only farmers but merchants, businessmen, and professional men also sought the new and better life in the young state of Iowa, where every-

13 Compiled by the author from the manuscript U.S. Census reports for Iowa for 1850 and 1860 and from the *Census of Iowa, 1856*, hereafter referred to as Nativities of Population.
14 Goodwin, *Occupation of Iowa*, 96–97.

one might start anew, on a better footing, it seemed, and on more nearly equal terms with each other. A serious outbreak of cholera in the Middle Atlantic states and a severe drought which gripped the entire Ohio Valley during the growing season of 1854 motivated thousands of Americans to leave the Northeast for happier and healthier regions.[15]

Great disappointments, however, sometimes awaited the newly arrived settler. In 1850 up and down the Mississippi, and especially along the portions of the river adjoining southern Iowa, an epidemic of the dread cholera raged along the water-front towns. During the intense heat of mid-July, a newspaper in Burlington reported that an average of six to eight persons was falling victim to the dreadful scourge daily and warned those living inland to remain out of town until the intensity of the disease had abated.[16]

If cholera could not deter the settler, natural calamities tried his mettle the following year. Starting in mid-May, heavy rains drenched the state for about two months. The gloom and sadness brought by the incessant storms which washed away much of the crops were reflected in the press. One journal pessimistically asserted that "we have before us not only the prospect but the certainty of hard times."[17] In the wake of the continued heavy rains came a more serious and destructive calamity. Floodwaters came surging over the lands to complete the dismal story of crop and property destruction. The Des Moines River at one time was miles in width; it inundated the fertile corn and wheat fields and swept away housing, sheds, fences, and livestock. Little of the corn and wheat, the two principal crops, remained to be harvested. So desperate was the condition of some people that a boat had to be sent to St. Louis to procure emergency provisions for the homeless and hungry survivors of the raging floodwaters.[18]

[15] *Ibid.*

[16] *Iowa State Gazette* (Burlington), July 24, 1850.

[17] *Burlington* (Iowa) *Daily Telegraph*, July 3, 1851; Cyrenus Cole, *A History of the People of Iowa*, 238.

[18] Cole, *A History of the People of Iowa*, 238.

Nor did the hard times of 1851 decrease with the receding waters. With the cessation of the rains came a severe drought which lasted the remainder of the summer, further ravaging what few crops had escaped destruction from the rains and floods. Once again cholera struck, as well as many other types of illnesses, finding many victims among the ill-fed, ill-clad, poorly sheltered sufferers from nature's capriciousness.[19]

Nonetheless, the pioneer of a century ago remained confident amid misfortune. Living as he did in the shadow of ever-present sudden death, the settler took his adversities in stride as he continued to eke out the life and existence he desired. Thus, in that very autumn of the "hard" year of 1851, one editor reflected that the fall had been favorable and that the Mississippi still remained open for free trade.[20]

The news of the natural disasters which struck Iowa did not discourage those who intended to migrate there. Indeed, a new flood of immigration came pouring across the Mississippi in 1851 and the following years, ceasing only temporarily during the Civil War. Iowa's population in 1851 increased by some 13,000 over the previous year's total, even though thousands had been lost to gold fever and to nature's harsh exactions. In 1852 the population climbed to 229,900, and two years later it stood at 326,500. From 1850 to 1854 the population increased by an average of about 40,000 a year.[21] After 1854 the upsurge became almost tidal, the population reaching 674,913 in 1860.

Up and down the Mississippi, in the towns bordering on the river and in those close to it, local editors kept their eyes on the influx of settlers. Even some of the inland towns took cognizance of the heavy travel, as more and more people moved into the interior to carve out their homes in the wild prairie regions. Oskaloosa reported that the streets of the town were clogged with travelers, their wagons, and their cattle. At all the principal

19 *Ibid.*, 238–39.
20 *Burlington Daily Telegraph*, November 29, 1851.

crossing points on the Mississippi the ferry boats plied from shore to shore endlessly in a vain effort to keep up with the tide of passengers and freight seeking to cross into Iowa. In Burlington the ferries lagged far behind their schedules, while the vehicles of the immigrants jammed the streets of the town.[22] At Prairie du Chien, Dubuque, McGregor, Davenport, Burlington, and Keokuk the congestion of traffic sometimes forced travelers to delay for two or three days. Nor were there any signs that the flow of human traffic would ever abate. Even out-of-state newspapers took notice of the mass of human beings heading for the state. A St. Louis paper reported that more than seventeen hundred wagons passed a certain point in Illinois, all bound for Iowa, and estimated that the increase in population during 1853 would amount to at least fifty thousand, a fairly accurate guess in the light of the actual census figures.[23]

The heavy traffic transformed some of Iowa's Mississippi ports into boom towns. Davenport and Keokuk reported unprecedented building activity as the citizens labored to provide the invading hordes with housing and supplies.[24] The *Morning Glory* of Keokuk, caught up in the fever of excitement, predicted that Iowa's population would reach the million mark by 1860. The *Keokuk Dispatch* reported that it was impossible to travel along the Mississippi "without being astonished at the immigration constantly pouring into Iowa from all parts of the country." From Dubuque the *Tribune* recorded that immigrants were streaming across the river "daily—yes, hourly."[25]

21 Hull, *Iowa Census*, 196–99.

22 *Oskaloosa* (Iowa) *Herald* quoted in *Iowa State Gazette*, May 21, 1851; *Burlington Daily Telegraph*, October 9, 1851, October 26, 1852, and September 28, 1853; *Iowa State Gazette*, October 22, 1851.

23 *St. Louis News* quoted in *Burlington Daily Telegraph*, November 30, 1853; Goodwin, *Occupation of Iowa*, 98.

24 William J. Petersen, "Population Advance to the Upper Mississippi Valley 1830–1860," *Iowa Journal of History and Politics*, Vol. XXXII (1934), 328; Nathan H. Parker, *Iowa as It Is in 1856*, 56–57.

25 *The Morning Glory* (Keokuk, Iowa), June 12, 1855; *Keokuk Dispatch* and *Dubuque* (Iowa) *Tribune* quoted in Nathan H. Parker, *Iowa as It Is in 1857*, 57, 62.

Iowa residents at first welcomed the newcomers with open arms, broadcasting to all who cared to listen that the soil of the state was the richest in the world and existed in plentiful quantities waiting to be improved. Before long overzealous editors began predicting that Iowa would soon move to the fore among the rich states of the Union. With a burst of pride characteristic of a frontier region, one editor proclaimed that not many days would pass before the selfish ascendancy in national affairs of the Middle and Northern states would be replaced by the freshness of the states in the "Valley of the Mississippi," which would "when the day of their predominance comes, put an end to that system of local and partial legislation which has done more to weaken the bond of union and obliterate the reverence of the people for the Constitution than all other causes combined."[26]

Until 1854, when a new wave of settlers moved to Iowa in massive numbers, largely from the Northeast, Iowans betrayed a definite Southern affinity, a mood that could be detected in the customs and attitudes of the people toward a variety of issues, especially politics and the Negro.[27] Iowa had been colonized to a considerable extent by Southerners working their way up the Mississippi and Missouri rivers. Many settled in what later became the counties of Fremont, Page, Appanoose, Davis, Decatur, Van Buren, and Lee, thinking they were still in the state of Missouri. Some even brought their slaves with them in the erroneous belief that they had settled upon slave soil.[28] Moreover, settlers who had come to Iowa in these early years from southern and western Pennsylvania and from the southern parts of Ohio, In-

[26] *Keosauqua* (Iowa) *American* quoted in *Burlington Daily Telegraph*, November 13, 1851; Petersen, "Population Advance," 333.

[27] Charles Roll, "Political Trends in Iowa History," *Iowa Journal of History and Politics*, Vol. XXVI (1928), 499–500.

[28] Nativities of Population, 1850; Wood Gray, *The Hidden Civil War: The Story of the Copperheads*, 21; *Biographical and Historical Record of Ringgold and Decatur Counties in Iowa*, 411; J. M. Howell and Heman C. Smith (eds.), *History of Decatur County Iowa and Its People*, I, 184.

diana, and Illinois were likewise bound to the South by ties of blood, tradition, and economic enterprise.[29]

A glance at the areas of first settlement helps to establish the Southern proclivities of the early settlers. Coming largely from forested areas, the people of the South shunned and feared the broad expanses of open, treeless prairies. Could land which supported only the tall prairie grass and flowers possibly possess any fertility? Was not the presence of timber a sure sign of the fertility of a parcel of land? Thus the first settlers avoided the open prairie lands and took up their residences along the streams where timber was available.[30]

Moreover, such a place of habitation was practicable. The timber could be put to use for shelters for human beings and animals, as well as for fencing and simple farm tools. The streams permitted ease in transportation and provided water for daily needs. And Iowa was blessed with an abundance of streams in addition to the two mighty rivers which formed her eastern and western boundaries. Most of the larger streams flowed from northwest to southeast, but several angled from northeast to southwest. The latter, however, were smaller and not nearly as navigable as the others. Along these rivers—for example, the Iowa and Cedar rivers in the east, the Des Moines and Raccoon rivers in the central region, and the Skunk and Nishnabotna rivers in the west—grew fairly fine stands of timber. Oak, walnut, ash, linn (linden), hickory, elm, and cottonwood were available at various places. These stands served to give the Southerners a feeling of security and well-being.[31]

According to the federal census of 1850, more than 16.5 per cent of the inhabitants of Iowa originated in the Deep South or

[29] Frank I. Herriott, "Whence Came the Pioneers of Iowa?" *Annals of Iowa*, 3d ser., Vol. VII (1906), 465.

[30] Paul W. Gates, "Land Policy and Tenancy in the Prairie States," *Journal of Economic History*, Vol. I (1941), 66.

[31] Gray, *The Hidden Civil War*, 22–23; Nathan H. Parker, *Iowa as It Is in 1855*, 35–36.

in the Border States. Another 16 per cent came from the Middle Atlantic or New England states. Still another 16 per cent came from Ohio, while the other states of the Old Northwest combined to contribute 17 per cent. About 20.5 per cent of the residents in Iowa in 1850 were born in the state; all others originated in other parts of the country or migrated from abroad.[32]

In the counties closest to Missouri the scales were heavily weighted by those with Southern backgrounds and traditions. Considering those who were born in the slaveholding areas of the United States, but not including those of Southern extraction who migrated from nonslave areas, Southerners totaled more than 38 per cent of the population of Appanoose County. Davis, Monroe, Decatur, Wayne, Fremont, Lucas, Page, Van Buren, and Taylor counties boasted similar or larger percentages. Certain of the interior counties, through which rivers ran, also contained large percentages of Southerners: Jasper, 31; Marshall, 38; Polk, 25; Dallas, 25; Keokuk, 21; Madison, 35; Warren, 26. In many more counties as much as 15 per cent of the inhabitants had Southern birthplaces. The statistics for those of Southern origin become even more impressive when they are enlarged to include those who entered Iowa from specific areas in Pennsylvania, Ohio, Illinois, and Indiana.[33]

Blood ties, however, were not the only bonds joining Iowa to the South. Stronger, perhaps, than sanguinary bonds were the links forged by trade and commerce. Until the railroads came to Iowa, most goods traveled down the rivers southward to be sold and transshipped to other areas. Even with the strengthening of the East–West facilities of travel and communication, even after the Northeast began to take the major share of the western trade, the economic ties with the South still remained firm.[34] Since the

[32] Nativities of Population, 1850.
[33] *Ibid.*; Gray, *The Hidden Civil War*, 21; Herriott, "Whence Came the Pioneers of Iowa?" 465.
[34] Gray, *The Hidden Civil War*, 20–21.

railroad did not enter Iowa until the mid-1850's, Iowans had fully twenty years to increase and strengthen their economic alliance with the South.

Truly indicative of the Southern frame of mind was the prevailing attitude toward the Negro and chattel slavery. While most of those who had migrated from the South did so because of the pressure of economic competition with the large plantation owners and their field crews of slave labor, as well as because of simple population pressure, these emigrants nevertheless came away with a loathing of the Negro. Most believed that slavery was the only natural condition for the Negro.[35] Most also opposed the advance of slavery into Iowa and elsewhere above the limits imposed by the Missouri Compromise—not, however, for moral reasons but from economic considerations. These people feared the unequal competition from slave labor or the cheap labor of free Negroes, competition which had motivated their departure from the South. Even the later arrivals in Iowa from the Northeast held similar views. This latter group might oppose slavery as a great moral evil, but no love for the Negro himself accompanied this attitude. Thus the people of Iowa, while opposing slavery for one reason or another, refused to permit the Negro to share the rights and privileges accorded to the white settler.[36]

This antagonism toward the Negro was translated into concrete action in 1850, when the General Assembly of Iowa passed a bill, subsequently signed by the governor, making it a penal offense for free Negroes to migrate into the state.[37] That this act had the full support of Iowans there can be no doubt. The disabilities under which the few Negroes already in Iowa had to live,

[35] See Joel H. Silbey, "Pro-Slavery Sentiment in Iowa, 1838–1861," unpublished M.A. thesis, State University of Iowa, 1956.

[36] Leola N. Bergmann, "The Negro in Iowa," *Iowa Journal of History and Politics*, Vol. XLVI (1948), 6–7. See also Eugene H. Berwanger, *The Frontier Against Slavery: Western Anti-Negro Prejudice and the Slavery Extension Controversy.*

[37] *Journal of the House of Representatives*, 3d General Assembly of Iowa, 1850, 88, 159; *Journal of the Senate*, 3rd General Assembly of Iowa, 1850, 295.

15

as well as the new prohibition against further Negro immigration, remained in effect until after the Civil War.[38]

The hostility to the Negro which was manifest in the state also found reflection in the public speeches of Iowa's representatives to the United States Congress. Senator Augustus C. Dodge, while stoutly protesting that he had no antipathy for any individual merely because of color, nevertheless firmly insisted that he was not *"l'ami des Noirs."* Three years later he reiterated his position when he told the Senate that "it must always be, in our Republic, that when living in the same community or family the negro will be denied, and justly denied, the political and social equality of the white man."[39]

Dodge's colleague in the Senate, George W. Jones, fully agreed with him. According to Jones, it was obvious that the white race was superior to the dark. Moreover, Jones denied that the Negro was included in the Declaration of Independence, especially in the clause that declared that all men were born free and equal. Even those few individuals who genuinely sympathized with the plight of the free Negroes conceded that it might be best if these freedmen were resettled in areas beyond the territorial confines of the United States.[40]

Though the Southern climate of opinion was a potent factor in the Iowa way of life, though evidence of Southern influence could be found throughout the state, though the early political leaders were Southerners by birth or inclination, Iowa contained other population groups whose importance, even during this early period, should not be minimized.

The Middle Atlantic and New England states contributed

[38] The prohibition against Negro immigration was rarely enforced, and the Negro population in Iowa grew from 333 in 1850 to 1,069 in 1860. Bergmann, "The Negro in Iowa," 15.

[39] 31 Cong., 2 sess., *Congressional Globe*, Appendix, 377; 33 Cong., 1 sess., *ibid.*, Appendix, 377.

[40] 34 Cong., 1 sess., *ibid.*, Appendix, 407–408; *Davenport* (Iowa) *Gazette*, March 11, 1852.

about 16 per cent of Iowa's settlers. In 1850, however, less than 3 per cent of Iowa's inhabitants came from New England, leaving about 13 per cent who had originated in the Middle Atlantic region. These individuals, reared in environments manifestly different from those of their neighbors, tended to settle in the northern portion of Iowa and along the Mississippi River. Later arrivals from the Northeast quickly moved inland away from the rivers and streams, a movement Southerners hesitated or feared to make. Perhaps the earlier settlers had already appropriated the best lands along the rivers and streams, or perhaps the difficulties encountered with the rocky soil of New England motivated settlers from that area to seek land which could be cleared and cultivated with ease. Whatever the reasons, it was the folk from the Northeast who first settled away from the rivers.[41]

Although persons of New England birth accounted for less than 3 per cent of the population in 1850, their numbers were considerably higher in certain sections, almost negligible in others. Where the Southerners predominated, for example, the New Englanders were scarce. Fewer than 1 per cent made their homes in Appanoose County. The same held true for Davis, Page, Marion, Madison, and other counties with sizable groups of Southerners. In the northeastern portion of the state, however, the opposite was true. New Englanders numbered more than 7 per cent of the population in Clayton and Clinton counties. In Delaware, Jackson, and Allamakee counties New Englanders made up more than 5 per cent of the population. Pottawattamie County, in the southwest, contained more than 8 per cent New Englanders in its population, but many of them were Mormons, soon to leave the state for Deseret.[42]

The settlers from the Middle Atlantic states also tended to live in the northeastern part of Iowa, though the entire area along the Mississippi was popular. More than 32 per cent of the inhabi-

[41] Nativities of Population, 1850.
[42] *Ibid.*

17

tants of Buchanan County originated in New York, New Jersey, or Pennsylvania. Iowans from the Middle Atlantic region comprised one-fifth to one-fourth of the population in Clayton, Clinton, Jackson, Delaware, Linn, Johnson, Muscatine, and Scott counties. Later in the decade the Northerners moved into many areas originally colonized by Southerners, but still religiously avoided the overwhelmingly Southern counties. The state of Ohio, alone, furnished over 16 per cent of Iowa's residents in 1850. Although Ohioans scattered throughout the state, large groups concentrated in two clusters of counties, one in the northeast, the other in the southeast. Buchanan, Cedar, and Fayette boasted 20 per cent or more natives of Ohio among their populations. Henry, Washington, Louisa, and Poweshiek counties contained similar percentages of Ohioans among their residents.[43]

The other states of the Old Northwest made up, collectively, about 17 per cent of the people of Iowa in 1850. Settlers from this area tended to congregate in the south-central portion of the state, where they comprised one-fourth to one-third of the inhabitants of Boone, Marshall, Benton, Dallas, Madison, Polk, Jasper, Warren, and Poweshiek counties. Likewise, there was a large concentration of natives of the Old Northwest in Lucas, Monroe, Wapello, Clarke, and Keokuk counties. Those who came from southern Illinois, Indiana, Ohio, and Wisconsin were strongly of Southern extraction and helped to swell the strong Southern element in the state.[44]

Before taking notice of the settlers of Iowa who came from the nations of Europe and the Western Hemisphere, it might be well to pause momentarily to examine the population of Pottawattamie County in southwestern Iowa. Until 1854 that county's residents were almost exclusively Mormons. Kanesville (later renamed Council Bluffs), on the Missouri River, became an important

[43] *Ibid.*; Harry Church and Katharyn J. Chappell, *History of Buchanan County Iowa and Its People,* I, 56.

[44] Nativities of Population, 1850; Herriott, "Whence Came the Pioneers of Iowa?" 465; Gray, *The Hidden Civil War,* 21.

rendezvous for Mormons preparing to trek to Utah to join Brigham Young. By 1854, with the departure of the Mormons, the population of Pottawattamie County declined to about 3,000 from the figure of 7,800 in 1850. A similar situation existed in Mills County, but, since that county had not yet been officially organized in 1850, the population figures are not available.[45]

While the settlers of Iowa were predominantly native Americans, the foreign-born population nevertheless comprised more than 10 per cent of the total in 1850. The foreign-born residents came mainly from Great Britain, Ireland, Canada, the Netherlands, Scandinavia, and the German States. Others, not so numerous, journeyed to Iowa from France, Switzerland, and the Austrian Empire. Immigrants from the German States, Ireland, and Britain combined accounted for more than 8 per cent of the total population. Germans held the lead, contributing 3.7 per cent of the total, while Britain and Ireland followed with 2.5 per cent each. All other nations yielded less than 3 per cent collectively. All told, of a total population of some 192,000, about 20,800 were not natives of the United States.[46]

Most of the foreign-born immigrants crowded into the eastern portion of the state, particularly in the settlements along the Mississippi River. In addition, they, like the Northeasterners, seemed to shun the areas of strong Southern attachments. Two important exceptions to this pattern of settlement were the British and the Hollanders.[47]

Owing to difficulties of language, as well as differences in culture and tradition, the Germans tended to be extremely clannish. Large numbers of Germans settled in the towns of the Mississippi, principally in Davenport, Burlington, Muscatine, and Dubuque. Clayton County, harboring a population which was more than 13 per cent German, contained colonies of German

[45] Jacob Van Der Zee, "The Mormon Trails in Iowa," *Iowa Journal of History and Politics*, XII (1914), 14–15; Hull, *Iowa Census*, 196–99.

[46] Nativities of Population, 1850.

[47] *Ibid.*

communists. Germans, moving from Davenport, founded Miden, Walcott, Avoca, Wheatland, and De Witt. New Wien was a solidly German and Roman Catholic town. Of the 7,101 Germans in Iowa in 1850, more than 5,400 established their residences in the six counties of Lee, Clayton, Des Moines, Scott, Dubuque, and Muscatine.[48] So numerous were they and so potentially powerful politically that the Iowa General Assembly continually made provision for printing the important legislative enactments and state documents in the German language. Perhaps their strong clannishness gave an exaggerated impression of political strength.[49]

These immigrants from the German States continued their custom of enjoying the Sabbath with fun and relaxation accompanied by heavy consumption of lager beer. Their native-born neighbors soon came to resent what they considered to be deliberate desecrations of the Sabbath and clamored for legislative enactments to preserve the sanctity of the traditional day of rest.[50] Later in the decade animosity toward the foreign-born, directed especially against the Germans and Irish, took political form.

The immigrants from Ireland in 1850 totaled 4,907 persons. Though the Irish spread throughout Iowa, they, like the Germans, concentrated more heavily in the towns along the Mississippi River. Later in the decade, when the railroads came to Iowa, many thousands of Irish entered the state as construction workers for the railroads and remained to settle in the state. During these early years the Irish swarmed into Dubuque County, where they formed 16 per cent of the population. The large concentration of Irish at Dubuque reinforced the already strong position of the Roman Catholic church in that city, which was large enough, even in 1850, to have its own bishop, Mathias Loras. Oth-

[48] *Ibid.*; Willard I. Toussaint, "The Know-Nothing Party in Iowa," unpublished M.A. thesis, State University of Iowa, 1956, 47–48.

[49] *Journal of the Senate*, 3rd General Assembly of Iowa, 1850, 245.

[50] *Ibid.*, 4th General Assembly of Iowa, 1852, 85; *Journal of the House of Representatives*, 4th General Assembly of Iowa, 1852, 79.

er substantial communities of Irish were located in Jones, Clayton, Jackson, Iowa, Clinton, Scott, and Winneshiek counties.[51]

The British, including those from Scotland and Wales, not being restricted by any language barrier and being far less clannish than the other foreign groups, scattered throughout the state in more or less equal diffusion. Pottawattamie County, however, contained a significant settlement of Britishers, but these were Mormons, newly arrived as converts and soon to leave for the sanctuary being carved out of the desert by Brigham Young and his followers. Otherwise, only Dubuque and Scott counties held any sizable numbers of Britishers, the former embracing about 6.5 per cent and the latter some 4.7 per cent. In 1850 the British in Iowa numbered 4,820.[52]

A not-inconsiderable group of settlers came from Canada. In 1850 these hardy pioneers amounted to 1,839 men, women, and children, or about 0.9 per cent of the population. Like the British, they scattered throughout the state, coming as they did from an environment which was not too dissimilar from that found in the United States. Nevertheless, substantial numbers of Canadians settled in the river-border counties of Dubuque, Jackson, Henry, Lee, Van Buren, and Pottawattamie.[53]

Settlers from Holland in Iowa totaled 1,096 in 1850, representing 0.5 per cent of the population. At Pella, in Marion County, one settlement of Hollanders, numbering 884 persons, comprised 16.2 per cent of the county's population. Other groups of Hollanders made their homes in Wapello, Lee, Mahaska, and Muscatine counties.[54]

The Scandinavians—Danes, Swedes, and Norwegians—comprised a mere 0.3 per cent of Iowa's population in 1850, number-

51 Jacob Van Der Zee, *The British in Iowa*, 42; Franklin T. Oldt (ed.), *History of Dubuque County Iowa*, 872–73; Nativities of Population, 1850.
52 Nativities of Population, 1850; Van Der Zee, *The British in Iowa*, 52–53.
53 Van Der Zee, *The British in Iowa*, 46–47; Nativities of Population, 1850.
54 Nativities of Population, 1850; see also Jacob Van Der Zee, *The Hollanders of Iowa*.

ing but 611 persons. Nevertheless, in Allamakee, Winneshiek, and Fayette counties, in the extreme northeastern corner of the state, they clustered in communities of some size. Many, of course, had crossed into the state from Wisconsin and Minnesota, as they were to do in increasing numbers later in the decade. Other Scandinavian settlements existed in Jefferson, Story, Lee, Henry, Polk, and Van Buren counties.[55]

Generally overlooked in any examination of the origins of the settlers of Iowa during its early history have been the immigrants from France, Switzerland, and the Austrian Empire. To be sure, immigrants from the last country were scarce in Iowa in 1850, but as the decade wore on, so too did their numbers increase. In Dubuque County, where the foreign-born elements comprised 39.5 per cent of the population, immigrants from France and Switzerland established homes in some strength. Lee, Davis, Jefferson, Des Moines, Johnson, and Washington counties also harbored people of French origin. In addition, Iowa had a few residents from Poland, Russia, Italy, Mexico, and Belgium, primarily in Dubuque, Wapello, Des Moines, and Pottawattamie counties.[56]

Iowans early became conscious of the increasing size of the foreign-born population and aware also that Wisconsin was the only western state actually encouraging settlement within her boundaries. To counteract the propaganda from Wisconsin, a bill was introduced in the Iowa Senate in 1853 providing for the appointment of an agent to promote immigration to Iowa, with headquarters in New York City. A special committee of the senate, to which the bill had been referred, reported back on January 12, 1853, just five days after the introduction of the measure, that it could not "from their present information recommend the

[55] Nativities of Population, 1850; see also George T. Flom, "The Growth of the Scandinavian Factor in the Population of Iowa," *Iowa Journal of History and Politics*, Vol. IV (1906), 268–85.

[56] Nativities of Population, 1850.

appointment of such commissioner of emigration."[57] Thus the first move to create such an office fell by the wayside.

The various groups of Iowa's residents, whether of Southern or Northeastern stock, whether of native or foreign origin, played important roles in the political history of the state during the convulsive decade of the 1850's. Because the influence of the Southerners was so strong during the earlier period of the state's history, politics tended to be shaped according to the prevailing Southern attitudes toward such issues as slavery, banking, and internal improvements. Indeed, the anti-Negro bias of the Southerners was largely shared by others even after the former had lost their dominance in the state. For the most part the Southerners voted with the Democratic party. Persistently loyal to the leaders and concepts that had early gained their allegiance, they did not give up their convictions very easily. Certain of the counties, where the Southern-born settlers continued to predominate, never departed from their loyalty to the Democratic party, even in the wake of the Lincoln sweep in 1860.[58]

When, after 1854, the immigrants to Iowa came increasingly from the Northeastern portion of the country, bringing with them all the prejudices and loyalties common to that section, the political complexion of the state began to undergo a significant change. Nor did the changes which were thus inaugurated proceed harmoniously. The Southerners and Yankees eyed each other suspiciously. The Eastern settlers brought with them a respect for education, a belief in the social proprieties, and a distinct antislavery attitude, notwithstanding that their feelings toward the individual Negro might have differed but little from those of their Southern brethren. The Yankees disdained the rough, ignorant appearance conveyed by the sturdy pioneers from the South. For their part the Southerners, accustomed to

[57] *Journal of the Senate*, 4th General Assembly of Iowa, 1852, 144, 187.
[58] *The History of Madison County Iowa*, 407; Gray, *The Hidden Civil War*, 23, 27.

the evangelism of the frontier religions, disliked, among other things, the colder piety of the Easterners. This mutual antagonism soon found expression at the polls.[59] Gradually an opposition coalition, which later helped to form the Republican party, displaced the Democrats from their position of political supremacy in the state.

The incoming human flood early stimulated a demand to the United States Congress for legislation to provide internal improvements at federal expense (the old cry of the Whig party) and for a measure offering the free disbursement of the immense holdings of government land within the state. The demand for homesteads, particularly insistent after 1850, became one of the standard political issues of the various campaigns during the 1850's. In Congress, Iowa's Democratic representatives energetically supported measures providing for free homesteads to actual settlers. In the Senate Augustus C. Dodge was equally friendly to such a measure.[60] These prohomestead and prointernal-improvements sentiments were merely the products of an ever-increasing population in Iowa which wanted the federal government to help the state in its growth. The Northern newcomers also clamored for changes in the state constitution, a document which embodied the Southern attitudes of its creators.

The population statistics for the second half of the 1850's reflect the rapid growth patterns in Iowa. According to the state census for 1854, Iowa's population stood at 326,500. Just two years later the figure read 512,000, and, as already noted, in 1860 there were 674,913 people in the state. Every county reported an increase in population. Pottawattamie County, too, gained in population after having suffered declines since 1850 owing to the Mormon departures.[61]

[59] Herriott, "Whence Came the Pioneers of Iowa?" 465; Gray, *The Hidden Civil War*, 24–25; *The History of Keokuk County Iowa*, 406.

[60] Louis Pelzer, *Augustus Caesar Dodge*, 153–54; 32 Cong., 2 sess., *Congressional Globe*, Appendix, 205.

[61] Hull, *Iowa Census*, 196–99; Nativities of Population, 1856, 1860. Secre-

Most of the immigrants came from the northeastern section of the nation, New England, the Middle Atlantic states, and Ohio. By 1856 people from these regions represented more than 38 per cent of Iowa's population, while in 1860 the figures declined somewhat, to 33.5 per cent. These newcomers not only settled in the more populous eastern counties but also streamed into the interior northern and western portions of the state, where land was plentiful and people few.[62] The immigrants from the East did not have the same distrust of the prairie regions which the early settlers manifested. They pushed into Iowa's unsettled interior areas until only the extreme northwestern corner of the state remained relatively free of human habitation at the outbreak of the Civil War.

During the latter portion of the 1850's settlements were established in Woodbury, Palo Alto, Emmet, Buena Vista, Clay, Dickinson, and Franklin counties, as well as in Sioux, O'Brien, Plymouth, and Cherokee counties. Only Lyon and Osceola counties were not listed in the federal census of 1860.[63] Residents of the Missouri slope began to tell of people coming in from the East, proudly announcing that not everyone was heading for Kansas or Nebraska or points farther west.[64] Of course, these newcomers to Iowa may not have come to the state directly from the places of origin which the census rolls show. The New Englander may have lingered for a number of years in, say, Ohio, before pushing on farther west. The Southerner may have paused for several years in Tennessee or Kentucky before proceeding north and crossing the Mississippi into Iowa. Palo Alto's first inhabitants

tary of State George McCleary reported to the legislature that the 1856 returns were "made in a very imperfect manner, and many important omissions have been made—some assessors omitting the nativity entirely." *Journal of the Senate, 6th General Assembly of Iowa, 1856*, 77.

[62] Nativities of Population, 1856, 1860.

[63] Cole, *A History of the People of Iowa*, 289, 292; *History of Franklin and Cerro Gordo Counties Iowa*, 224–25; Dwight G. McCarty, *History of Palo Alto County Iowa*, 22.

[64] *Sioux City* (Iowa) *Eagle*, May 8, 1858.

were Irish who had originally settled in Kane County, Illinois, before deciding to locate in Iowa.[65]

By 1856 persons of New England origin in Iowa had quadrupled since the federal census of 1850. Though New Englanders comprised merely 4.1 per cent of Iowa's population, such newer counties as Mitchell, Grundy, Audubon, and Kossuth boasted a population that was more than ten per cent of New England background. The older counties of Fayette, Black Hawk, and Buchanan also reported an increase in the number of Yankees. In Fayette, for example, New Englanders totaled more than 22 per cent of the population. But these same counties contained ever-larger numbers from the Middle Atlantic states or from Ohio. By 1860 settlers from Ohio and the Middle Atlantic region had tripled or quadrupled since 1850. In 1856 former Ohioans numbered 90,000 persons, or 17.5 per cent of the total population, while natives of the Middle States totaled 85,564, or 16.7 per cent of the whole. In 1860 settlers from Ohio and the Middle States comprised 100,117 and 101,541 persons, or 14.8 per cent and 15 per cent, respectively.[66]

In contrast to the increased immigration from the Northeast was the decreased flow from the slaveholding states. Although the number of Southerners did increase numerically after 1850, the percentage in relation to the total population declined. In 1850, Southerners comprised 16.7 per cent of the population; in 1856 they accounted for only 10.8 per cent of the total, while in 1860 they fell to a mere 4.6 per cent.[67] In cold statistics, and in truth, Easterners replaced Southerners in numbers and in influence in all but the southernmost tier of counties, and even in that area their numbers were not entirely negligible.

Although natives of Indiana and Illinois more than doubled in 1856 in contrast to their numbers in 1850, their percentage fig-

---

[65] McCarty, *History of Palo Alto County*, 22.
[66] Nativities of Population, 1856, 1860.
[67] *Ibid.*

ures decreased. The situation persisted in 1860. Persons born in Indiana represented 11.2 per cent of the total population of Iowa in 1850; they accounted for 10.4 per cent in 1856 and 8.5 per cent in 1860. Natives of Illinois declined from 5.6 per cent in 1850 to 4.5 per cent in 1856 and 4.2 per cent in 1860. Residents of Iowa from Wisconsin, Michigan, and Minnesota numbered only 6,021 persons in 1856, or 1.1 per cent of the population of the state. In 1860 the figures rose to 9,837 individuals, or 1.5 per cent.[68] Since many of the newcomers from the western areas of the Old Northwest came from families which were originally Southern, their decreasing totals further underscored the decline and waning influence of the Southern element in Iowa.

Immigrants of foreign origin also joined in the great movement to Iowa. These groups, too, increased in numbers during the same period. Germans and Irish quadrupled, British tripled, while the Scandinavians increased almost sevenfold. Settlers from France, Canada, Austria, Switzerland, and Holland likewise registered sizable gains. All told, the foreign-born residents of Iowa comprised over 15 per cent of the population in 1856 and 1860 in contrast to 10.9 per cent in 1850. Germans, Irish, and British continued to lead all other groups.[69]

While the British and Canadians, escaping the usual difficulties occasioned by language and custom differences, scattered fairly evenly throughout the state, the Germans continued to concentrate in the Mississippi counties and in the central eastern counties. The Irish also congregated in the towns of the eastern portion of the state, but absence of a language barrier enabled them to spread also into the interior regions. For the most part the Hollanders gravitated to Marion County, which was home for three-fourths of them. Johnson, Winneshiek, and Linn counties contained more than half of the immigrants from the Austrian Empire, while a like percentage of the Scandinavians settled in

[68] *Ibid.*
[69] *Ibid.*

Allamakee, Clayton, Jefferson, and Winneshiek counties combined. Of the 7,676 Scandinavians, Winneshiek held 2,923 in
1860. Lightly sprinkled here and there throughout the state were
immigrants from several other foreign lands.[70]

The wagon trains that rumbled along the well-worn trails leading to the Mississippi from the East, as well as the railroads, carried the antislavery attitudes of the new arrivals in addition to
their tangible possessions. The New Englanders were sincerely
convinced that slavery was a great moral sin in the eyes of God.
Newcomers from Ohio and the Middle Atlantic region held somewhat similar views. Generally, however, they were not outright
abolitionists, but on the question of the expansion of slavery they
could be as fanatic in their opposition as the most outspoken
radical.[71]

Moreover, the New Englanders were leaving an area where for
many years the Democratic party had not been flourishing. Vermont had never cast a presidential electoral vote for a Democrat;
Rhode Island and Connecticut had voted for Whigs in the last
three presidential elections. Only New Hampshire and Maine
had remained tenuously in the Democratic camp of late.[72] Thus
the new arrivals in large part transported voting habits unfavor-
able to Democratic candidates.

During the late 1850's one population group, the freed Negroes, still received no welcome in Iowa. Even after the machinery of the state government fell into the hands of the antislavery
elements, the same men who had inveighed so loudly against
slavery opposed just as vehemently the elimination of the barriers
to Negro settlement in the state. Nevertheless, some petitions to
eradicate this injustice began to reach the state lawmakers.[73] It

[70] *Ibid.*

[71] Bergmann, "The Negro in Iowa," 7.

[72] Roy F. Nichols, *The Democratic Machine 1850–1854*, 80.

[73] 32 Cong., 1 sess., *Congressional Globe*, Appendix, 408; *Journal of the House of Representatives*, 5th General Assembly of Iowa, 1854, 317.

would remain for the Civil War, however, to remove the obstructions to Negro migration into Iowa.

The foreign-born residents in Iowa, as noted earlier, provoked friction with the native-born settlers. Not only the clannishness but also the customs, habits, language, and dress of the foreign groups were objects of suspicion to the Americans, characteristics of an unknown nature that could—so ran the fear—undermine the foundations of the American system of government.[74]

Before long, criticism of foreigners and of their habits began to appear in the newspapers. According to the *Burlington Daily Telegraph*, Europe's displaced people were responsible for difficulties hitherto unknown in Iowa. The *Western Gazette* of Bloomfield charged that some of the German States were deliberately shipping "their convicts to our shores." The same paper voiced the fear that the increased number of Catholics—for the Irish almost wholly and most of the Germans professed Roman Catholicism—would "transfer to this happy land Popery in all of its lurid forms." Something should be done immediately to stop this threat. Furthermore, these foreigners were involved in most of the drunken brawls that were noticeably increasing in the state.[75] The *Davenport Gazette* disdainfully noted that the Germans especially were quick to oppose certain state laws, such as prohibition and the Sabbath law, which most Iowans had favored. The paper condemned these people in the aggregate "for their excesses and their infidel principles."[76] Precisely what they had done the editor failed to disclose. Most of the antiforeign editorials appeared in Whig journals or in papers friendly to the Whig cause. Few if any of the Democratic organs attacked the foreign-born settlers.

The growing antiforeign sentiment very soon found expression

[74] Marcus L. Hansen, "Official Encouragement of Immigration to Iowa," *Iowa Journal of History and Politics*, Vol. XIX (1921), 163.

[75] *Western Gazette* (Bloomfield, Iowa), January 20 and June 28, 1854; see also Toussaint, "The Know-Nothing Party in Iowa," 7–8.

[76] February 15, 1855.

in a political party which mushroomed in 1854 and later. In the elections in the East this party won more political offices than either the Democrats or Whigs cared to admit. Officially entitled the American party but more popularly called the Know-Nothing party (from the refusal of its members to divulge details of meetings), this unique political organization first appeared in Iowa late in 1854. By early the following year it had begun to attract an impressive following, and until 1857 it entered candidates in Iowa's political contests.

Several factors lay behind the increasing popularity of the Know-Nothing party in Iowa. One was the pressure of economic competition from the overseas immigration, which undoubtedly impelled many Easterners to journey to less populous areas. Another was the fear of Roman Catholicism. Anti-Catholic prejudice came in part from the refusal of native Americans to accept foreigners, with their cultural differences, as social equals. Anti-Catholicism did not get out of hand in Iowa, however. As workers, the foreigners were readily welcomed in communities suffering from a shortage of labor.[77] Irish laborers also played a significant role in the construction of railroad lines across Iowa.

German fondness for beer and Irish predilection for whisky also played into the hands of the Know-Nothings. During the middle 1850's Iowa was in the throes of a temperance crusade. Needless to say, the Irish and Germans energetically opposed prohibition legislation. Hence it was not a difficult step for temperance men to join the Know-Nothings against the foreign anti-temperance elements.[78]

By late fall of 1854 the Know-Nothings had made enough progress in Iowa to enter the newspaper battles with their own journals. These included the *Muscatine Tri-Weekly Journal* and the *Keokuk Whig*, whose sympathies, however, were suspect.

[77] Toussaint, "The Know-Nothing Party in Iowa," 44–46; *Eddyville* (Iowa) *Free Press*, March 2, 1855.

[78] Toussaint, "The Know-Nothing Party in Iowa," 44–45.

Later the Know-Nothings could boast of papers in Des Moines, Dubuque, and Oskaloosa.[79]

In order to capitalize on the nativist sentiment within Iowa, as well as to reap the benefits of the unsettled political atmosphere, the Know-Nothings broadened their appeal to the voters. The party offered a platform with two major planks: one, of course, reflected the antiforeign, anti-Catholic stand of the Know-Nothings; the other was an antislavery position. The national meeting of the American party had split over the slavery issue in 1855, and the Iowa group backed the antislavery wing of the party.[80] But the Republican party, which rose in Iowa after 1856, ultimately captured its adherents.

Toward the end of 1857, Iowans began to feel the pinch of economic distress brought on partly by the Panic of 1857 and partly by a series of natural disturbances. The economic crisis which engulfed the East and later spread westward began on August 24, 1857, when Charles Stetson, president of the New York branch of the Ohio Life Insurance and Trust Company, announced that his firm would suspend monetary payments. Instead of helping Stetson's firm meet its financial obligations, other New York banks began a policy of contraction which proved to be contagious. Economic distress was one product of this policy.[81]

Although many firms in Iowa were forced to close their doors in 1857, severe economic hardship did not develop until 1858. As late as October, 1857, for example, Charles Aldrich, editor of the *Hamilton Freeman*, reported that "things are still moving on satisfactorily" in north-central Iowa, but during the early months of 1858 Iowans began to suffer.[82] The collapse of real-estate values, the decline in grain prices, and the lack of banks of issue with

[79] David S. Sparks, "The Birth of the Republican Party in Iowa, 1848 to 1860," unpublished Ph.D. dissertation, University of Chicago, 1951, 127.

[80] *Democratic Banner* (Davenport, Iowa), June 22, 1855; *Des Moines Valley Whig* (Keokuk, Iowa), November 21, 1855.

[81] George W. Van Vleck, *The Panic of 1857*, 64–66.

[82] October 22, 1857.

a consequent shortage of circulating media combined to inflict financial hardships on scores of Iowans. Too many, moreover, had overextended themselves by purchasing stocks in railroads, as well as by buying land for speculation. Railroads lay behind most of the land speculation. Although out-of-state buyers had swarmed into Iowa during the 1850's, many Iowans also had dabbled in real estate.[83]

Complicating the distressing financial picture was a series of natural disasters which struck Iowans about the same time. The winter of 1856–57 was the most severe in the memory of the settlers and took hundreds in western Iowa by surprise. Many suffered from shortages of food and fuel.[84] To add to the miseries of the cruel winter, the summer and autumn of 1858 brought further distress. Heavy rains and intermittent frosts caused crop failures over two-thirds of the state. Caught between the Panic of 1857 and the wrath of the elements, many Iowans suffered extreme privation. In the more recently settled portions of the state, pioneer families barely managed to survive, subsisting on diets of wild game and a little flour. And wheat sold for only forty cents a bushel. The inability to pay taxes compelled thousands to yield their land holdings to tax-title purchasers.[85]

In addition to the many families hurt by the crop failures, low prices for grain, and the panic, many business establishments experienced financial difficulties. In 1857, Iowa firms with total liabilities of over two million dollars closed their doors. The next year firms with liabilities totaling more than three million went out of business. Other Middle Western states—Michigan, Wiscon-

[83] Van Vleck, *The Panic of 1857*, 33, 83, 92; 35 Cong., 2 sess., *Congressional Globe*, 767–68; Gates, "Land Policy and Tenancy in the Prairie States," 70–71.

[84] Robert Robinson to George W. Jones, February 19, 1857, in the George W. Jones Correspondence at the Iowa State Department of History and Archives in Des Moines; Enos Lowe to George W. Jones, February 14, 1857, *ibid.*; George W. Fitch, *Past and Present of Fayette County Iowa*, I, 93; R. A. Smith, *A History of Dickinson County Iowa*, 52.

[85] Charles E. Payne, *Josiah Bushnell Grinnell*, 53–54; *Hamilton Freeman* (Webster City, Iowa), July 29, 1858; Cole, *A History of the People of Iowa*, 308.

sin, Minnesota, Illinois, and Missouri—exhibited similar trends. Indeed, long after Eastern companies had recovered from the panic or were well on the road to recovery, the Middle West continued to suffer.[86] Before long, suffering Iowans began to look to the state legislature for relief. The press was divided on the question of relief legislation. The *Montezuma Weekly Republican*, for example, held that existing laws sufficed to meet the situation. Nevertheless, the demand for relief measures grew strong enough to persuade the General Assembly to yield to the anguished appeal of the hard-pressed Iowans. Iowa lawmakers enacted such relief measures as stay and appraisement laws and extended the redemption times.[87]

The ravages of the panic also greatly impeded railroad building in Iowa; construction was all but halted throughout the state. Despite the incentive of the Iowa land grant of 1856, fewer than 500 miles of railroad were in operation in the state by 1859. The *Hamilton Freeman* wondered whether railroad construction crews would ever resume their work.[88]

Regardless of their personal problems, however, throughout the final antebellum decade the residents of Iowa, both native-born and foreign-born, came to grips with what they conceived to be the important issues of the day, local and national. These included temperance, constitutional reform, nativism, internal improvements, transcontinental railroad routes, speculation, homestead legislation, slavery, the Kansas-Nebraska Act, Dred Scott, John Brown, civil strife in Kansas, and the nature of the federal Union, to name some of the most significant ones. Participating in these concerns and making various critical and some-

[86] Van Vleck, *The Panic of 1857*, 84, 91.

[87] *Montezuma* (Iowa) *Weekly Republican*, February 27, 1858; *Iowa State Journal* (Des Moines), February 12, 1858; Des Moines *Session Journal*, February 12, 1858; *Journal of the Senate*, 8th General Assembly of Iowa, 1860, 745–46.

[88] Cole, *A History of the People of Iowa*, 284; *Hamilton Freeman*, February 25, 1858.

times fateful choices with the indefatigable energy and decisiveness characteristic of inhabitants of the frontier, Iowans played prominent roles in the drama which preceded the ultimate tragedy of the Civil War.

The Great Compromise

THE OPENING of the last antebellum decade witnessed the climax of a multifaceted political struggle whose arenas of confrontation included, but also extended far beyond, the confines of the Legislative chambers of Congress.[1] The battle was largely a sectional one between the mutually antagonistic North and South, but it was complicated by the intrusion of important western factors: California clamored for admission into the Union as a free state, and Utah and New Mexico pressed for territorial status. To add further to the already difficult and complex situation, Texas demanded certain adjustments, both financial and territorial while the South as a whole called for strong federal legislation to aid in retrieving runaway slaves who were fleeing from bondage in ever-increasing numbers. On its part the North with equal determination insisted upon the elimination from the na-

[1] See Holman Hamilton, *Prologue to Conflict: The Crisis and Compromise of 1850.*

tion's capital of what it considered nothing less than barbarous eyesores, the slave auctions and markets.

Any of these urgent matters would have been sufficient to inflame tempers in both North and South, for the sectional controversy had already become so heated that any congressional bill sponsored by one side appeared certain of being opposed by the other. In the 1840's on issues involving matters other than slavery or slavery extension the political parties in Congress had generally voted without regard to sectional divisions.[2] Whether or not this demonstration of ostensible political party unity could be maintained during the 1850's, however, was quite another matter.

Amid the warring passions and conflicting viewpoints shared by his congressional colleagues, Henry Clay introduced bills which he earnestly hoped would soothe aroused feelings and furnish an equitable settlement of the problems which the country faced. The omnibus package, however, had to contend with a legislative ambush established by the disruptive elements of sectionalism, factionalism, and individualism, an ambuscade from which Clay's proposals could not successfully emerge. Consequently, other dedicated and more politically astute legislative moderates, especially Stephen A. Douglas, hammered out the measures which became known to contemporaries and in history alike as the Compromise of 1850.

Iowa reflected in a strong degree the issues which then stirred the nation, but the Hawkeye State also had its own problems to consider. The year 1850 was an important election year for Iowans. A new governor, a new assembly, other state officers, and representatives from the state's two congressional districts were to be selected in the coming elections. Moreover, a special election was to be held during the year to fill an unexpired term in Congress from the First Congressional District, an investigating

2 Joel H. Silbey, *The Shrine of Party: Congressional Voting Behavior 1841–1852*, 144.

committee in the House of Representatives having declared the seat vacant. Control of the machinery of government in the state rested on the outcome of these elections.

When Henry Clay introduced his compromise resolutions in the United States Senate in late January, 1850, he gave the Democratic party in Iowa the vital political ammunition it needed for the ensuing electoral campaign. Democratic party leaders, as subsequent events would soon demonstrate, intended to exert all their energy and talents to secure the success of the compromise, support of which became the cardinal tenet of the Democratic program of 1850.

Quick to take a cue, the Democratic state convention assembled to nominate candidates, as well as to provide the voting public with a statement of its principles. The platform wholeheartedly endorsed the compromise bills as introduced into the Senate and hoped for the success of the measures.[3] While giving its traditional approval to the retiring state Democratic administration, the platform condemned the national administration, principally because it was in the hands of the opposition party. Certain removals of Democrats from federal office in the state and the subsequent appointment of Whigs to succeed them had stung many of the party leaders, who gave expression to their feelings in the platform of their party.

On the question of internal improvements, that tested rallying call of the Whig party, the Democrats added a plank to their platform calling the attention of the voters to the action of the secretary of the interior, Thomas Ewing, who had recently declared illegal Iowa's title to a portion of the original Des Moines River land grant which the state had received during the late 1840's. Ewing ordered that the land revert to federal jurisdiction.[4] To be sure, Ewing was a Whig in a Whig administration.

[3] Roy V. Sherman, "Political Party Platforms in Iowa," unpublished M.A. thesis, State University of Iowa, 1926, 106–10.
[4] *Iowa Weekly Republican* (Iowa City), June 5, 1850.

Finally, the state Democratic platform called for universal support of the party's nominees for state offices and for the two congressional seats. To succeed the retiring Democratic governor, Ansel Briggs, the convention nominated Stephen B. Hempstead. George W. McCleary was nominated for secretary of state, while William Pattie and Israel Kister obtained the convention's endorsement for auditor and treasurer.

The nomination of Hempstead for governor was a wise move. As a native of New England, he would appeal to the Northern element in the state; as a loyal Democrat he would receive the support of the Southern group. His was a record of long service to the state, dating back to 1838, when he had won election to the First Legislative Assembly of Iowa Territory. His nomination was a fitting reward for loyal service to the Democratic party as well as to the people of Iowa.[5]

The Democratic press applauded the selection of Hempstead as his party's standard-bearer. The Democratic *Iowa State Gazette* of Burlington, perhaps one of the two or three most influential papers in the state, hailed Hempstead as a man of "talent . . . and valuable experience. Possessed of enlarged and comprehensive views, . . . his nomination . . . gives general satisfaction."[6]

The Whig party, striving to wrest the state from the Democrats for the first time, held its convention in May.[7] The Whigs nominated James Harlan for governor, Isaac Cook for secretary of state, William H. Seevers for auditor, and Evan Jay for treasurer. Harlan, not yet thirty years old, a native of Illinois and recently arrived in the state, later declined the nomination because of his age (according to the state constitution a governor had to be thirty years old at the time of election, and Harlan would not

[5] Benjamin F. Shambaugh (ed.), *The Messages and Proclamations of the Governors of Iowa*, I, 423–24.

[6] *Iowa State Gazette* (Burlington), June 19, 1850.

[7] *Iowa Weekly Republican*, January 9 and April 7, 1850.

reach that age until eleven days after the election).[8] His with-drawal forced the Whig executive committee to make a substi-tute nomination one month later in the person of James L. Thompson, of Johnson County.[9]

The Whig platform betrayed evidence of a divided organiza-tion which leaned very strongly to, or was dominated by, the free-soil or antislavery elements in the party. The platform con-tained a forceful plank on "Free Men, Free Territory, and Free States."[10] The same sentiment was reflected in the platform plank dealing with the compromise bills pending in the Senate. While calling for the immediate admission of California into the Union as a free state, the platform remained awkwardly silent on the other compromise resolutions. Perhaps silence provided the only solution for the unfortunate dilemma facing the Whigs. To con-demn the other measures would be tantamount to a disavowal of the national party stalwarts, Henry Clay and Daniel Webster, who had so strongly endorsed the compromise. On the other hand, unqualified acceptance of the bills would have invited, and un-doubtedly reaped, abuse from the free-soil wing of the party.

Other planks in the Whig platform lauded the administration of Zachary Taylor and called for the election of a Whig Congress to sustain his program. Another plank demanded an amendment of the Iowa constitution, which had been largely a Democratic creation. At this early date such an appeal fell upon deaf ears, but within a year or two it would receive a wider endorsement. On the matter of internal improvements the Whigs, in order to prevent further disruptions in the party, said absolutely nothing.

[8] James Harlan to Whig State Executive Committee, May 25, 1850, *ibid.*, May 29, 1850.

[9] *Ibid.*, May 29 and July 3, 1850. The Dubuque (Iowa) *Tribune* described Thompson as "an exemplary Christian, a friend to more liberal constitutional provisions in behalf of companies chartered within the State for objects of Public Improvement, and a tiller of the soil." Quoted in *Iowa Weekly Republican*, July 24, 1850.

[10] Sherman, "Political Party Platforms in Iowa," 110–12.

Thus the Whigs prepared to wage political battle with their heretofore victorious opponents armed with a slate of candidates weakened by the withdrawal of their principal nominee and with a platform distinguished mainly by its irresolute position on the most popular issues of the day. For the Whig party the battle would be an uphill struggle.

For Congress, the Democrats of the First Congressional District (which embraced the southern half of Iowa) with a minimum of haggling nominated Bernhart Henn, a native of New York and a resident of Iowa since its territorial days.[11] His Whig opponent was George G. Wright, an Indiana native.[12]

In the Second Congressional District (covering the northern portion of the state but including the southeastern counties as far as Des Moines County) the Whigs nominated William H. Henderson,[13] who was to conduct his campaign on the basis of the time-honored Whig tenets of internal improvements and high tariff, accompanied by a general condemnation of slavery.[14] To run against him the Democrats designated Lincoln Clark, of Dubuque, at their June district convention, but not without a good deal of internal bickering and a long session of balloting.[15]

The representatives from central Iowa, principally those from Johnson, Scott, and Cedar counties, opposed the party's first choice, Judge Thomas Wilson, from Dubuque. With Muscatine and Des Moines counties casting the deciding ballots, Lincoln Clark emerged as the "compromise" candidate of the convention.[16] Nevertheless, several bitterly disappointed delegates from

---

[11] *Iowa State Gazette*, June 5, 1850; *Biographical Directory of the American Congress 1774–1949*, 1299.

[12] *Iowa Weekly Republican*, April 17, 1850; Edward H. Stiles, "Prominent Men of Early Iowa," *Annals of Iowa*, 3rd ser., Vol. X (1912), 255.

[13] *Iowa Weekly Republican*, June 26, 1850.

[14] Dubuque (Iowa) *Telegraph* quoted, *ibid.*, July 11, 1850.

[15] *Iowa State Gazette*, May 15 and June 12, 1850.

[16] James Grant to Laurel Summers, June 15, 1850, in the Laurel Summers Correspondence at the Iowa State Department of History and Archives in Des Moines.

central Iowa delivered hostile speeches to the convention condemning the Dubuque party leadership.[17] Clark's selection was, however, popular in the district as a whole.

Lincoln Clark, a native of Massachusetts, had made something of a name for himself in Alabama before moving to Iowa in 1848.[18] It was perhaps his former residence in that slaveholding state which prompted one of the leading Whig papers in the state to brand Clark as a man "too deeply tainted with a love for the music of the lash, the clanking chains, and the heavy sighs and groans of slavery, to receive the aid and comfort of a freeman's vote."[19]

The resolutions adopted by the Democratic Second District convention followed the lead of the state party platform in warmly approving the compromise measures. A plank likewise condemned Secretary Ewing's decision concerning the Des Moines River land grant. Finally, the platform called for future donations of land to the state for use in internal improvements.[20] The latter was a cry that would become very popular in Iowa during the coming years, especially in connection with railroad construction.

A third party to enter the field was the small but vocal Free-Soil party, officially known as the Free Democracy, which campaigned chiefly upon an antislavery platform and had little else to offer to the voters. Formed in 1848 in time to offer candidates in the election of that year, the Iowa Free-Soilers, practically all of whom were abolitionists, included among their numbers remnants of the old Liberty party and some antislavery Democrats, but were chiefly men with Whig antecedents. Leaders of the Free-Soil group included William Penn Clarke, Jonathan W. Cattell, George Shedd, and Samuel A. Howe. Howe edited the organ of the party, the *Iowa True Democrat*, at Mount Pleasant.

[17] *Davenport* (Iowa) *Gazette*, June 13, 1850.
[18] *Biographical Directory of Congress*, 982.
[19] *Iowa Weekly Republican*, July 31, 1850.
[20] *Iowa State Gazette*, June 12, 1850.

41

Later the Reverend Asa Turner and George Magoun assumed positions of leadership in the organization.[21]

Since the Whigs, too, cherished known antislavery sympathies and, indeed, counted among their supporters many who would have done better to wear the label of the Free-Soilers, there was some talk of a union or coalition between the two parties. No fusion occurred, however, for the Whigs demanded as their price for cooperation, let alone union or coalition, unqualified support from the Free-Soilers. The latter, however, did not intend to drop their own slate of candidates.[22]

The Free-Soil party entered candidates for all the state offices, as well as for the congressional seats. William Penn Clarke carried his party's banner in the gubernatorial contest. Born in Maryland, Clarke had emigrated to Iowa in 1844 by way of Pennsylvania and Ohio. A former Whig, he had aided the cause of that party until he formally joined the Free-Soilers in 1848. He was an appropriate choice, particularly in view of his later efforts on behalf of John Brown and the Free State men in Kansas in the mid-1850's. No more ardent antislavery advocate than Clarke could be found in Iowa.[23] To run for the congressional seats, the Free-Soilers picked George Shedd for the First District and John H. Dayton for the Second District. Neither man rose to political prominence in Iowa.

The voters in the First Congressional District were also asked in 1850 to select a representative, at a special election to be held in September, to fill out the term of William Thompson, who had lost his seat as a result of a ruling by a special investigating committee in the House of Representatives.[24] The controversy over Thompson's seat dated back to 1848, when he had won a narrow

21 Theodore C. Smith, *The Liberty and Free Soil Parties in the Northwest*, 157, 216–19, 266, 321.

22 *Ibid.*, 218; *Davenport Gazette*, February 14, 1850.

23 Benjamin F. Gue, *History of Iowa*, IV, 53; Erik M. Eriksson, "William Penn Clarke," *Iowa Journal of History and Politics*, Vol. XXV (1927), 4–9, 38.

24 *Iowa Weekly Republican*, September 18, 1850.

victory over his Whig opponent, Daniel F. Miller. The latter had immediately protested the election. The original quarrel had involved the legality of certain electoral returns in Pottawattamie County, the right of the Mormons to vote, and charges concerning stolen election ledgers.[25] The House of Representatives, unable or unwilling to decide the argument on the merits of the evidence presented, had merely declared the seat vacant after procrastinating over the issue for more than a year. Both Thompson and Miller again opposed each other for the short term of Congress that remained.[26]

One Delazon Smith, however, complicated the Democratic side by refusing to accept the verdict of the special convention which had nominated Thompson again. Smith decided to run as an independent candidate for the post. Whether he really believed he could win is, of course, unknown, but his candidacy caused the Democrats no little concern. He was a good speaker and had an outstanding political personality. A Methodist minister, he had gained some earlier notoriety following his dismissal from Oberlin College in 1837, when he had published a tract, *Oberlin Unmasked*, a diatribe accusing faculty and students of Negro adoration and miscegenation. He left Iowa after the election and in 1852 reached Oregon, where his political career blossomed, first as a member of the territorial legislature and later as a United States senator.[27] That the Democrats were worried about Smith was evident in the virulent attacks which appeared in the Democratic press, one such organ christening him "Delusion" Smith.[28]

Once the various contesting parties had selected their candi-

[25] Muscatine (Iowa) *Journal*, July 20, 1850, quoted in Louis B. Schmidt, "The Miller-Thompson Election Contest," *Iowa Journal of History and Politics*, Vol. XII (1914), 121.

[26] *Ibid.*, 121–23.

[27] Robert Johannsen, *Frontier Politics and the Sectional Conflict: The Pacific Northwest on the Eve of the Civil War*, 65n.

[28] *Ibid.*, 124; *Iowa State Gazette*, August 28, 1850.

dates and published their platforms, they began to campaign in earnest. The Democrats had only one issue to carry to the voters of Iowa. This they proceeded to do with energy and efficiency. The leaders of the party believed that the people were very much alarmed over the growing bitterness which had been increasing between the sections during the past several years. They believed, too, that Iowans desired nothing more than to preserve the Union and to restore harmony to the nation as a whole. Finally, they believed that virtually everyone in the state save the most fanatic was enthusiastic about the compromise measures designed to allay the erupting passions which threatened to destroy the Union. Hence, when the Democrats determined to stake their bid for office exclusively on the single issue of the Compromise of 1850, they felt certain that such a maneuver would be a popular one with voters and nonvoters alike.[29]

While the extremists in the North and South raged and fumed, the moderate leaders from both sections struggled to discover the formula which might resolve the controversial issue to the satisfaction of both sides. The press in Iowa sincerely prayed that some "master spirit" would cool hostile tempers so that harmony could be restored once again to the councils of the government. One journal called upon the "Great West" to settle the quarrel which the other sections seemed incapable of deciding.[30]

An editorial which appeared in the columns of the influential *Iowa Democratic Enquirer* of Muscatine best expressed the position of the Iowa Democrats on the compromise. In a note of careful restraint the editor advised his readers: "Every good citizen should overlook the little of evil that may result, and be satisfied with the vast amount of good to flow from a definite and per-

[29] David S. Sparks, "The Decline of the Democratic Party in Iowa, 1850–1860," *Iowa Journal of History*, Vol. LIII (1955), 9–10; *New York Daily Times*, October 23, 1851.

[30] *Frontier Guardian* (Council Bluffs, Iowa), March 6, 1850; *The Iowa Weekly Republican*, May 15, 1850.

manent adjustment of questions which have always proved too much for American equanimity."[31]

The "little of evil" undoubtedly referred to one of the measures drawn up to placate the interests of the South, a bill which became the Fugitive Slave Act. This law provided that slaveowners pursuing their fleeing charges into the free states could demand, and expect to receive, aid from the local federal and state authorities in recovering the fugitives. Another section stipulated that anyone aiding and abetting a fugitive slave would be liable to fine and imprisonment.[32] The law was drafted to eliminate one of the chief sources of grievance which the South harbored against the North, for Northern collusion with the escaping Negroes was causing serious financial losses to Southern slavemasters.

Nevertheless, the Fugitive Slave Act provoked most of the opposition to the compromise measures. All the other acts—those dealing with the admission of California into the Union as a free state, the abolition of the slave trade in the District of Columbia, the organization of Utah and New Mexico as territories, the settlement of the financial and boundary claims of Texas—were accepted by Iowans with little or no animosity. Indeed, many had long clamored for California's admission as a free state. Still, at least one journal charged that a coalition of Northern and Southern senators had deliberately impeded the admission of California by introducing other issues or by granting needless concessions to the South.[33] Apparently the Fugitive Slave Act was one of these "needless concessions" to slavery.

Newspaper opposition to the Fugitive Slave Act was not, however, unanimous. While one editor raged about a "scheme of infamy," others found nothing wrong with the act and announced

[31] *Iowa Democratic Enquirer* (Muscatine), May 30, 1850.
[32] *The Statutes at Large and Treaties of the United States of America*, Vol. IX (1854), 462–65.
[33] *Iowa Weekly Republican*, May 15, 1850.

themselves "utterly opposed to open, organized resistance" to the measure. They cautioned the North against advocating contravention to a lawful enactment, lest the Union be destroyed and the states be subjected to a bath "in American Blood."[34] The *Daily Telegraph* of Burlington chided papers which opposed the law: "The North got what it wanted ... and this attitude is wrong. It sets a bad example of ignoring the law and endangers the compromise. If a negro runs away he knows the risk. Runaway slaves are objects of pity, but armed resistance to the law is wrong."[35]

In the United States Senate, Iowa's Democratic senators, Augustus C. Dodge and George W. Jones, worked indefatigably to secure the passage of all five of the compromise resolutions distilled from those originally introduced by Henry Clay. Unlike many of their senatorial colleagues whose home-state legislatures had issued instructions at one time or another to uphold the principles of the Wilmot Proviso, or to protect the institutions and interests of the South, Dodge and Jones were free to exercise their best judgment and vote according to the dictates of their consciences.[36] Jones, declaring his opposition to slavery in principle, nevertheless defended the right of the institution to exist where "the constitutions and laws of my country have placed it." Still, he would strive with all his power "to give quietus to this distracting question." Thus, since "the bill now before us will effect that object ... I shall record my vote for it with unmixed pleasure."[37]

Dodge likewise took his place beside the supporters of all the compromise measures, including the Fugitive Slave Act. Con-

[34] *Ibid.*, May 15 and November 6, 1850; *Daily Hawk-Eye* (Burlington, Iowa), November 14, 1850.

[35] Quoted in George A. Boeck, "An Early Iowa Community: Aspects of Economic, Social, and Political Development in Burlington, Iowa, 1833–1866," unpublished Ph.D. dissertation, University of Iowa, 1961, 225–26.

[36] Hamilton, *Prologue to Conflict: The Crisis and Compromise of 1850*, 114.

[37] 31 Cong., 1 sess., *Congressional Globe*, Appendix, 1716.

cerning the latter Dodge declared without hesitation or equivocation that "the southern states and people have a right to the enjoyment of their property, and to the security and protection guaranteed to it and to them under the Federal Constitution; and neither my State nor its Representatives seek to interfere with either." While he could not state without reservation that the laws would be "destined to effect the good results which those who voted for them intended," he believed that "they have done good, are doing good, and should be religiously lived up to and carried out in good faith."[38]

Both Dodge and Jones blamed a few fanatics for trying to obstruct the beneficial operation of the compromise in general and of the Fugitive Slave Act in particular. Jones attributed the so-called evils of slavery to the fanaticism of the Free-Soilers and abolitionists rather than to any actual suffering endured by the slaves themselves. Dodge severely took to task those who sought to induce slaves to flee from their bondage and then ceased to care for the fugitive Negroes.[39]

The voting in the Senate on the various compromise proposals clearly demonstrated that the Democrats more consistently and more faithfully backed the measures than did the Whigs. Moreover, Iowa's senators favored all the bills on every ballot. Only Democrats Sam Houston of Texas and Daniel Sturgeon of Pennsylvania and Whig John Wales of Delaware could boast of similar voting records. Eight other senators cast ballots approving four of the acts and abstained from voting on a fifth. Thus only thirteen senators gave what could be termed full support to the Compromise of 1850.[40]

While Whig opposition nationally was more pronounced than

[38] 31 Cong., 2 sess., *ibid.*, Appendix, 310.

[39] 31 Cong., 1 sess., *ibid.*, Appendix, 1716; 31 Cong., 2 sess., *ibid.*, Appendix, 311.

[40] Holman Hamilton, "Democratic Senate Leadership and the Compromise of 1850," *Mississippi Valley Historical Review*, Vol. XLI (1954), 407–409; Roy F. Nichols, *The Democratic Machine 1850–1854*, 82; 33 Cong., 2 sess., *Congressional Globe*, Appendix, 382.

that of the Democrats, in Iowa the Whigs could do nothing but express general approval of the legislation or remain silent. The Whig party organ in Burlington, for example, averred:

> We wish to express no opposition to the general features of Mr. Clay's plan. It is our wish as much as his to put an end to all causes of future disquiet among our people. Perhaps there are some portions that we might not entirely agree to—but as a whole, we would be willing to see them adopted rather than matters should remain in their present condition.[41]

The same journal even went so far as to praise the work of Senator Dodge on behalf of the compromise. Indeed, the paper included all of Dodge's congressional colleagues from Iowa (all Democrats) in its general commendation of their labors.[42] Nevertheless, the paper did propose changes in the Fugitive Slave Act; the editor was "against the features which compel freemen to be slave catchers and offer rewards for catching fugitive slaves, some who have lived a long time in freedom."[43]

Other Whig papers also applauded the compromise bills, for with their passage "all fears of a dissolution of the Union or of a hostile coalition between any of its members will doubtless cease, and, we trust, peace, harmony, and fraternal feelings will again be the order of the day."[44] Actually the Whig press had little choice but to accept the compromise, for it was undoubtedly one of the most popular issues ever introduced into Iowa politics, at least up to that time.[45] Nor did the Democrats shrink from accepting the plaudits of the public for the measures, regardless of the fact that they had originated in the fertile mind of Henry Clay.

While the Democrats sought to achieve victory by promoting

[41] *Daily Hawk-Eye,* June 13, 1850.
[42] *Ibid.,* March 14, 1850.
[43] Quoted in Boeck, "An Early Iowa Community," 225.
[44] *Iowa Weekly Republican,* September 25, 1850.
[45] David S. Sparks, "The Birth of the Republican Party in Iowa, 1848 to 1860," unpublished Ph.D. dissertation, University of Chicago, 1951, 52.

the compromise, the Whigs vainly attempted to remind Iowans that they ought to consider other issues during the campaign. For one thing, as the Whigs pointed out, the Democrats had been in control of the national government for the better part of twenty years and of the machinery of the state government since its organization as a territory.[46] The state of Iowa ought to be "redeemed from that thraldom under which she has groaned ever since her existence," wrote one editor.[47] Furthermore, Whig government would be safer than Democratic government: the latter "exhibits a recklessness of character, tending to unwarrantable extremes that endanger the peace and prosperity of the nation," was the opinion of another.[48]

Whig papers also rehashed the old issue of internal improvements or demanded an amendment to the state constitution. After all, the editors asserted, the Whigs had long advocated the use of federal funds to clear away the barriers obstructing internal commerce throughout the nation and in Iowa. Yet the Democrats continued to vote down such proposals, either through congressional action or by presidential veto.[49]

The Whigs, too, attacked Iowa's congressional delegation in an attempt to demonstrate that Iowans in Congress were too prone to accept the position of the South on the question of slavery.[50] Here clearly was a maneuver to capture the votes of the Free-Soilers as well as of Democrats who opposed the "peculiar institution" on moral grounds.

But the efforts of the Whigs to inject their favorite issues into the campaign, to divert attention from the popular compromise, and to malign Iowa's Democratic officials proved useless in the

[46] *Iowa Weekly Republican*, July 3, 1850.
[47] Dubuque *Telegraph* quoted, *ibid.*, February 6, 1850.
[48] *Frontier Guardian*, May 29, 1850.
[49] Cincinnati *Gazette* quoted in *Iowa Weekly Republican*, January 16, 1850. Iowa's Democratic congressional delegation labored zealously to procure federal funds to aid projects of internal improvements, especially river and harbor improvements. 31 Cong., 1 sess., *Congressional Globe*, 210.
[50] *Daily Hawk-Eye*, February 7, July 25, and November 21, 1850.

49

face of the great national crisis which the compromise seemed destined to resolve. Cries for internal improvements and for amending the state constitution could not compete effectively with the compromise as a campaign issue. In the end the polls told the story.

August 5, 1850, was the day of reckoning for the candidates. Some 25,500 voters went to the polls to cast their ballots. Once again, as in previous elections in Iowa, the Democrats carried the day. Their success, however, could by no means be termed overwhelming, for the margins of victory received by the successful candidates were relatively narrow in virtually all instances. Nevertheless, the Democratic sweep of the offices at stake was complete.[51]

In the gubernatorial contest Hempstead defeated his substitute Whig rival, Thompson, by a vote of 12,486 to 11,452. Free-Soiler Clarke ran a poor third with but 570 votes, more than 300 of which came in three southeastern counties, Lee, Henry, and Washington. Hempstead's final tally represented 52.85 per cent of the total votes cast, while Thompson received 44.88 per cent and Clarke a mere 2.23 per cent.[52]

In the congressional race in the First District, which contained a somewhat larger voting population than that of the Second District, Henn eked out a narrow victory over his Whig opponent, Wright. The former received 7,437 votes to the latter's 6,985 votes. Shedd brought up the rear with 301 votes, most of which he won in Henry and Lee counties. Henn's majority was a slim 50.51 per cent of the total votes recorded. Wright attracted 47.44 per cent, and Shedd's total netted him 2.04 per cent. A shift

[51] The election returns from which the percentage statistics were compiled are on file in the Office of the Secretary of State, Capitol Building, Des Moines, and are entered in a ledger entitled "Election Records, 1848–1860." A microfilm copy of these returns is on file at the Library of the University of Iowa at Iowa City.

[52] *Ibid.*

of fewer than 230 votes from Henn to Wright would have cost the former the victory.[53]

In the contest held in the Second Congressional District, the picture was far more favorable for the Democratic aspirant, Lincoln Clark. Clark polled 5,745 votes, while his Whig rival, Henderson, received 4,775 votes. John H. Dayton, the Free-Soil candidate, scraped together 107 votes in his hopeless quest for office. Clark's 53.73 per cent of the total votes was the highest for his party in the important races. Henderson attracted 44.66 per cent of the total, while Dayton had to console himself with but 1 per cent.[54]

The extent of the Democratic sweep, albeit on the basis of slender margins, is best illustrated in the returns of the races for the assembly. Here the Democratic achievement was no less than overwhelming. Of the nineteen senate vacancies, the Democrats captured thirteen, while in the balloting for Iowa's lower house the Democrats took thirty-five of the thirty-nine seats.[55]

In the contests for the other state offices the Democrats attracted totals very much in keeping with that won by Hempstead. The honor of heading the Democratic list with the most votes fell to the newly elected auditor, William Pattie, who received 13,529 ballots.[56]

The following month, on September 24, the run-off election was held among candidates William Thompson, Daniel F. Miller, and Delazon Smith for the unexpired term in Congress. Although the Democrats had already captured the seat for the coming full term, interest in the election was surprisingly strong. Nevertheless, for what it may have been worth to him as a moral victory,

[53] *Ibid.*

[54] *Ibid.* Running independently, one Alex McEad received 63 votes from Washington County and 2 votes from Johnson County.

[55] Louis Pelzer, "The History and Principles of the Democratic Party of Iowa, 1846–1857," *Iowa Journal of History and Politics*, Vol. VI (1908), 192.

[56] Election Records, 1848–1860.

Miller defeated his Democratic opponent by a vote of 5,463 to 4,801. Smith received 365 votes. Since more than 2,600 voters had remained away from the polls, Miller's task was somewhat lightened and his success somewhat tarnished.[57]

Hempstead carried all but ten of the forty-two counties which returned votes. His party's congressional candidates fared almost as well, taking twenty-nine of the forty-two counties. The only two counties in western Iowa that went to the Whigs were Fremont and Pottawattamie, both of which would shift to the Democratic ranks in later elections.

The Free-Soil party, while failing to carry a single county in any of the contests, rolled up its largest totals in Henry, Washington, Lee, Louisa, Linn, and Jones counties. In Henry and Washington counties the Free-Soilers attracted more than 10 per cent of the votes recorded there. These counties contained not only large settlements of Southern-born Whigs but also sizable communities of Quakers, whose antislavery position was exceedingly strong. Many of the Quakers were already beginning to make local reputations for themselves as operators of the Underground Railroad. Hence Free-Soil sympathy could be expected to be intense in this region of the state.

In the state as a whole, it is difficult to discern any significantly peculiar voting patterns, for the Democrats in 1850 displayed considerable strength in all sections of Iowa. Areas with heaviest Democratic voting returns were concentrated in the central counties bordering on the Mississippi River, along the western fringes of settlement inland from the Missouri River, and along the Iowa border counties just north of Missouri. Generally speaking, the Democrats averaged about 53 to 55 per cent of the total votes in most of the counties.

If the leaders of the Iowa Democratic party examined closely

[57] *Ibid.* A comparison of the results of the regular election with the returns of the special election reveals that the Democratic totals decreased by 2,636 at the special election. Whig totals declined only 1,529 for the same contest.

the returns for their state, they doubtless viewed them with mixed feelings rather than unbridled joy. From the southern half of Iowa the Mormons would soon journey to their Zion from their temporary home in Pottawattamie County, decimating the population of that county. With the departure of the Mormons would go a source of Whig strength, for Pottawattamie, through the bloc voting of the Mormons, gave the Whigs a majority of more than 370 votes which, had these been subtracted from Wright's totals, would have given Henn a more comfortable margin of victory. In the First Congressional District, then, the Democrats had every reason to be optimistic about their party's political prospects.

The Second District, however, should have caused the Democrats no little concern, for it was in this district that signs of party discord were evident. Even after Clark's nomination delegates from the central counties had remained morose, bitter, hostile, and largely unplacated. Unless the breach could be healed, Clark's political career could very well be abortive. Swirling beneath the surface, such disagreement could erupt to wreck the party in a year when the tremendously popular compromise issue would no longer unite the majority of Iowans behind the Democratic banner.

For the present, however, the Iowa Democrats, victorious throughout the state, having endorsed the labors of their senators in behalf of the compromise and having won a display of confidence from the voters, could agree with the *Iowa State Gazette* which boasted that Iowa and the Democratic party were "invulnerable to the attack of the combined forces of whigism, abolitionism, Mormonism, and in fact all other isms put together."[58] But the real danger, at the moment at least, lay from within rather than without the party.

The Compromise of 1850, more than any other issue or combination of issues, enabled the Democratic party of Iowa to retain

[58] August 21, 1850.

its power in the state. Astute Democratic politicians, correctly analyzing the preelection sentiment of the voters, had parlayed the popular compromise laws into another Iowa party triumph. In 1850 the people of Iowa were not especially aroused by moral arguments directed against the existence of slavery in the United States, although most would have opposed any further geographic extension of slavery. But they were deeply and immediately concerned about the preservation of a harmonious federal Union which extremists in the North and South threatened. The compromise measures, and the Democratic party which had so resolutely supported them, held out the promise of restoring peace to the nation. For this reason Iowa voters gave Democratic candidates their support in 1850.

Politics as Usual

Tнɛ people of Iowa demonstrated the characteristics usually associated with the residents of frontier cities, towns, and outlying areas. They were ambitious, industrious, energetic, aggressive, hospitable, largely self-reliant, serious in their politics, active in support of their principles and ideals, and dedicated to the prevailing democratic political system in which they placed their faith. The election of 1850 had been hard-fought, exciting, and emotional principally because of the fury generated by the promulgation of the Compromise acts. Nevertheless, Iowans also enjoyed themselves immensely, for they delighted in attending rallies, feasting at well-supplied barbecues, and devouring the endless words delivered by sonorous speakers.[1]

Emotionally drained by the events of 1850, Iowa voters wel-

---

[1] *Burlington* (Iowa) *Daily Telegraph,* June 21, 1851; Clement Eaton, *Henry Clay and the Art of American Politics,* 153; *Iowa State Gazette* (Burlington), January 15, 1851.

comed the respite from politics which the new year offered, for political activity was decidedly limited and of little more than local importance. Indeed, the *Iowa State Gazette* complained about the apathy of the voters as the election for superintendent of public instruction, as well as for many county offices, drew near in the spring of 1851. Democrat Thomas H. Benton, described by a friendly paper as a "candidate confessedly worthy and popular . . . a gentleman of approved ability," easily defeated his Whig rival, William G. Woodward, for the state's principal educational position.[2]

Iowa's politicians of all parties, however—the strongly entrenched Democrats, the aspiring Whigs, the highly vocal Free-Soilers—eagerly awaited and mapped plans for the approaching elections in 1852, a year of no little political significance in the state. Presidential, congressional, and state contests would take place in 1852. Moreover, the election to fill the vacancies in the legislature was of more than usual importance, for the new state assembly would face the responsibility of selecting a United States senator. The term of the Democratic incumbent, George W. Jones, was scheduled to expire in 1853.

The Whigs launched their election campaign during the waning months of 1851. They endeavored, among other things, to increase popular support for their long-cherished program of internal improvements with federal aid. Theirs was the task of convincing Iowans that a vote for a Democrat would be a wasted ballot, for the national Democratic party continued to oppose internal improvements at federal expense.[3] This was the only line of attack which the Whigs could have adopted on the issue of internal improvements. Even the Whigs' own newspapers conceded that Iowa's congressional delegation had been working diligently to persuade Congress to make appropriations for river

[2] March 19, 1851; Election Records, 1848–1860, Office of the Secretary of State of Iowa, Des Moines.
[3] *Iowa Weekly Republican* (Iowa City), June 11, 1851.

and road improvements in the state. That Senators Dodge and Jones had been especially industrious in their efforts to secure federal funds for use within the state not even the most partisan Whig could deny. That the senators had been unsuccessful could not have been disputed either.

Dear to the hearts of Iowans, especially those who lived along the banks of the Mississippi, was the project to improve the navigation of the upper portions of the river. Just above Keokuk a series of rapids considerably hampered navigation and during certain times of the year made ship passage impossible. Iowa's senators continually sought to win funds from Congress to improve the river channel.[4] Nor was Democratic press support for certain projects entirely absent. In the words of one of the more influential papers, the *Iowa State Gazette*, the West required a "permanent system of internal improvements."[5] Consequently, all the Whigs could do was to hammer away at the obvious inconsistency between the programs of the state and national Democratic organizations.

The Whigs also toiled to win public acceptance of their tariff position. They painted a glowing picture of an industrialized state which could become a reality only through "adequate and constant protection—to our industry, against the half-paid laborers of Europe."[6] They chided the Democrats for continuing the Walker Tariff of 1846, for everyone knew that Democrats professed "to believe in *free trade*."[7]

With another issue the Whigs could be hopeful of greater success in their appeal to the voters. The state constitution, adopted in 1846, essentially embodied all the Jacksonian principles valued by the Democratic party, which, dominating the

[4] 32 Cong., 1 sess., *Congressional Globe*, 41; 33 Cong., 2 sess., *ibid.*, 580, 782, 850, 525; Richard M. Young to George W. Jones, December 26, 1851, in the George W. Jones Papers at the State Historical Society of Iowa in Iowa City.
[5] *Iowa State Gazette*, March 26, 1851.
[6] *Des Moines Valley Whig* (Keokuk, Iowa) quoted in *Iowa Weekly Republican*, June 11, 1851.
[7] *Ibid.*

57

constitutional convention, wrote the provisions of the document. As early as 1850, Whig journals began to criticize the constitution, particularly the section which prohibited the establishment of public banking facilities in the state. The only public bank incorporated in the state from the earliest settlement to the adoption of a new constitution in 1857, was the Miner's Bank of Dubuque. This institution, however, had received its charter of incorporation from the Wisconsin territorial legislature in 1836 and had remained active only until 1844. Thus, so far the citizens of Iowa had been without public banks.[8]

The absence of public banks, the Whigs carefully pointed out, was creating much hardship and inconvenience for Iowa's farmers and businessmen. Paper currency from other states flooded Iowa in ever-increasing quantities, drawing the hard currency, gold and silver, out of the state. The adoption of a free banking system would, Whigs believed, remove the objections of monopolistic control but at the same time carry with it all the practical advantages of public banking.[9] Moreover, the Whig press added, other states had erected proper barriers to prevent or guard against the few evils that might arise in connection with banking.[10]

The chartering of public banks, however, called for a revision of the state constitution, a step the Democrats were as loath to take as the Whigs were quick to advocate.[11] In his inaugural address late in 1850, Governor Hempstead stated the official Democratic position on the question of public banks and, in-

---

[8] Ruth A. Gallaher, "Money in Pioneer Iowa 1838–1865," *Iowa Journal of History and Politics*, Vol. XXXII (1934), 13.

[9] *Frontier Guardian* (Council Bluffs, Iowa), March 7, 1851.

[10] Louis Pelzer, "The History and Principles of the Democratic Party of Iowa, 1846–1857," *Iowa Journal of History and Politics*, Vol. VI (1908), 201–202; *Des Moines Valley Whig*, March 11 and May 20, 1852; *Iowa Weekly Republican*, January 28, 1852; *Davenport* (Iowa) *Gazette*, May 20, 1852; *Burlington Daily Telegraph*, October 12, 1852.

[11] *Des Moines Valley Whig*, May 15, 1851; *Iowa Weekly Republican*, December 11, 1850.

directly, on the issue of revising the constitution to effect this objective. He declared that without banks in Iowa "to create distress or panic by their failures, contractions, and expansions ... our citizens relying on their own industry and frugality ... [are] showing to the world that bank indulgences, paper money, and special privileges are unnecessary to secure to a people happiness and prosperity."[12] Supporters of changes in the constitution could be certain that as long as Hempstead remained in office the constitution would be undisturbed. Still, it was an area in which the Democrats, while they continued to maintain an increasingly unpopular position, might prove to be vulnerable to criticism. Nor did the Whigs spare their opponents from embarrassment when they called attention to the fact that the latter, while claiming to favor "*an exclusive metallic currency*," nevertheless did nothing to prevent the circulation in Iowa of paper currency from banks in other states.[13]

The Whigs probed to discover other spheres where the Democrats might be susceptible to effective attack. Shrewdly assessing the difficulties that had occurred during the Democratic convention in the Second Congressional District in 1850, the Whigs sought to fan any lingering embers into real flames of party discord. The press, for example, pointedly remarked that both Dodge and Jones, while visiting various parts of the state before departing for Washington to attend the opening of Congress, had neglected to visit the counties of central Iowa. At the nominating convention in 1850 several delegates from central Iowa had expressed bitter feelings to the assembly because of their dissatisfaction with the nomination of Lincoln Clark for Congress. Whigs wryly noted that while southern Iowa had benefited from Dodge's exertions, and while Jones had faithfully served northern Iowa, the central sections of the state derived no benefits from

[12] Benjamin F. Shambaugh (ed.), *The Messages and Proclamations of the Governors of Iowa*, I, 426.
[13] *Iowa Weekly Republican*, June 11, 1851.

these gentlemen.[14] Coincidentally, Dodge made his home in Burlington, which was in the south, and Jones lived in the north in Dubuque. Whether any restive elements continued to lurk among the Democrats of central Iowa remained to be seen; Whigs kept watering any seeds of dissension which the Democrats themselves might have sown.

While the Whigs tried to generate support for their program, raised a question or two for Iowans to ponder, and endeavored to stir discontent in the ranks of their opponents, the Democrats late in 1851 selected the issue that became the basis for the party's presidential campaign in 1852. On December 16, Senator Jones introduced in the Senate the resolutions of the Iowa General Assembly in support of the Compromise of 1850. Jones himself added that he believed that "these resolutions . . . reflect the sentiments of the Democratic party of Iowa."[15] Thus the state of Iowa officially informed the nation that she fully supported the compromise measures. Three months later, on March 8, 1852, Lincoln Clark introduced the same resolutions in the House of Representatives.[16] The Democratic party of Iowa intended to adopt as its main issue for the approaching campaign the Compromise of 1850, which the organization had so successfully promoted two years earlier.

The Whigs began their political activity in the important election year of 1852 by calling a state convention for February, primarily to select delegates for the Whig national convention due to meet in mid-summer to choose the party's presidential and vice-presidential candidates. Nominees for the minor offices of the state, also selected by the Whig convention, were J. W. Jenkins, secretary of state; Asbury B. Porter, auditor; and Hosea B. Horn, treasurer.[17] None of the delegates chosen to represent Iowa at the national Whig conclave—D. W. Kilbourn, S. M. Bal-

[14] *Ibid.*, October 15, 1851.
[15] 32 Cong., 1 sess., *Congressional Globe*, 103.
[16] *Ibid.*, 700.
[17] *Iowa Weekly Republican*, January 21, 1852; *Burlington Daily Telegraph*,

lard, G. L. Nightingale, and Archibald McKenny—achieved prominence in Iowa political circles. They would journey to Baltimore unpledged to any of the aspiring presidential candidates, but with a known sympathy for Millard Fillmore, perhaps because of his close identification with the Compromise of 1850.[18]

The platform the Whigs adopted at their February meeting differed little from the official statement of the parent organization drawn up four months later. The national platform, a rather innocuous statement of principles in keeping with the vague and unknown sentiments of the party's nominees, Winfield Scott and William A. Green, affirmed the adherence of the Whigs to the tenets of the federal Constitution and to states' rights and reaffirmed the party position regarding the tariff and internal improvements. On the question of the Compromise of 1850 the Whig attitude was, at best, lukewarm. Owing to the presence of strong antislavery adherents in the organization, the party merely "acquiesced in" that series of laws and promised to "maintain them and insist upon their strict enforcement until time and experience shall demonstrate the necessity of further legislation to guard against the evasion of the law on the one hand, and the abuse of their powers on the other." Clearly the Whigs did not intend to accept the Compromise as a "finality."[19]

The Whig state platform praised the Fillmore administration, called for the usual tariff and internal improvements, and pledged to support the nominees of the party, whoever they were. On the compromise issue the state platform adopted a more favorable plank than did the national convention. One plank declared that the Whigs of Iowa considered the slavery question "as settled now and forever."[20]

March 1, 1852. Whig alternates were H. T. Reid, James Noster, T. D. Crocker, and W. G. Woodward.

[18] *Iowa Weekly Republican,* July 30, 1851.

[19] Kirk Porter (comp.), *National Party Platforms,* 36–37.

[20] Roy V. Sherman, "Political Party Platforms in Iowa," unpublished M.A. thesis, State University of Iowa, 1926, 116–18.

61

The state convention of the Democratic party met in May. Like the Whigs, the Democrats selected their delegates to the party's national convention, scheduled to gather in Baltimore on June 1, without encumbering them with official instructions. It was no secret, however, that the delegates—William F. Coolbaugh, A. W. Carpenter, George Gillaspie, and Philip B. Bradley—leaned strongly toward Stephen A. Douglas, the popular senator from neighboring Illinois, because he was, in the words of a partisan journal, the "Young Giant of the West." Indeed, Douglas had been hopeful that Iowans would support his candidacy: "All that is necessary now to enable me to succeed is to show that the West is ready to unite on me. It becomes important therefore that Missouri and Iowa should speak out." For the state's minor offices the convention renominated two incumbents, George W. McCleary for secretary of state and William Pattie for auditor. Martin L. Morris, a newcomer, received the nomination for the treasurer's post.[21]

The national Democratic platform reiterated the party's official views on the chief issues of the day, supporting a low tariff and opposing a national bank, internal improvements, and federal interference in the local affairs of states. Concerning the Compromise of 1850, the national Democratic party promised to "abide by and adhere to a faithful execution of the acts known as the compromise measures." Other planks reminded the voters that the war with Mexico had been a just conflict, upheld the Virginia and Kentucky Resolutions of 1798, vowed to maintain the rights of the states, and pledged continued resistance to "all monopolies and exclusive legislation for the benefit of the few at the expense of the many."[22] The refusal of the national convention to endorse the compromise as final reflected the failure

[21] *Jackson County Democrat* quoted in *Burlington Daily Telegraph*, May 12, 1852; Stephen A. Douglas to Samuel Treat, December 15, 1851, in Robert Johannsen (ed.), *The Letters of Stephen A. Douglas*, 233.
[22] Porter, *National Party Platforms*, 28–32.

of the Democratic congressional caucus to declare the measures final.[23] To head its ticket, the Democratic party selected a dark horse with Southern sympathies, Franklin Pierce of New Hampshire. William R. King of Alabama became his running mate.

The Iowa Democratic state platform was briefer than the document of the national party but similar in tone and content. It opposed a national bank and a protective tariff, but a carefully worded plank announced that the state organization favored internal improvements of a national character as opposed to the "wasteful, extravagant, and corrupt system of internal improvements" advocated by the Whigs. On the Compromise of 1850 the state platform was unequivocal: "We are in favor of the 'Compromise' as a *final* settlement of the questions which have so long agitated the country upon the subject of domestic slavery." Concerning the proposed revision of the state constitution, the local Democratic party assured the voters that it would endorse such a move "when the people shall manifest a desire for an alteration of the present constitution." Other planks opposed any change in the naturalization laws, called for a strict construction of the federal Constitution, and condemned "nullification" by any state, North or South.[24]

Adding to the excitement a presidential election normally generated was the presence on the ballot of the Free-Soil party with its own slate of candidates and its own platform. The Free-Soilers, however, did not enter candidates in the congressional races, preferring to concentrate on the county as well as the presidential contests. The Free-Soil candidates planned to conduct their electioneering on a platform of undisguised opposition to the Fugitive Slave Act coupled with a demand for the eradication of slavery from American soil. Various county gatherings pledged support to the Free-Soil presidential ticket of John P. Hale and George

[23] Roy F. Nichols, *The Democratic Machine 1850–1854*, 88.
[24] Sherman, "Political Party Platforms in Iowa," 113–15. Italics added.

W. Julian. Thus the stage was set for a three-party fight for Iowa's presidential electors.[25]

A few weeks after the close of their state convention, the Whigs published "An Address to the People of Iowa" in which they attacked the Democrats for their views on internal improvements, state banking, and constitutional revision. The address, to be sure, favored a change in the constitution to permit banking. In addition, it demanded federal aid "to improve the navigation of our rivers, harbors, and lakes; and make all needful appropriations for the general welfare, prosperity, and improvement of the country." Moreover, the Whigs taunted the Democrats for attempting to maintain a ridiculous, weak, absurd, and inconsistent position: the local party favored internal improvements, but the national organization opposed them.[26] Undoubtedly this charge disturbed some of the local Democratic leaders. Actually, however, the state Democratic platform had indeed been rather vague on the question of internal improvements, for the party had tried to steer clear of the issue.

The Whigs also continued to labor on behalf of a higher tariff. They insisted that a protective tariff would be beneficial not only to the interests of national industry but also to the Western farmer. A tariff would enable manufacturers to be certain of a home market for their goods and would increase employment, thus providing an expanded market for the produce of farms.[27] Here was another attempt to link the farmers of the West to the industrialists of the East in support of a protective tariff. Such a union was still about ten years away from realization.

But the efforts of the Whigs to stimulate interest in their time-honored issues seemed to meet with little or no success. Discussions of the tariff stirred few persons. Remarks favoring internal

[25] *Burlington Daily Telegraph*, June 7, 1852; *Davenport Gazette*, October 28, 1852.

[26] *Davenport Gazette*, April 22, 1852.

[27] *Ibid.*, October 28, 1852; Dubuque (Iowa) *Tribune* quoted in *Iowa Weekly Republican*, April 21, 1852.

improvements, though somewhat embarrassing to the Democrats, caused little concern. Even an appeal to the pocketbooks of Iowans regarding the lack of public banking facilities in the state did not seem to provoke the voters as much as the Whigs might have desired.[28]

An issue that could have been troublesome for the Democrats was the question of homesteads. Iowans were already beginning to call upon the federal government to give a portion of the public domain to bona fide settlers free of charge. There was a divergence of opinion, however, between the state and national organizations on the matter of homesteads. Although the state party favored homestead measures and sought congressional enactment of such legislation, the national party opposed homestead bills. Fortunately for the Democrats, none of the state's party platforms took official cognizance of the overtures for homesteads. The Democratic party of Iowa was thus spared another source of embarrassment.

All the issues which the Whigs sought to promote fell short of the mark when measured against the mainstay of the Democratic campaign, the Compromise of 1850. Two years earlier the compromise had demonstrated its extreme popularity. Although some of its appeal had worn off, it still held a hypnotic power over the voters of Iowa. That the slavery problem had been settled once and for all, as they believed, was a source of deep gratification to Iowans who had earlier feared for the preservation of the Union.

One historian of the period contends that the Democrats of Iowa were badly divided over the question of homesteads and internal improvements. To prevent damage to the party's cause in 1852, the Democrats, he suggests, decided to close ranks behind the compromise, a move which all factions could support.[29] There may be some validity to this contention, but the fact remains that the Iowa Democratic party was not alone in omitting

[28] David S. Sparks, "The Birth of the Republican Party in Iowa, 1848 to 1860," unpublished Ph.D. dissertation, University of Chicago, 1951, 52.
[29] *Ibid.*, 29–30, 55.

a homestead plank from its platform. The Whigs, too, failed to mention homesteads in their platform, but there is no evidence that they were split over this issue. Actually, Democratic solidarity behind the compromise had served the party well in 1850; such a move could prove to be valuable again.[30]

Everything considered, the presidential campaign of 1852 in Iowa, as elsewhere in the nation, was devoid of inspiring issues.[31] No one seemed greatly excited by any of the Whig policies, while the compromise, except for the Fugitive Slave Act, received general public approval. Before long the campaign degenerated into a series of personal attacks against the major candidates. Whigs ridiculed Pierce as unfit to hold the presidential office. Some attacked him for being too friendly to Southern interests. Democrats castigated Winfield Scott for harboring antiforeign views, as well as for supporting abolitionism and free-soilism.[32]

The Democrats tried to vitalize their campaign by inviting Senator Stephen A. Douglas, always popular with Iowans, to speak in the state in the fall. Douglas accepted the invitation and on October 4 appeared in Burlington, where he shared the speakers' platform with Iowa's Democratic illustrious—Dodge, Jones, and Lincoln Clark—as well as other local party officials. The audience, numbering five thousand or more, patiently listened to at least six hours of political haranguing. German-speaking persons at the meeting heard speeches in their native tongue. But aside from this brief stimulant, the presidential campaign appeared to lack the enthusiasm usually characteristic of frontier politics.[33]

[30] *Iowa Capital Reporter* (Iowa City), May 19, 1852, quoted in *Iowa Weekly Republican*, May 26, 1852; 32 Cong., 1 sess., *Congressional Globe*, Appendix, 1118–19.

[31] Nichols, *The Democratic Machine 1850–1854*, 153–54.

[32] Pelzer, "History of the Democratic Party of Iowa," 198; *Des Moines Valley Whig*, October 14, 1852.

[33] Charles Waters to George W. Jones, September 20, 1852, in the George W. Jones Correspondence at the Iowa State Department of History and Archives in Des Moines; *Iowa State Gazette*, October 6, 1852; Pelzer, "History of the Democratic Party of Iowa," 198.

A similar indictment could not be made concerning the congressional elections, especially in the Second District, where Lincoln Clark sought another term. In the First District the Democratic incumbent, Henn, again won his party's endorsement to run against the Whig, Philip Viele. The latter, a native of New York and an alumnus of Union College, left the Democratic party in 1840, three years after arriving in Iowa.[34] Delazon Smith, disappointed as an office-seeker and extremely dissatisfied, bolted the Democrats as he had done in 1850 and organized what he called "The Young Democracy of Van Buren County."[35] What he hoped to gain for himself is not quite clear, but perhaps revenge was his principal motive. If the Democrats persisted in being unfriendly to his candidacy, he would work to secure the defeat of the regular party nominee. Thus, as in 1850, Smith became a thorn in the side of the Democratic party in the First Congressional District.

Trouble came early for the Democrats in the Second District. At the nominating convention of the district, held in Muscatine on June 30, several delegates were critical of Lincoln Clark's record in Congress. Clark had worked hard for the Dubuque and Keokuk Railroad, a north–south line running along the Mississippi, while the central counties preferred their own favorite east–west route across the center of the state. Nevertheless, Clark succeeded in winning renomination, despite the grumbling of the delegates from the central counties.[36]

Clark also attracted some opposition from the Dubuque delegation, men from his own county, a strong indication that all was not serene in the Dubuque organization. Difficulties involved a clash of personalities and feuding among the leadership which dated back to 1848, when George W. Jones was elected United

---

[34] *Frontier Guardian*, June 18, 1852; Benjamin F. Gue, *History of Iowa*, IV, 273.

[35] *Autobiography of Charles Clinton Nourse*, 23.

[36] *Davenport Gazette*, July 15, 1852; 32 Cong., 1 sess., *Congressional Globe*, 672–75.

States senator. The victory won for him the lasting enmity of Judge Wilson, who had been the chief Democratic contender for the senatorial vacancy before Jones entered the picture. Also at odds with Jones was Dennis A. Mahoney, editor of the *Dubuque Herald*. Wilson and Mahoney became the leading figures of an anti-Jones faction which emerged in Dubuque. Clark leaned toward the Wilson-Mahoney camp, thus accounting for some opposition from the Dubuque delegation. Later, when the Jones group became stalwart supporters of the Buchanan administration, the anti-Jones faction, save for Mahoney, became antiadministration men. Clark, too, would be numbered among the leaders of the antiadministration Democrats in the state.[37]

The unreconciled dissenters of the Second District called a convention of their own to meet in Cedar Rapids on July 15 to nominate a man of their own choice for Congress. On the appointed date representatives from Johnson, Cedar, Linn, Iowa, and Benton counties convened at Cedar Rapids. Le Grand Byington, railroad promoter from Iowa City, was one of the leaders of the gathering. This rump group picked a Judge Carlton to run for Clark's seat, but Carlton declined the honor.[38]

So serious did the Democratic leadership deem the situation in the Second District that they published an address to the voters there, imploring them to stand together behind the regular party nominee, lest the opposition be able to capitalize on the Democratic schism. The leaders called upon the voters to lay aside sectional jealousy and close ranks behind Clark.[39] It was a stirring appeal, but whether the voters would listen was quite another matter.

Meanwhile, the Whigs worked diligently to take advantage of

[37] *Dubuque* (Iowa) *Herald*, quoted in the *Burlington Daily Telegraph*, July 14, 1852; David S. Sparks, "The Decline of the Democratic Party in Iowa, 1850–1860," *Iowa Journal of History*, Vol. LIII (1955), 11–12; John C. Parish, *George Wallace Jones*, 34, 44–45, 50–51.

[38] *Burlington Daily Telegraph*, July 21 and 24, 1852.

[39] *Iowa State Gazette*, July 21, 1852.

the Democratic rupture. Very early in the campaign they had accused the Democrats of neglecting the central counties. Now the Whigs intended to profit at their opponents' expense. To run against Clark they chose John P. Cook, a long-term resident of Davenport known to possess "safe" ideas on the railroad issue which had so aroused Byington and his friends. Cook, it was hoped, would receive the votes of the Democratic bolters.[40]

Democratic party regulars, meanwhile, strove to make Clark acceptable to the voters of his district. They characterized him as a friend to all sectors of his district, not merely to a particular area. He was described as "a faithful, talented representative" who merited the votes of all true Democrats.[41] Whether or not the Democrats could persuade the voters only the results on August 2 would reveal.

The outcome of the race in the Second District was a decided shock to the Democratic party. With 74 per cent of the electorate casting ballots, John P. Cook defeated Lincoln Clark by a vote of 7,767 to 7,194. Cook received 51.9 per cent of the total vote to Clark's 48.09 per cent, the latter figure representing a decline of 5.64 percentage points from his share of the vote two years earlier. Clark lost his race for reelection in Linn, Cedar, Iowa, and Johnson counties. In these four counties, which would benefit from a railroad west from Davenport, Cook amassed 1,120 more votes than his competitor.[42] In 1850, Clark had carried these central counties without any difficulty. Thus the Democrats suffered defeat because they failed to mend their political fences in the Second District, despite knowledge of trouble there. Much credit, of course, must go to the Whigs for successfully exploiting Democratic dissension.

Reviewing the election, the Democratic press described Clark

[40] *Ibid.*, July 28, 1852; *Biographical Directory of the American Congress 1774–1949*, 1014. Cook joined the Democratic party after the formation of the Republican party. Gue, *History of Iowa*, IV, 59.
[41] *Iowa State Gazette*, July 7, 1852.
[42] Election Records, 1848–1860.

as a victim of fraud and treachery within the ranks of the Democrats.[43] Local interests, however, such as the railroad projects of the different sectors, contributed more to his defeat than political disloyalty.

In the First District, where Delazon Smith was busy creating as much trouble for the Democrats as he could, Henn experienced no difficulty in defeating his Whig opponent, Philip Viele, by a vote of 9,714 to 7,874. Henn received 55.23 per cent of the total vote, an increase of 4.72 percentage points above his record in 1850. The departure of the Mormons from Pottawattamie County contributed substantially to Henn's victory. There the Whig totals declined from 457 to 68 votes.[44]

The returns from the presidential balloting sharply pointed up the Democratic loss in the Second District. The Democratic electors ran ahead of Clark in seventeen of the twenty-three counties of the district. Cedar, Linn, and Johnson counties wound up in the Democratic column in the presidential voting.[45]

In a close contest Franklin Pierce defeated Winfield Scott in the state by a vote of 17,823 to 15,895. The Free-Soil party attracted 1,612 votes, more than double the number of votes given to the Free-Soil candidate in the gubernatorial election of 1850. Evidently the antislavery impulse was gaining momentum in Iowa. Pierce received 50.45 per cent of the total votes cast, while Scott obtained 44.99 per cent and Hale won 4.56 per cent. Since the Democrats had so narrowly squeezed through to victory, the opposition had good reason to look forward to the future with renewed optimism.[46] A coalition of opposition elements could well spell disaster for the Democratic party in future elections.

Pierce's slim margin in Iowa accurately reflected his narrow triumph in the rest of the nation. Although he carried all the states except Vermont, Massachusetts, Kentucky, and Tennessee

---

[43] *Iowa State Gazette*, August 11, 1852.
[44] Election Records, 1848–1860.
[45] *Ibid.*
[46] *Ibid.*

and accumulated a tremendous majority in the electoral college, his margin of victory over all other candidates combined was barely 30,000 votes in a total of 3,100,000 votes cast. The national Whig party in Iowa, as well as the Iowa Whig organization, was still alive.[47]

The Free-Soil party maintained or increased its following in the areas where it had exhibited considerable strength in 1850. In eleven counties the party polled 6 per cent or more of the votes. Three counties—Cedar, Henry, and Washington—gave the Free-Soilers 12 per cent of the votes, and Louisa County almost matched this figure. The party registered gains throughout the entire eastern portion of the state. For the most part the Free-Soilers were strongest in the Whig counties, but they also made inroads into centers of Democratic popularity, such as Lee, Scott, and Monroe counties. In the latter two counties, however, the Democratic party was beginning to betray signs of weakness. The same was true for several other counties which once had been "safe" Democratic strongholds, including Des Moines, Jefferson, Jones, Iowa, Muscatine, and Clinton counties.[48]

In the other state contests the Democratic hopefuls were swept into office by margins of 1,000 votes or better. George W. McCleary and William Pattie received popular approval for second terms as secretary of state and auditor, and Martin L. Morris was equally successful in his bid for the treasurer's office. In the important races for the Iowa legislature, the Democrats elected twenty of the thirty-one senators and forty of the sixty-two members of the lower house, thus assuring that a Democrat would be returned to the United States Senate.[49]

Nevertheless, the returns of the voting for the assembly affirmed what the congressional and presidential results indicated, namely, that the popularity of the Democrats was beginning to

[47] Nichols, *The Democratic Machine 1850–1854*, 167.
[48] Election Records, 1848–1860.
[49] *Ibid.*; Pelzer, "History of the Democratic Party of Iowa," 198.

wane. Partly it was a matter of Whig persistence in hammering away in favor of such issues as internal improvements, the tariff, and public banking, whose adherents were increasing in numbers. Partly it occurred because the Democratic party was too closely identified with the South and slavery, whereas the late election reflected the growing antislavery sentiment in the state. Partly the decreasing Democratic appeal could be attributed to a split within the organization, a schism provoked by disagreements over conflicting railroad projects, as well as by intramural squabbles in Dubuque.

The growing restiveness within the Democratic party manifested itself again during the voting in the Iowa legislature for senator of the United States. The term of George W. Jones was soon to expire and he eagerly sought to be returned to Washington. Support for Jones's candidacy, however, was not universal. One paper, the *Telegraph* of Burlington, reputedly a "neutral" organ, made Jones its favorite whipping boy and worked hard to secure his defeat. Nor did Jones's delayed departure for the Capital,[50] causing him to miss the opening of Congress, endear him to his foes. Said to be seeking the senatorial seat which Jones coveted were Joseph Williams, Stephen B. Hempstead, Thomas S. Wilson, James Grant, and Ver Planck Van Antwerp. Hempstead still had two years to serve as governor and hence could not be considered a serious candidate for the Senate.[51]

Strong opposition to Jones came also from the southern portion of the state. This area charged that Jones, a resident of the north, was more partial to the interests of his own region than to the state at large. Railroad interests in Des Moines County especially felt aggrieved at Jones for failing to champion their favorite railroad project, a line from Burlington to Fort Des Moines, as energetically as he pushed the Dubuque and Keokuk

---

[50] *Burlington Daily Telegraph*, November 10 to 30 and December 3, 1852.
[51] Dan E. Clark, *History of Senatorial Elections in Iowa: A Study in American Politics*, 55.

line.[52] Jones denied that he had been working against the interests of the Burlington people. Unfortunately for his position, the bill to grant land to aid in the construction of the Burlington road failed to make any headway in Congress, and Jones had to shoulder the blame for its lack of success. Nevertheless, he assured a Burlington leader, Charles M. Mason, that *"each one* of the Iowa delegation will exert himself to the utmost for the accomplishment of the wishes of our constituents in the south in relation to their favorite R.R. project." He could make this promise, he insisted, not because he was a candidate for reelection but because he was "bound by every principle and every feeling of gratitude to serve my constituents everywhere & particularly those about Burlington & everywhere in the southern part of the state who on all occasions have sustained me."[53] In the end the regular Democrats, urged on by Dodge and Henn, kept the recalcitrants in line. The assembly reelected Jones to another six-year term in the United States Senate over his Whig rival, George G. Wright, by a vote of 59 to 31.[54]

Everything considered, the Democrats of Iowa had no reason to view the election results of 1852 with unmitigated satisfaction. The frontier voter was, at best, an uncertain and unpredictable voter who switched political allegiance readily, depending upon the urgency of his immediate needs. Failure to accommodate the desires of Iowa's central counties for a railroad contributed heavily to the Democratic defeat in the Second District's congressional race. Continued failure to gratify the growing aspirations of Iowans for public banking facilities, internal improvements, and homestead legislation, as well as the lack of success in stilling the controversy over slavery, would eventually lead to the dislodgement of the Democrats from their positions

[52] *Ibid.*, 52; James Grimes to Charles Mason, February 13, 1852, in the Charles M. Mason Papers at the Iowa State Department of History and Archives in Des Moines; Parish, *George Wallace Jones,* 44.

[53] George W. Jones to Charles M. Mason, May 18, 1852, in Mason Papers.

[54] *Journal of the Senate,* 4th General Assembly of Iowa, 1852, 79–80.

73

of power, prestige, and authority in the state. The democratic process, particularly as it operated on the frontier, acted as a relentless check upon the empire-building ambitions of local politicians and their political organizations.

The year following Pierce's victory was another political off year in which only a few minor state offices and some county positions were to be filled. Officials to be elected included the attorney general, and the commissioner and the register of the Des Moines River Improvement. The Democrats picked David C. Cloud for the attorney general vacancy to oppose Whig Samuel A. Rice. For the offices in the Des Moines River Improvement, the Democrats selected Josiah A. Bonney and George Gillaspie, while the Whigs chose Uriah Briggs and R. H. Warden.[55]

The main item of significance in the Democratic state platform for 1853 was the plank asking Congress to pass a law "giving the public domain, in limited quantities, to actual settlers at a price covering the cost of survey and other necessary expenses."[56] Thus, after warding off the issue for more than three years, the Democrats officially recognized the growing and persistent demand of Iowans for homestead legislation.

Aside from the usual invective hurled at the various candidates, the major issue of this election, judging from the platform and the newspapers, was the homestead question. In Congress, Dodge and Henn had repeatedly argued in favor of homestead legislation but with little success. Henn had spoken in behalf of such a measure during the previous session of Congress. At that time he had declared that the granting of homesteads would result in moral, social, political, and economic benefits to the nation. In the Senate, Dodge tried to secure passage of a homestead bill in January but the measure was defeated. Whig editors, as

[55] *Iowa State Gazette*, March 30, 1853; Gue, *History of Iowa*, IV, 55; *Burlington Daily Telegraph*, February 14, 1853. See also Leonard F. Ralston, "Railroads and the Government of Iowa, 1850–1872," unpublished Ph.D. dissertation, University of Iowa, 1960.

[56] Sherman, "Political Party Platforms in Iowa," 118–20.

in the matter of internal improvements, were quick to taunt the Democrats about their unfortunate dilemma: state leaders again seeking legislation which the national leaders opposed.[57]

Yet little excitement could be aroused, and only about half of Iowa's eligible voters exercised their franchise privileges to record another Democratic sweep.[58] Rumblings of party discord, however, continued to emanate from Dubuque and from the central counties. Although the Democrats carried Dubuque, the margins of victory were cut considerably.[59]

A major factor behind many Iowans' lack of interest in the political activities of 1853 was their absorption in the progress of their favorite railroad projects. Everybody seemed involved in one railroad project or another, planning, meeting, discussing, selling, doing everything possible to induce this or that railroad to build along this or that route.[60]

In 1850, Iowa's favorite routes ran across the state from the Mississippi to the Missouri: one from Davenport, through Iowa City, and westward; the other from Burlington to the Missouri. A third line was the Dubuque and Keokuk Railroad, running north–south. This company seemed to have the most determined group of backers of any line. Lucius Langworthy journeyed to Washington to lobby for a grant of land to aid construction of the Dubuque and Keokuk line, paying special attention to Senator Jones of Dubuque.[61] The latter did indeed introduce a bill to aid the Dubuque and Keokuk company but failed to secure its passage. Congressman Thompson had previously, and also without success, introduced a bill designed to provide gifts of

[57] 32 Cong., 1 sess., *Congressional Globe*, Appendix, 495–99; 32 Cong., 2 sess., *ibid.*, 321; *Des Moines Valley Whig*, March 17, 1853.

[58] Election Records, 1848–1860.

[59] Franklin T. Oldt (ed.), *History of Dubuque County Iowa*, 333–34.

[60] S. H. Bonham to Le Grand Byington, October 8, 1850, in the Le Grand Byington Letters on microfilm at the State Historical Society of Iowa in Iowa City; Robert McKee to Le Grand Byington, November 23, 1850, *ibid.*

[61] John King to John L. Taylor, January 16, 1850, in the Lucius H. Langworthy Papers at the State Historical Society of Iowa in Iowa City; L. H. Langworthy to George W. Jones, January 3, 1850, in the Jones Correspondence.

federal land to other covetous railroad companies in Iowa. The Iowa City interests, led by Le Grand Byington, also looked to Senator Jones, among others, to aid their pet schemes. The latter, of course, pledged to do all he could to further the projects.[62]

Railroad activity continued unabated throughout 1852 and 1853, intensifying as each month passed. Railroad meetings were held in Fairfield, Anamosa, and Iowa City, as well as in numerous other towns in the state, for the purpose of promoting various railroad enterprises. In the central counties railroad planners, convinced that Lincoln Clark would do them little good, had successfully unseated him. Clark had introduced a bill to secure a land grant for their line, but it was overshadowed by his exertions in behalf of the Dubuque and Keokuk company.[63]

So feverish had railroad activities become that as early as 1851 the Iowa legislature had appointed a committee to investigate the stockholders of the various infant railroad organizations within the state to determine which elected officials, if any, held stock in these companies and to what extent. The committee reported that it could not ascertain the names of the stockholders or of any elected officials because "the means within the control of your committee as yet do not afford any authentic information in relation to the matter of which they were appointed to enquire."[64] This was the last attempt by the legislature, during the 1850's at least, to discover the extent to which railroads and politics were entangled. With the threat of state investigations thus removed, the field was left clear for the business interests and the politicians to "cooperate" with each other.

Meanwhile, petitions continued to pour into the General Assembly asking the legislature to seek federal land grants for a

[62] 31 Cong., 1 sess., *Congressional Globe*, 294, 391–92, 1240–41; Louis Pelzer, *Augustus Caesar Dodge*, 172; Le Grand Byington to George W. Jones, February 6, 1850 and December 7, 1851, in Jones Correspondence; George W. Jones to Le Grand Byington, December 20, 1851, in Byington Letters.

[63] *Des Moines Valley Whig*, May 15 and August 21, 1851; *The Iowa Weekly Republican*, August 27, 1851; 32 Cong., 1 sess., *Congressional Globe*, 56.

[64] *Journal of the Senate*, 3rd General Assembly of Iowa, 1850, 126, 218, 223.

myriad of projects. The Iowa lawmakers dutifully sent off a bundle of memorials to Congress. And Iowa newspapers, while sniping at the projects of rival towns, helped to stimulate interest in the various schemes. Burlington, in particular, considered itself the leading center of business in Iowa, but Keokuk, Muscatine, Davenport, Iowa City, and Dubuque vehemently disputed its claim.[65]

Members of Iowa's congressional delegation had no choice, of course, but to continue their efforts to secure a land grant to aid railroad construction. It was an unhappy task which befell Iowa's congressmen. Though precedent for a land grant existed, Congress still refused to yield to the entreaties of Iowans for gifts from the public domain. Moreover, if any of Iowa's congressional delegation labored for one railroad line to the exclusion of another, the wounded interests usually undertook to unseat the offending congressman. Nevertheless, Dodge and his colleagues from Iowa continued to fight for land grants in the face of congressional hostility. Even Senator Cass of Michigan marveled at the "zeal, energy, and talent" displayed by Iowa's senators.[66]

By 1853 railroad fever had reached the mania level. Towns and counties subscribed public funds to aid railroad construction, the Iowa Supreme Court having declared such action legal. Many railroad companies never laid any track. The city and county of Dubuque voted $300,000 to build the Dubuque and Pacific Railroad; Linn County supported a bond issue of $200,000 for the Iowa Central Air Line Road; Mahaska, Keokuk, Warren, Marion, and Muscatine counties voted upwards of $55,000 each to pro-

[65] *Ibid.*, 4th General Assembly of Iowa, 1852, 48, 105, 110, 113; *Journal of the House of Representatives*, 4th General Assembly of Iowa, 1852, 44, 49, 54–55, 79; James W. Grimes to A. C. Dodge, December 24, 1852, quoted in Charles J. Fulton, *History of Jefferson County Iowa*, I, 273; *Burlington Daily Telegraph*, January 24, March 29, and July 31, 1852.

[66] 32 Cong., 1 sess., *Congressional Globe*, Appendix, 497–98, 674–75, 495–99; L. H. Langworthy to George W. Jones, February 7, 1852, in Jones Correspondence; copy of a letter by George W. Jones and A. C. Dodge to *Washington* (D.C.) *Union*, May 28, 1852, *ibid.*; Pelzer, *Augustus Caesar Dodge*, 180.

mote the Iowa Western Railroad.[67] One paper appraised the situation with ill-concealed concern:

> The Railroad mania in Iowa presents some developments which to a quiet looker on must appear more ridiculous than any "manifestation" of the spirit rappers. Every town, cross roads, and blacksmith shop in the state has held public meetings and passed resolutions demonstrating to all the world . . . the peculiar advantages of said village, cross roads, or blacksmith shop for a railroad route. . . . So furious has the zeal of each locality become in favor of itself, and so venemous against every other point coming in competition, that even *political ties are sundered* and the "cohesive power of public plunder" proves too weak for the repulsion of railroad mania.[68]

Nevertheless, the journal continued to advocate its own favorite railroad line; it, too, was overcome by "railroad mania."

The great problem for the Democrats was that, just as in the matter of internal improvements and homesteads, so also with the question of securing land grants from Congress, the state leaders were unstinting in their efforts to satisfy the demands of their constituents but faced unyielding opposition from other parts of the nation, as well as from the national party. Since the Democrats controlled the federal government, they of course had to bear the blame, in Iowa at least, for failing to give the state what it desired. Moreover, the railroads managed to figure prominently in the changing fortunes of the national and state Democratic organizations.

[67] *Des Moines Valley Whig*, July 7 and 14, 1853.
[68] *Ibid.*, April 14, 1853. Italics added.

"The Nebraska Outrage"

O N DECEMBER 5, 1853, when Iowa's Senator Dodge announced his intention to introduce a bill providing for the establishment of a territorial government for Nebraska, he had not the slightest notion of the furor his action would ultimately provoke. He simply believed that he was acceding to the desires of most of his constituents, some of whom were eager to cross the Missouri River to settle upon the virgin lands beyond. Moreover, the organization of Nebraska would certainly please railroad entrepreneurs, as well as speculators, who were avid to push their lines across the Mississippi, thence to the Missouri, and eventually westward to California. Such an apparently popular act, in addition, would undoubtedly enhance the image and prestige of the Democratic party, for which Senator Dodge had labored long and diligently. Indeed, most Iowa Democrats would readily have agreed with William H. Merritt, editor of Dubuque's *Daily*

Miners' Express, and a leading spokesman for the party, when he exulted:

> It is a matter of high congratulation that the State of Iowa from the day of her inception as a member of the great American Confederacy has been, so far as the sentiment of her people was concerned, thoroughly Democratic. On no marked occasion has her faith faltered or wavered. This constant unity, this unbroken current has at last borne down and swept away all regular organized opposition. This fact, existing in no other state, has been most strikingly manifest in our state elections occurring lately.[1]

Unhappily for the Iowa Democrats, however, Senator Dodge's maneuver would generate a tide of opposition powerful enough to topple the local party from its lofty position in the state.

Iowans had long been intrigued by the territory just across the Missouri River. The reasons for this interest appear to have been twofold. In the first place, Nebraska contained a vast area of land dearly coveted by eager, land-hungry Westerners. Title to the land, however, still reposed in the hands of the Indians, and unless the territory was organized by the federal government, it would remain there. Organization of Nebraska not only would clear the land of its Indian titles but also would open that vast tract to white settlers, many from or passing through Iowa. Businessmen, among others, could expect to reap large profits supplying Nebraska-bound travelers.[2]

The railroad was another important reason for the desire of Iowans to secure the organization of Nebraska. If the national leaders of the party in power could be shown that Iowa lay on a

---

[1] Quoted in Frank I. Herriott, "A Neglected Factor in the Anti-Slavery Triumph in Iowa in 1854," *Deutsch-Amerikanische Geschichtsblätter: Jahrbuch der Deutsch-Amerikanischen Historischen Gesellschaft von Illinois*, Vol. XVIII–XIX (1918–1919), 174–75.

[2] *Iowa State Gazette* (Burlington), December 8, 1853; David S. Sparks, "The Decline of the Democratic Party in Iowa, 1850–1860," *Iowa Journal of History*, Vol. LIII (1955), 15.

direct route for the keenly desired railroad to the Pacific, perhaps they would approve grants of land for the state. Such a line would, of course, run across Iowa and Nebraska, but the latter must first be organized. Even if a main line for a Pacific railroad did not pass through the state, track construction in Iowa could feed into a Pacific route. Indeed, the agitation for a transcontinental route was a strong motivation for Iowa's congressmen to seek the organization of Nebraska.[3]

As early as 1850 the Iowa legislature had passed a memorial and joint resolution requesting Congress to organize Nebraska. No action was taken in Washington at that early date. Iowa itself was barely occupied. Most of her residents lived in the eastern portions of the state along the Mississippi, in the southern counties just north of the Missouri line, and in small clusters on the Missouri slope, principally at Council Bluffs. Elsewhere the vast acreage of the state remained uninhabited. Since Iowa was only sparsely settled, the organization of a territory directly to her west still seemed unnecessary.[4]

Agitation in Iowa for the organization of Nebraska, however, recurred in 1853. Meetings held at Glenwood, Mills County, in October, and at Sidney, Fremont County, in November asked for the elimination of the Indian titles in Nebraska and called for its organization as a territory. A Democratic convention early in January, 1854, in Pottawattamie County declared that "the immediate organization of Nebraska and the establishment of a territorial government over its citizens is a question of national importance and greatly affecting the interests of western Iowa."[5]

[3] Frank H. Hodder, "Genesis of the Kansas-Nebraska Act," State Historical Society of Wisconsin *Proceedings* for October 24, 1912, 69.

[4] *Journal of the House of Representatives*, 3rd General Assembly of Iowa, 1850, 255; "The Seventh Census of the United States," manuscript census reports for Iowa at the Iowa State Department of History and Archives in Des Moines.

[5] *Iowa State Gazette*, January 11, 1854; *Burlington* (Iowa) *Daily Telegraph*, November 4, 1853; P. Orman Ray, *The Repeal of the Missouri Compromise*, 176–77.

If an additional incentive was needed to arouse Iowans over Nebraska, the people of Missouri supplied it. They, too, were interested in Nebraska, for much the same reasons as the Iowans. A mass meeting, held in St. Louis presumably by the friends of Missouri Senator Thomas H. Benton, included among its resolutions one which stated that the assembly "was in favor of a territorial government for Nebraska . . . and regarded all who oppose it upon *whatever pretext* as hostile to the best interest of the state."[6]

While Iowans were drawing up resolutions and petitions, Missourians were acting. In the fall of 1853 a Methodist missionary to the Shawnee Indians, Thomas Johnson, was elected delegate to Congress from the unorganized territory of Nebraska and set out for Washington. A rival, Abelard Guthrie, also claimed the office and headed for Washington to present his case.[7]

The people of Iowa, however, were not to be outmaneuvered. As soon as the settlers along the Missouri slope learned of the call which resulted in the selection of Thomas Johnson, they crossed the river at Council Bluffs to conduct their own balloting. Hadley D. Johnson journeyed to Washington as the delegate of this "election." There he joined his Missouri namesake in pressing Congress to organize Nebraska, as well as to recognize the legality of his election.[8]

On December 14, Senator Dodge fulfilled his announced intent by introducing his bill, which was promptly referred to the Committee on Territories, of which Stephen A. Douglas of Illinois was chairman and George W. Jones of Iowa one of the members. Significantly, Dodge had visited his constituents in western Iowa just before the opening of Congress. There he learned about the desires of the border residents concerning Nebraska and about the election of the two Johnsons.[9]

[6] Quoted in Ray, *The Repeal of the Missouri Compromise*, 173.

[7] George F. Milton, *The Eve of Conflict: Stephen A. Douglas and the Needless War*, 107; James C. Malin, *The Nebraska Question 1852–1854*, 182.

[8] Milton, *The Eve of Conflict*, 107.

On January 23, 1854, Chairman Douglas, reporting for the Committee on Territories, recommended that Congress split Nebraska into two territories. The necessity for a division of Nebraska stemmed in part from the election of the two Johnsons. Both men wanted to be seated as duly elected delegates, and each had the support of his congressman. Moreover, Iowa's Johnson demonstrated that it would be to the state's best interests to split Nebraska instead of permitting the organization of one territory, as proposed in Dodge's original bill. The title of the Omaha Indians, directly west of Iowa, had not yet been extinguished. If Nebraska was organized as one large territory, the center of population would likely fall to the south of Iowa. This could result in a Pacific railroad running south of the state, thereby jeopardizing the interests of Iowa in her competition with Missouri for the route. The possibility of securing additional patronage for distribution among loyal Iowa Democrats may have been further motivation for a division. Iowa's senators, therefore, decided to ask for a split and conveyed this decision to Senator Douglas. Nebraska was divided along the fortieth parallel, and the Kansas-Nebraska Bill took concrete form, as Dodge and Jones became its most ardent champions.[10]

In addition to the establishment of the territories of Kansas and Nebraska, the most significant feature of the bill was the repeal of that part of the so-called Missouri Compromise which prohibited slavery in the area that lay north of the line of $36° 30'$. Congress thereby, in effect, not only announced that it would not legislate on the question of slavery in the territories but also encouraged the actual settlers of Kansas and Nebraska to determine for themselves the resolution of this thorny matter. Ignoring the moral crusade being waged against slavery by the abolitionists and their supporters, advocates of the measure an-

[9] 33 Cong., 1 sess., *Congressional Globe*, 1, 44; Ray, *The Repeal of the Missouri Compromise*, 177, 195.

[10] Milton, *The Eve of Conflict*, 148; 33 Cong., 1 sess., *Congressional Globe*, 221.

ticipated the eventual admission of Kansas into the Union as a slave state, while Nebraska would enter as a free state.[11]

Although Iowans both in and out of Congress had supported the bill, the publication in Iowa of the provisions provoked sharp reactions, and proponents of the measure and its critics formed their lines of battle. While the Whig press almost universally condemned the bill, the papers which supported the Democratic party were divided over the issue. Such influential journals as the *Daily Miners' Express* and the *Daily Herald* of Dubuque, the *Iowa Sentinel* of Fairfield, and the *Iowa State Gazette* of Burlington backed the bill. Other papers, including the Iowa City *Capital Reporter*, the Muscatine *Democratic Enquirer*, the Davenport *Democratic Banner*, the Cedar Rapids *Progressive Era*, and the *Lee County Plaindealer*, opposed the measure.[12] Acting as unofficial spokesman for this group of dissenting newspapers, the organ in Muscatine declared:

> We believe it to be wrong and undemocratic to override a solemn national compact—to open again the bleeding wounds of the country—to violate the pledge of the democratic party, made at Baltimore in 1852 to discountenance the slavery question.
>
> We believe these things to be undemocratic and all these things the supporters of the Nebraska Bill are doing.[13]

An influential but politically neutral newspaper, the *Daily Telegraph* of Burlington, also came out in vigorous opposition to the Kansas-Nebraska proposal, a posture from which it never

[11] *The Statutes at Large and Treaties of the United States of America,* Vol. X, 277–90. For a good but somewhat dated study of the historiography of the Kansas-Nebraska Act, see Roy F. Nichols, "The Kansas-Nebraska Act: A Century of Historiography," *Mississippi Valley Historical Review,* Vol. XLII (1956), 187–212; cf. Robert W. Johannsen, "The Kansas–Nebraska Act and the Pacific Northwest Frontier," *Pacific Historical Review,* Vol. XXII (1953), 129–41.

[12] *Burlington Daily Telegraph,* January 23 and February 20 and 21, 1854; Herriott, "A Neglected Factor in the Anti-Slavery Triumph in Iowa in 1854," 198.

[13] *Iowa Democratic Enquirer* (Muscatine) quoted in *The Iowa Weekly Republican* (Iowa City), March 8, 1854.

wavered. In March this journal published nine reasons why it believed Iowans should condemn the Nebraska bill:

1. It reverses a policy regarding the territories which originated with the fathers of our country, i.e., to prohibit rather than legalize slavery.

2. It re-opens the slavery question in violation of the Baltimore platforms and disturbs the Compromise of 1850.

3. It violates a "solemn compact" of 30 years between the North and South; a compact which has been of benefit solely to the South.

4. It will lead to excitement and disunion.

5. It is humiliating to Northern pride.

6. It will destroy public confidence in compromise.

7. It will extend slavery under governmental patronage.

8. It will be a moral blight on Nebraska and bring slavery into competition with white labor.

9. It will put a slave state west of Iowa, affect our hopes for railroads, etc., and our interior will suffer as a result.[14]

Keokuk's Whig paper, the *Gate City*, strongly concurred:

The Kansas-Nebraska difficulties had their origin in Congress. They need not and they should not ever have existed. There was no population which demanded the organization of the territories, no public sentiment which required the repeal of the Missouri Compromise, and there was no need and no excuse for public tumult and public danger.[15]

The *Iowa State Gazette*, the Democratic organ in Burlington, condemned the *Telegraph* as a turncoat journal. It also accused the latter of being the personal paper of the Whig party leadership of the state.[16]

[14] George A. Boeck, "An Early Iowa Community: Aspects of Economic, Social, and Political Development in Burlington, Iowa, 1833–1866," unpublished Ph.D. dissertation, University of Iowa, 1961, 238–40.

[15] Quoted in Faye E. Harris, "A Frontier Community: The Economic, Social, and Political Development of Keokuk, Iowa, 1820–1866," unpublished Ph.D. dissertation, University of Iowa, 1965, 312.

[16] Boeck, "An Early Iowa Community," 239–40.

One Democratic paper based its defense of the measure on the ground that the question of slavery or free soil should be left to the actual settlers of the new territories. As for the Missouri Compromise, which critics of the bill hastened to defend, the Compromise of 1850 had virtually terminated its operation. In any case, to make the act of one Congress binding forever on its successors is "radically wrong and an outrage on all free institutions; and the attempt to give imperative validity to the compromise of 1820 is nothing less."[17]

Though the Democratic party at home was divided, the Democratic members of Congress from Iowa were unanimous in their support of the Kansas-Nebraska legislation. Apparently unconcerned about the sudden protests emanating from his state, Senator Dodge vigorously endorsed the bill before the Senate. He defended popular sovereignty as "the noblest tribute which has ever yet been offered by the Congress of the United States to the sovereignty of the people." To win friends for the act, Dodge endeavored to identify it with the Compromise of 1850 and Manifest Destiny, both ever popular in the West. At the same time he justified the repeal of the Missouri Compromise. The latter, he declared, represented, with similar measures, "dangerous assumptions of power" and were "as manifest usurpations as a law would be which should require all settlers to purchase and hold one or more negroes as slaves." Opponents of the bill, Dodge insisted, were merely using the issue of slavery as a means to gain political power. Concluding his remarks, Dodge declared that "the passage of the bill before us will, in my judgment, confer great benefits upon the nation, the West, and especially upon the State which I in part represent. The settlement and occupation of Nebraska will accomplish for us what the acquisition and peopling of Iowa did for Illinois."[18]

Dodge's speech in behalf of the bill was perhaps the most force-

[17] *Iowa State Gazette*, February 15, 1854.
[18] 33 Cong., 1 sess., *Congressional Globe*, Appendix, 376–82.

ful and eloquent address he ever delivered to the Senate. Regardless of whether his words swayed any of his colleagues, they were reprinted in Democratic papers in various parts of the country. The *Boston Statesman,* for example, reviewed his speech as "strong, manly and straight-forward." The *Daily Delta* of New Orleans, commenting on Dodge's remarks, employed the occasion to praise the entire state of Iowa for her "fidelity to the Federal Compact" and for her sustenance of the "Constitutional rights of the South. On no occasion within our recollection has this noble Northwestern state disgraced itself through its legislature by the passage of resolutions intended to warp Congressional action in relation to Slavery." And Hempstead, Iowa's outgoing governor, wrote that Dodge's speech was "the best speech on that question."[19]

Senator Jones confined his remarks to an attack on the Clayton amendment, sponsored by Senator Clayton of Delaware, which limited the right of suffrage and of officeholding to citizens of the United States. Even had Jones gone farther, he would have contributed little to what Dodge had already expressed.

Iowa's congressmen in the House of Representatives were divided over the bill. John P. Cook, the lone Whig from Iowa, based his opposition to the bill on the three points commonly made by its critics: it repealed the Missouri Compromise and opened the way for the extension of slavery; it reopened the slavery argument; it was contrary to the principles of the Compromise of 1850. The views of his colleagues in the Senate, Cook insisted, did not "represent the sentiments of Iowa when they consent to the renewed agitation."[20]

Four days later Congressman Henn rose to reply to Cook. He countered the latter's slavery argument by pointing out that, regardless of the repeal of the Missouri Compromise, the two

[19] *Iowa State Gazette,* April 12, 1854; Louis Pelzer, *Augustus Caesar Dodge,* 321–22; Herriott, "A Neglected Factor in the Anti-Slavery Triumph in Iowa in 1854," 176.

[20] 33 Cong., 1 sess., *Congressional Globe,* Appendix, 670–73.

territories would, of necessity, become free states, because the pattern of settlement would favor immigration from non-slaveholding states. The organization of Nebraska, Henn averred, would benefit Iowa and the whole North by adding "to the commerce, wealth, and prosperity of the whole country."[21]

The consistent support which Iowa's congressional Democrats gave to the Kansas-Nebraska Bill, particularly in the Senate, motivated the *National Era* of Washington, D.C., to brand Iowa as

> another of the Free Slave States. From the hour of its admission to the present, its influence and its votes have been given in favor of slavery. Augustus Caesar Dodge's vote has always been as certain for any villainous scheme of slavery propagandism, as those of Butler and Atchinson. Where the special blame of this state of things lies, we do not pretend to say . . . but there is no disguising the fact that Iowa is now, and has been from the outset, so far as her action in the Confederacy is concerned, to all intents and purposes, a Slave State.[22]

Another journal in the capital, however, the *Daily Union*, had nothing but praise for Iowa's political stance:

> The Democrats of Iowa may boast, with some justice, that the state is the soundest Democratic Free State on the compromises of the Constitution. They have never yet been known to evade the responsibility of accepting the boldest issue on the slavery question. The consequence has been, that they have become impregnable to the assaults of the Whigs, and that no true Democrat of Iowa ever waits to see how the current runs before taking his position.[23]

While the battle over the Nebraska Bill raged in Congress, political tempers began to erupt among the rank-and-file Iowa

---

[21] *Ibid.*, 885–88.

[22] Quoted in Herriott, "A Neglected Factor in the Anti-Slavery Triumph in Iowa in 1854," 177–78.

[23] *Ibid.*, 176–77.

Democrats. The various county conventions, meeting to select delegates to attend the state Democratic convention at Iowa City on January 9, generally expressed a desire to work for party unity. Most voted resolutions approving the efforts of the Democratic members of Iowa's congressional delegation and praising the administration of Franklin Pierce. Some criticized what they termed "renegade journals and disappointed office seekers" for attempting to disrupt the harmony of the party. The Democratic convention in Pottawattamie County, especially concerned about Nebraska, adopted a resolution asking for its ultimate organization.[24]

After the usual preliminaries the state Democratic convention selected Curtis Bates to head the party's ticket. A native of Connecticut, Bates entered local politics in Ohio, where he was elected to the state senate in 1831. Ten years later he migrated to Iowa. The other state nominations went to George W. McCleary, secretary of state; Martin L. Morris, treasurer; David C. Cloud, attorney general; and P. L. Sharp, auditor. For superintendent of public instruction the convention selected James D. Eads, a choice not supported by all Democrats at the convention. One local party luminary, Ver Planck Van Antwerp, believed that Eads was totally unsuited for the position, and that the nomination was merely an attempt to undermine the current Democratic leadership.[25]

The state Democratic platform included the usual resolutions lauding the Pierce administration and reaffirming the national party platform of 1852. The most strongly worded resolution asked for a speedy organization of Nebraska. Other planks called for party harmony and disclaimed any sectionalism. To attract the foreign element, the Democrats added that the party looked

---

[24] *Iowa State Gazette*, January 4 and 11, 1854.

[25] Charles E. Snyder, "Curtis Bates," *Iowa Journal of History and Politics*, Vol. XLIV (1946), 297–99; V. P. Van Antwerp to Laurel Summers, December 18, 1853, in the Laurel Summers Correspondence at the Iowa State Department of History and Archives in Des Moines.

with disfavor upon efforts to hamper foreign-born persons from becoming citizens and owning land.[26]

Missing from the Democratic platform were resolutions expressing the party stand on such issues as homesteads, internal improvements, and temperance. Failure to mention the first two reflected the dilemma of the party; time and again the local organization advocated congressional action in favor of internal improvements and homestead laws, but the national leadership, emanating principally from the South, blocked these measures, leaving the local party in a precarious political position. Supporters of the national administration apparently preferred to ignore these issues. Silence on the temperance question was the only way to avoid intraparty feuding, for the rank and file were divided on this issue. In addition, there was no plank stating the party's attitude on another local issue, the question of amending the state constitution. Thus the Democrats of Iowa entered the political contests of 1854 with a vaguely worded, weak platform which was uncomfortably silent on most of the vital problems of interest to the voters of the state.

Meantime, the Whigs and Free-Soilers convened to select their candidates. The Whigs of Iowa met in convention virtually for the final time under this label. The party was torn by factionalism, principally as a result of the slavery question. There were Seward Whigs, Cotton Whigs, Conscience Whigs, and Silver Greys. All differed on the problem of slavery, but all more or less opposed its extension into the territories.

The Whig gathering in Iowa City on February 22 selected James W. Grimes for the office of governor. A native of New Hampshire and a graduate of Dartmouth, Grimes moved to Iowa in 1836. His previous experience included terms in the territorial and regular legislatures of the state. Other Whig candidates were

---

[26] Roy V. Sherman, "Political Party Platforms in Iowa," unpublished M.A. thesis, State University of Iowa, 1956, 124–27.

Simeon Waters, secretary of state; Eliphalet Price, treasurer; A. P. Stevens, auditor; James W. Sennett, attorney general; and George Shedd, superintendent of public instruction. This ticket was not a solid Whig lineup but included some of the nominees of the Free-Soil party, such as George Shedd and Simeon Waters.[27]

In their platform the Whigs demanded a revision of the state constitution in order to permit the establishment of banks, called for a change in the educational system of the state, pledged passage of a prohibition law, and supported legislation for homesteads and internal improvements. In addition, they endorsed Congressman John P. Cook and excoriated the Nebraska Bill and its authors, calling upon Iowans to oppose the act.[28]

The Whig platform represented an attempt by certain leaders, headed by Grimes, to persuade various splinter groups to coalesce into a single body. Only a unified opposition could hope to defeat the Democratic party in the approaching elections. Thus the platform tried to appeal to Free-Soilers, abolitionists, Whigs, temperance groups, and anti-Nebraska Democrats, as well as to voters who were becoming increasingly disaffected by the failure of the Democrats to secure land grants, railroad franchises, and other internal improvements for the state. Though the foreign element would undoubtedly oppose the Whig stand on prohibition, they might favor the party's position on banking and homesteads.

Among Iowa's Netherlands-born immigrants, however, this strategy backfired. This group strongly condemned prohibition as an unwelcome intrusion into their private lives as well as an unwarranted violation of their traditional manner of living. Led by their principal spokesman, the Reverend Henry P. Scholte,

[27] *Biographical Directory of the American Congress 1774–1949*, 1239; Snyder, "Curtis Bates," 291–92.
[28] Sherman, "Political Party Platforms in Iowa," 124–27.

the Hollanders defected en masse from the Whig party and gave their allegiance to the Democrats, whom they continued to support throughout the remaining years of the 1850's.[29]

Whig unity, moreover, was not to be readily achieved. The antislavery, anti-Nebraska platform adopted by the party under Grimes's driving leadership was too strong for the Silver Greys, the conservative wing of the party. The abolitionist faction of the party had dominated the convention, much to the disgust of the conservatives, many of whom refused to support Grimes as the party's nominee. The Burlington *Daily Hawk-Eye*, one of the leading Whig papers in the state, attacked Grimes and criticized the Whig platform. Even more disconcerting was the refusal of three of the Whig nominees—Simeon Waters, George Shedd, and Eliphalet Price—to run for office under that label. The first two men were strong Free-Soilers. Signs of this Whig discord, of course, were heartening to the Democrats. One paper invited the conservatives among the Whigs to join the Democrats to fight "the fanatical disunionists of the north."[30]

The Free-Soil party met in convention in early February as the Free Democracy of Iowa party and chose a full slate of candidates. Simeon Waters was nominated for governor and George Shedd for superintendent of public instruction. Accompanying the usual Free-Soil resolutions was a plank condemning the Nebraska Bill. If they could have united the various antislavery, anti-Nebraska elements, the Free-Soilers might well have held the balance of power in the state.[31]

29 Robert P. Swierenga, "The Ethnic Voter and the First Lincoln Election," *Civil War History*, Vol. XI (1965), 32–33.

30 Cyrenus Cole, *A History of the People of Iowa*, 271; Frank I. Herriott, "James Grimes Versus the Southrons," *Annals of Iowa*, 3d ser., Vol. XV (1925–1927), 326–27; *Daily Miners' Express* (Dubuque, Iowa), May 13, 1854; *Iowa State Gazette*, July 5, 1854, quoted in Louis Pelzer, "The History and Principles of the Democratic Party of Iowa, 1846–1857," *Iowa Journal of History and Politics*, Vol. VI (1908), 179–80.

31 David S. Sparks, "The Birth of the Republican Party in Iowa, 1848 to 1860," unpublished Ph.D. dissertation, University of Chicago, 1951, 79–80.

At this point Grimes moved to win the Free-Soilers to his banner. He approached the leaders of the movement, the Reverend Asa Turner and Dr. George F. Magoun, and arranged to secure their support. Accordingly, a new convention of the Free Democracy met at Crawfordsville, Washington County, and adopted a resolution endorsing James W. Grimes for governor. Thus the Whigs and the Free-Soilers essentially fused to oppose the Democrats.[32]

The Democrats of the First Congressional District picked Augustus Hall to oppose Whig Rufus L. B. Clarke. Hall, a New Yorker by birth, had settled in Keosauqua after winning some local repute in Ohio. Later he would become chief justice of Nebraska Territory. His opponent was a Connecticut Yankee who had come to Iowa in 1849 but never had won much popularity even among his own party colleagues.[33]

In the Second District the Democratic Party selected the retiring Governor Hempstead in an effort to recapture the congressional seat lost to the Whigs in 1852. To oppose him the Whigs nominated James Thorington, a North Carolinian who had been reared in Alabama. Moving to Davenport in 1839, Thorington had risen rapidly in local politics and become mayor of the town. A strong temperance advocate and Know-Nothing, he was an excellent choice to attract the splinter groups to his standard.[34]

On April 8, Grimes published a pamphlet entitled *To the People of Iowa*, presenting his personal political creed. The pamphlet was reprinted in Whig journals throughout the state. The endorsement which he had earlier received from the Free-Soilers at their Crawfordsville convention had come as a result, in part at least, of their favorable impression of his message, which they

[32] *Ibid.*, 88–89; *Des Moines Valley Whig* (Keokuk, Iowa), April 20, 1854; Mount Pleasant (Iowa) *Weekly Observer*, April 6, 1854; *Iowa State Gazette*, April 12, 1854.

[33] *Biographical Directory of Congress*, 1251; David S. Sparks, "The Birth of the Republican Party in Iowa, 1854–1856," *Iowa Journal of History*, Vol. LIV (1956), 5.

[34] *Biographical Directory of Congress*, 1917.

had seen in draft and had thoroughly discussed at their meeting. Grimes was planning a trip to the East and apparently published the pamphlet to compensate for his absence. Evidently he was fully confident of his ability to capture the gubernatorial office without conducting an intensive personal tour of the state, at least not so early in the campaign. Five days before the publication of his address, he wrote that he could "carry Des Moines County by a larger majority than any man ever got it, and so far as I can learn the chances are that I can be elected." About a week or so later Grimes departed for the East.[35]

Grimes's pamphlet was designed to furnish a common ground upon which the discordant elements in Iowa could unite in support of his candidacy. In addition, he made a strong effort to attract the foreign-born voters, particularly the Germans. Grimes advocated the popular election of judges of the state supreme court, called for an amendment of the state constitution to permit the establishment of banks, and asked for federal aid for internal improvements. On the temperance issue he trod softly, not wishing to alienate the antitemperance vote, but at the same time desiring to demonstrate his friendly attitude toward temperance legislation. On this point he merely stated that if the legislature passed a prohibitory law he would not veto the measure unless it was manifestly unconstitutional.[36]

On the matter of homesteads Grimes could not successfully attack the Democrats of the state for failing to work to secure such legislation, but he could and did point out to the Germans and other foreign groups that the most recent homestead bill, introduced by Congressman Henn, contained certain discriminatory clauses which, by implication if not by intent, prevented

[35] Herriott, "A Neglected Factor in the Anti-Slavery Triumph in Iowa in 1854," 265, 272; James Grimes, "To the People of Iowa," in the William Salter Collection at the Iowa State Department of History and Archives in Des Moines; James Grimes to William Penn Clarke, April 3, 1854, in the William Penn Clarke Correspondence at Iowa State Department of History and Archives in Des Moines.

[36] Grimes, "To the People of Iowa."

foreigners from participating fully in a homestead program.[37]

Finally Grimes came to the central issue of his address, the denunciation of the Nebraska Bill. He reviewed most of the arguments advanced against the repeal of the Missouri Compromise and the attempts to spread slavery, vowing that "the Nebraska outrage shall receive no aid or comfort from me."[38]

It was partly on the Nebraska question that Grimes sought to lure the German voters to his banner, not by appealing to their antislavery impulses but by emphasizing an item which had appeared in the *Burlington Daily Telegraph* on March 21. This paper had noted that in a Senate speech A. P. Butler of South Carolina had made references to Iowa which, at best, were indiscreet and unfortunately timed. Butler allegedly had asserted that

> the slaveholder, with his slaves well governed forms a relation that is innocent enough, and useful enough. I believe that it is a population which Iowa tomorrow would prefer to an innundation of those men coming as emigrants from a foreign country, wholly unacquainted with the institutions of this country—and nearly all continental comers are of this class. This same remark cannot be made of those, who like the Irish and English, have lived under the administration of the common law.[39]

With a pen dripping with sarcasm, Grimes denounced Butler's remarks: "In the boastfulness of anticipated triumph, the citizens of Iowa have been told by a Southern Senator how much better would be the condition of our State with negro slaves than with our foreign population." Further to arouse the antislavery segments of Iowa's population, Grimes added that "a distinguished Representative from Georgia has announced that in fifteen years, Iowa will be a slave state."[40]

[37] *Ibid.*
[38] *Ibid.*
[39] 33 Cong., 1 sess., *Congressional Globe*, Appendix, 333.
[40] Grimes, "To the People of Iowa."

Grimes's pamphlet received the usual laudatory reception from friendly journals locally and nationally. For example, Horace Greeley's *New York Tribune*, widely circulated throughout the North, strongly approved of it:

> The Address is marked by great clearness and ability, and shows Mr. Grimes to be a man of abundant talent. . . . It is a plain and manly appeal to the people. The views he advocates are so undeniably sound, that did no partisan hindrances exist, one would suppose they could hardly fail to receive the endorsement of every citizen of the state.[41]

The Democratic press, however, raked the message and its author over the coals. One paper described his address as "a miserable piece of the lowest kind of electioneering trickery, filled with the grossest falsehoods and misrepresentation."[42] Another declared that his remarks were not really addressed to all Iowans but merely to certain factions, principally bankers and abolitionists. The Washington, D.C., *Union* also excoriated the Whig gubernatorial candidate. Among other things, the *Union* questioned Grimes's sincerity concerning his friendly feelings toward the foreign-born:

> Our would-be-governor of Iowa was, doubtless, a few years ago, if he is not now, with most of his party, *a native American.* Like General Scott, he had doubtless cursed the foreigners *after* the election, though he coaxed them most affectionately before the election. The adopted citizens have always been a stumbling block to the Whigs.[43]

Stung by Grimes's reference to Butler's speech and to the alleged remarks of a Georgia representative, Iowa Democrats queried Butler as well as the entire Georgia congressional delega-

---

[41] Quoted in Herriott, "A Neglected Factor in the Anti-Slavery Triumph in Iowa in 1854," 273–74.

[42] *Iowa State Gazette*, April 19, 1854.

[43] Quoted in *Des Moines Valley Whig*, May 25, 1854; *Iowa Sentinel* (Fairfield), April 20, 1854.

tion in order to prove that Grimes's statements were pure fabrications. Henn communicated with Georgia's representatives, while Senators Dodge and Jones wrote to Georgia's senators and to Butler himself. Georgia's House delegation flatly denied having made any such assertion as charged by Grimes, dismissing his accusation as a "part of the general system of wholesale *misrepresentation* which so many of the enemies of the equal, just, and republican principles of the Kansas and Nebraska bill have resorted to, for the purpose of misleading the minds of the people of the Northern States upon them." Georgia's senators agreed with their colleagues in the House.

Senator Butler, on his part, insisted that he "never said anything that could authorize such a remark." Continuing further, he assured his friends from Iowa that his earlier statements were "intended to illustrate the opinion that a gentleman of good character in Missouri and Nebraska, notwithstanding he held slaves, would be as good a neighbor as a newly immigrated foreigner from Germany," and nothing else.[44] But whether or not Butler and the Georgia delegation had satisfactorily vindicated themselves to the Iowa Democrats, the damage had already been done.

One day before publication of Grimes's pamphlet, the voters of Iowa went to the polls to select a superintendent of public instruction. While the Whigs had advocated a change in the state's educational structure, the Democrats did not mention the matter. Although a last-minute substitute Whig candidate, Isaac Stevens, did appear, the withdrawal of George Shedd as the regular Whig nominee left the field virtually clear to the Democratic hopeful, Eads. The latter carried the election by a vote of 17,793 to 13,462, a manifest indication that the power of the Democrats in Iowa was still formidable despite the excitement which the Kansas-Nebraska debate was generating.[45]

[44] The letters and the responses to them were published in the *Iowa State Gazette*, May 10 and 24 and June 14, 1854.

[45] Election Records, 1848–1860, in the Office of the Secretary of State of Iowa, Des Moines.

Disturbed by the news of the Democratic victory in the contest for the educational post, wounded by the attacks of the Washington *Union,* and cautioned by the antislavery leaders he undoubtedly met during a side trip to Washington while on his eastern travels, Grimes decided to cut short his stay in the East and return to Iowa to take to the stump. The news from Iowa had apparently tempered his earlier optimism.[46]

Arriving in Iowa in mid-May, Grimes penned another address to Iowans in which he endeavored to soften the darts hurled at him by the *Union* by attacking Dodge and Jones. He accused them of voting for the Clayton amendment, of driving Northern railroad investors from Iowa by catering to the South, and of encouraging the spread of slavery. To the charges that he constantly shifted his views to suit the occasion, Grimes rather weakly replied that experience had prompted him to modify certain of his earlier views.[47]

Following the publication of his second address, Grimes issued an itinerary for thirty-one speeches which he intended to deliver throughout the state. At the same time he challenged his Democratic adversary, Curtis Bates, to join him on his tour to debate the various issues with him. The Democratic nominee, however, refused to accept the gauntlet. Nevertheless, Grimes had determined to seize and hold the initiative.[48]

Democratic newspapers hammered at Grimes for deciding to stump the state after he had already declared that his first address had precluded such activity. The *Iowa Capital Reporter* of Iowa City accused him of taking to the stump because of a belated realization that his initial pamphlet had failed to deceive the public. The *Iowa State Gazette* of Burlington charged that Grimes had always intended to canvass the state. The Mount Pleasant *Weekly Observer,* however, friendly to Grimes, ex-

[46] Herriott, "James Grimes Versus the Southrons," 353, 404.
[47] *Des Moines Valley Whig,* June 1, 1854; *Davenport* (Iowa) *Gazette,* June 8, 1854.
[48] Herriott, "James Grimes Versus the Southrons," 404.

plained that he had returned to Iowa solely to respond to the unwarranted animadversions of the Washington *Union*.[49]

Grimes opened his tour of Iowa at Mount Pleasant on May 29,
remained in the southwestern portion of the state for about a
week, and then headed for the western counties. Writing to his
wife from the Missouri slope, he reported that he had met with
strong opposition from pro-Nebraska men, especially in Pottawattamie County, and from antitemperance partisans. Toward the
end of June, Grimes began to work his way eastward through the
central counties. Despite his energetic stumping, Democrats remained confident of victory. About three weeks before election
day Grimes himself acknowledged the strength of these sentiments as his own optimism waned. On July 13 he sent a call for
aid to Salmon P. Chase and Elihu Washburne, asking for letters
to assist him in his campaign.[50]

In the meantime, meetings were held in several counties in
Iowa to protest against the Nebraska Bill. These gatherings were
attended by abolitionists, Free-Soilers, Whigs, temperance supporters, and anti-Nebraska Democrats. Some of the opposition
to the Kansas-Nebraska Bill stemmed from the Clayton amendment which almost had become part of the bill. Because of the
antiforeign nature of the amendment, abolitionists sought to convince the Germans, whom the amendment especially antago-
nized, that the real purpose of the entire Douglas bill was to
prevent foreign-born persons from migrating to Nebraska. One
Whig paper thought it only natural for the Germans to resent the
measure and explained that the Irish remained silent only because
they had grown accustomed to years of oppression at the hands
of the English. Theodore Guelich, the editor of *Der Demokrat*,

[49] *Iowa Capital Reporter* (Iowa City), May 31, 1854; *Iowa State Gazette*,
June 14, 1854; *The Davenport Gazette*, June 8, 1854; *Des Moines Valley Whig*,
June 21, 1854.

[50] James Grimes to Mrs. Grimes, June 4, 16, and 18, 1854, quoted in William
Salter, *The Life of James W. Grimes*, 51–52; *Des Moines Valley Whig*, June 1
and 12, 1854; A. W. Carpenter to Laurel Summers, July 16, 1854, in the Summers Correspondence; Sparks, "The Birth of the Republican Party in Iowa, 1854–
1856," 103.

the influential German-language paper in Davenport, was outspoken in his denunciation of Senator Douglas and the Nebraska
Bill. He called for a realignment of the parties because the existing organizations were unable to cope with the important issues
of the day.[51]

Grimes's efforts to lure the Germans away from the Democratic banner may have been meeting with some success despite
their dislike of the temperance plank in the Whig platform. Editors of German-language newspapers encouraged this political
defection among their readers. Indeed, in several counties German voters were irate because they believed that they had been
prevented from exercising a proper role in the selection of delegates to the state Democratic convention. James Grant, a prominent Democrat from Davenport, pessimistically warned that
many German voters would desert the Democrats. He noted in
open alarm that Grimes was scheduled to visit Davenport just
before the general election.[52]

In Washington, meanwhile, the Senate passed the Kansas-
Nebraska Bill on March 4, 1854, by a vote of 37 to 14. Dodge and
Jones cast affirmative ballots. On May 22 the House concurred by
a vote of 113 to 100—Henn responded, "Yea"—and President
Franklin Pierce signed the act on May 30. The enactment of the
measure intensified the protests in Iowa against its passage.

Anti-Nebraska meetings at Davenport, Muscatine, Anamosa,
Elkader, and Burlington and in Washington, Henry, and Linn
counties adopted resolutions condemning the Nebraska Act for
repealing the Missouri Compromise and for conspiring to extend
slavery into the free territories of the United States. The assembly
in Washington County also passed a resolution vowing to with-
hold votes from any man running for public office "who is not

[51] *Des Moines Valley Whig*, March 23, 1854; Sparks, "The Birth of the Republican Party in Iowa, 1848 to 1860," 72.

[52] *Burlington Daily Telegraph*, January 6 and 8, 1854; James Grant to Laurel
Summers, August 2, 1854, in the Summers Correspondence; *Davenport Gazette*,
August 10, 1854.

decidedly in favor of a prohibitory liquor law." Other meetings endorsed Grimes, attacked such renegade Whig journals as the *Daily Hawk-Eye* of Burlington, and applauded the Muscatine Democratic paper for opposing the Douglas measure. The anti-Nebraska gathering in Linn County adopted a plank endorsing the Democratic national platform of 1852 and insisted that persons in attendance were loyal Democrats who wanted no part of "unjust or despotic measures." In Muscatine a segment of the Democratic party split from the parent body on the Nebraska issue and came out against a pro-Nebraska ticket in that county. The meeting at Elkader, claiming to be the first anti-Nebraska convention in the state, urged the repeal of the Fugitive Slave Law and nominated an anti-Nebraska ticket dominated by former Whigs.[53]

That the Nebraska controversy was a significant issue during the campaign of 1854 in Iowa cannot be denied, and that the Iowa Democratic party was divided on this issue is equally beyond question. Actually, the schism within the Democratic organization ran deeper than the Nebraska problem. Other areas of friction and sources of disagreement contributed to the disruption of party unity. Two years earlier disputes over railroad projects had resulted in the defeat of the Democratic candidate in the Second Congressional District. The question of state constitutional revision provoked considerable intramural strife, as did the matter of the incorporation of banks and the authority of the latter to issue bank notes to replace the confusion of currencies then in circulation in the state. Internal improvements and homestead proposals also produced serious friction within the ranks.[54]

[53] 33 Cong., 1 sess., *Congressional Globe*, 532, 1254; John Cook was absent from the House and did not vote. See also Allan Nevins, *Ordeal of the Union*, II, 136–59; *Burlington Daily Telegraph*, March 21, July 18, 19, 21, 25, and 27, and August 19, 1854; *Des Moines Valley Whig*, March 30, 1854; *History of Clayton County Iowa*, 419–20.

[54] Herriott, "A Neglected Factor in the Anti-Slavery Triumph in Iowa in 1854," 185–86.

The temperance movement in Iowa had increased in intensity and momentum during the years immediately preceding the events of 1854 and was a popular cause with most Whigs and not a few vocal Democrats throughout the state. Early in December, 1853, temperance advocates had circulated an *Address to the Total Abstinence Societies and to the Friends of Total Abstinence in the State of Iowa* to promote their cause. Later in December the State Temperance Society convened in Iowa City, where the delegates adopted a number of resolutions, two of which warned of the political significance of the temperance issue:

> Resolved that the temperance question as agitated at this day, with reference to a prohibitory law, involves all the best interests of Society, and while it is not our design to disturb existing political parties or organizations, yet we do intend to have and to enforce a law, prohibiting the manufacture and traffic of intoxicating liquors as a beverage, whatever may be the consequences to any or all political parties.
>
> Resolved that as men of all parties and no party, we will vote for no man to make and execute laws who is not decidedly and unequivocally in favor of the passage and enforcement of a law prohibiting the sale of intoxicating liquors as a beverage.[55]

Moreover, the temperance issue was political dynamite to the Democratic party. The Reverend Henry Clay Dean, a fiery Methodist preacher of the Gospel, frontier style, and a firm supporter of temperance, addressed letters to the gubernatorial candidates requesting their views on the subject. Not wishing to reveal their sentiments too plainly, Grimes and Bates both replied that they would not veto a measure of the legislature which provided for prohibition. Dean decided to endorse and campaign for the Democrats and became a source of no little embarrassment to the party, especially in the antitemperance areas.[56]

[55] *Ibid.*, 210–11.

[56] Curtis Bates to Henry Clay Dean, March 8, 1854, quoted in the *Burlington Daily Telegraph*, March 27, 1854; James Grimes to Henry Clay Dean, March 2, 1854, quoted in Salter, *The Life of James W. Grimes*, 50.

The press of both parties, of course, continued to flail at each other. The *Tribune* of New York praised Grimes as "a man of abundant talent" and lauded his first address. Conversely, Democratic papers hailed Curtis Bates as "an amiable, honorable, and intelligent man." Bates was a worthy Democrat because he was loyal to the party and above the squabbles of the past few years. Grimes, on the other hand, was a thorough abolitionist, and the Whigs were captives of the radical elements with whom Grimes had made his bargain.[57]

Whig journals also continued to press for constitutional changes to permit banking, but Democratic papers, still frightened by the specter of Eastern financiers and speculators, opposed such changes. The need for banking, averred one paper, was spurious and unfounded. These institutions were established merely to enrich bankers at the expense of the rest of society. The printing of paper money, which would accompany the legalization of banks, was "not only unnecessary but vicious" and was useful only to bankers. Most editors, however, were willing to permit the voters to decide whether they wanted a revision of the constitution.[58]

Nor did the state press overlook the growing demand for homestead legislation. Whig journals charged that the passage of the Nebraska Bill had doomed homestead legislation. They asserted that Democrats would never enact homestead legislation because the party was controlled by slavery interests who had no desire to see free labor encouraged to migrate to the territories. But the Whigs could not with honesty accuse Iowa's congressional delegation of laxity on this score, for Iowa Democrats had been working indefatigably for a homestead law. The state Democratic press also welcomed a homestead act, for such legislation, it was

[57] *New York Tribune* quoted in *Des Moines Valley Whig*, May 11, 1854; *Davenport Gazette*, July 13, 1854; *Iowa Weekly Republican*, July 7, 1854; *Iowa State Gazette*, January 18, 1854; Davenport *Democratic Banner*, April 14, 1854.
[58] Dubuque (Iowa) *Express and Herald* quoted in *Iowa Capital Reporter*, October 4, 1854; *Eddyville* (Iowa) *Free Press*, December 22, 1854.

claimed, would benefit the country by draining the surplus population from the cities.[59]

To counter absurd Whig charges that they were antiforeign, as
manifested by their support of the Kansas-Nebraska Act, Democrats strove to identify Grimes and other Whigs with the newly
formed Know-Nothing organization, a group whose *raison d'être*
was a strong antipathy to foreigners and Roman Catholics. Except during political campaigns, Democrats declared, Whigs and
Know-Nothings worked hand in hand against the foreign-born
population. In an election year, however, the former pretended
to sympathize with the immigrants from other nations. And this
was the Whig game during the current campaign:

> Mr. Grimes and others, who heretofore have turned up their
> aristocratic noses at our fellow citizens of foreign birth, pre-
> tend to be wonderfully concerned about the rights and inter-
> ests of those who happen to have been born on the banks of
> the Rhine or Shannon. It is astonishing how liberal Whig can-
> didates become toward foreigners just about election time.[60]

The question of relocating the state capital also played a role
of some importance in the campaign. Sentiment in favor of re-
moving the capital to Des Moines, a place more suitably situated
than Iowa City, had been gathering momentum. Because Curtis
Bates was a Des Moines resident, the friends of the Iowa City
location viewed him with suspicion. Moreover, in Des Moines
itself there was a ridiculous struggle between the east and west
portions of the town over the actual site of the capitol building.
Residents of the eastern side suspected that Bates, who lived on
the western side, favored his own sector as a site.[61]

While the gubernatorial contest raged throughout the state,

[59] George M. Stephenson, *The Political History of the Public Lands,* 221;
Burlington Daily Telegraph, July 27, 1854; *Des Moines Valley Whig,* March
9, 1854; 33 Cong., 1 sess., *Congressional Globe,* 1667; *Iowa State Gazette,* January 4, 1854.
[60] *Iowa State Gazette,* June 14, 1854.
[61] Snyder, "Curtis Bates," 304.

the congressional races were disputed with equal vigor. In the First District, Augustus Hall, campaigning on a strong pro-Nebraska platform, had a distinct advantage over his lesser-known rival, Rufus L. B. Clarke, in that normally Democratic sector. In the Second District the Whigs sought to retain the seat which John P. Cook had wrested from the Democrats in 1852. Here Hempstead ran as a pro-Nebraska, antitemperance candidate against James Thorington, who took the opposite position on both issues. The Know-Nothing association of the latter had not yet come to light. Both candidates engaged in a series of debates which extended throughout the district. In Thorington the Whigs had a man who could unite temperance advocates, abolitionists, anti-Nebraska men, and nativists.[62]

When the smoke of political battle had at least cleared and the votes cast on August 7 had been tabulated, the results indicated that the Whigs had scored an impressive victory in the state. In the battle for the legislature the Whigs took forty of the seventy seats in the House of Representatives, but the Democrats captured the Senate sixteen to fifteen. On a joint ballot, however, the Whigs would control the General Assembly. The Democrats carried all the lesser state offices except auditor.[63]

The Whigs retained their control in the Second Congressional District, where Thorington trounced Hempstead by a vote of 11,424 to 9,772. In the First District, Augustus Hall defeated his Whig rival Clarke by 171 votes, 11,213 to 11,042. James Grimes's tireless campaigning was not in vain, for he defeated Bates by 23,325 votes to 21,202.[64]

The Whigs naturally rejoiced at the outcome of the election. For the first time in the history of the state the Democrats had lost

[62] *Iowa Weekly Republican*, July 12, 1854; *Davenport Gazette*, July 27, 1854; *Dubuque Miners' Express*, quoted in *Des Moines Valley Whig*, July 26, 1854; R. Christie to Laurel Summers, July 18, 1854, in the Summers Correspondence; George W. McCleary to Laurel Summers, July 20, 1854, *ibid.*

[63] Pelzer, "The History and Principles of the Democratic Party of Iowa, 1846–1857," 211; Election Records, 1848–1860.

[64] Election Records, 1848–1860.

the gubernatorial office, as well as one branch of the assembly. One Whig paper, carried away by its own exuberance, exclaimed that "the recent election of Iowa can only be properly expressed by styling it a *revolution*." According to this journal, the reason for the Whig victory was evident: the repeal of the Missouri Compromise had brought the downfall of the Democratic party.[65] Grimes himself was only slightly more modest in his appraisal of the results. To Salmon P. Chase he wrote: "I fought the battle nearly alone. My colleagues on the congressional ticket were dead weights; I was too much of a Free Soiler; and I had the *Burlington Hawk-Eye*, a professedly Whig paper, and the *silver-grey* interest openly against me."[66]

In New York, Horace Greeley examined and assessed the results of the election in the Hawkeye State and offered his readers his own evaluation of its outcome:

> We observe in some quarters a disposition to represent the late triumph of the Anti-slavery and Anti-grog-shop ticket in Iowa as a victory of the Whigs. This is erroneous and unjust. The Whig Party, as such, never could have gained that success. It was achieved by a fusion of all honest parties—by the combination of men previously entertaining differing or antagonistic sentiments on political questions who came together on the same common ground of Slavery restriction and Liquor prohibition, and fought the glorious battle of Freedom as one man, with the result at which we now rejoice. It was not done by either of the old organizations but by that new party of the People which the Nebraska outrage has brought to life in all Northern States and which, we do not doubt, is destined substantially to triumph elsewhere.[67]

The defeat of Bates stunned the Democratic press. One journal

---

[65] *Cincinnati Gazette* quoted in *Des Moines Valley Whig*, August 30, 1854.
[66] James W. Grimes to Salmon P. Chase, October 3, 1854, printed in Salter, *The Life of James W. Grimes*, 54.
[67] Quoted in Herriott, "A Neglected Factor in the Anti-Slavery Triumph in Iowa in 1854," 216.

blamed the failure of the ticket, and of Hempstead in particular, upon the temperance issue.[68] The *Iowa Democratic Enquirer* of Muscatine, a foe of both nativism and of the Kansas-Nebraska legislation, observed:

> One more element entered actively into the contest in some localities. The old Native American party, newly revived, and freshly organized, has extended its influence to Iowa, and in some portions of the state wields considerable power. The support of this proscriptive faction was of course given to the Whigs.[69]

Moreover, lamented the Muscatine newspaper, *"the leaders of the Democratic party abandoned the Baltimore platform of 1852; and violated the fundamental principles of Democracy."*[70]

In Washington the *Union* weighed the results and decided that

> the causes are apparent and unquestionable. The Whigs took ground against that clause in the radical constitution of the State prohibiting all banking in the State, and made that an issue, while they rallied on the temperance question with all their force. Of course, the Nebraska bill was made the pretext of excitement, although the element had less to do with the canvass than is supposed.[71]

Another Democratic paper pointed out that Whig control of the Iowa legislature would end the career of Senator Dodge, whose term was to expire in 1855. That a Whig would replace him was now a foregone conclusion.[72]

The factors underlying Grimes's victory were, of course, complex. No single issue alone can explain his triumph. Employing

---

[68] *Iowa State Journal and Sunbeam*, September 1, 1854, quoted in Dan E. Clark, "The History of Liquor Legislation in Iowa, 1846–1861," *Iowa Journal of History and Politics*, Vol. VI (1908), 71.

[69] Herriott, "A Neglected Factor in the Anti-Slavery Triumph in Iowa in 1854," 343–45.

[70] *Ibid.*, 344.

[71] Quoted in *Iowa Capital Reporter*, September 6, 1854.

[72] *Milwaukee News* quoted in *Iowa Capital Reporter*, September 6, 1854.

the Nebraska question with consummate skill, Grimes presented a moral canopy under which several dissimilar groups could unite politically. Disdaining the support of old-line national Whigs, Grimes relied upon the more radical segments of the party and combined them with anti-Nebraska men, Free-Soilers, Know-Nothings, abolitionists, temperance advocates, and disgruntled Democrats. The latter had grown dissatisfied with the Democratic party because of quarrels over internal improvements, constitutional revision, railroad projects, and homesteads. The matter of relocating the state capital also operated to the disadvantage of the party. Among the foreign-born voters, especially the Germans, however, aside from the assertions of certain editors of German-language newspapers, scant evidence exists that Grimes was successful in converting them to the views of his party. As the elections of 1859 and 1860 would later reveal, and as the Hollanders had already demonstrated, the immigrant voters were too strongly opposed to nativism and temperance to support Grimes and his ticket.

The Democrats, in part, contributed to their own downfall. Believing that the state would remain safely under their control, they did not wage as active and as thorough a campaign as did Grimes and his supporters. Only excessive overconfidence can explain the failure of party leaders in Washington—Dodge and Jones, for example—to return to Iowa to work for the party ticket. To be sure, Congress was in session during a good part of the time, but even in the crucial stages of the canvass no one returned to Iowa to assist the state ticket.[73]

But more than anything else, Grimes's victory was a personal triumph, a fitting reward for his tireless labor and energetic stumping, as well as his political acumen. A more intensive effort on Bates's part might well have given him the election, for, even

[73] Cf. Milton, *The Eve of Conflict*, 173; Herriott, "James Grimes Versus the Southrons," 428; Sparks, "The Birth of the Republican Party in Iowa, 1854–1856," 17.

with the moral and emotional heat which Grimes had generated, the outcome was exceptionally close and far from fully decisive.

Had the Iowa Whigs conducted their campaign solely on the basis of their opposition to the Kansas-Nebraska Act, they might well have been defeated by their opponents. Local issues of vital concern to the citizens of the state motivated the voters as effectively and decisively as the Nebraska agitation. What the Nebraska law did do was provide the adhesive element which enabled the Whigs to fuse the various special interest groups into a solid unit of opposition to the Iowa Democratic party and thereby initiate the beginning of the latter's political demise in the state.

Of Legislature, Liquor, and Land

THE DEMOCRATIC party which emerged from the 1854 elections bled from many wounds. The Nebraska question tried even the party stalwarts and produced a deep cleavage among the rank and file. The temperance issue likewise rent the party. Moreover, the old feud in Dubuque and the discord in the east-central counties remained unresolved. A respite from politics might have allowed peacemakers in the organization to soothe ruffled feelings and reestablish unity, but the Democratic party obtained no such pause. The Whigs, by now merely an amorphous collection of individuals loyal to old principles, along with the other opposition splinter groups temporarily united under Grimes's fusionist appeal, by no means remained idle while the Democrats worked to repair their party. Indeed, the political battle was resumed with renewed vigor even before the close of 1854, when the state legislature convened to elect a full-term United States senator.

The August balloting had given the Whigs and their allies a

majority of ten in the House. Although the Democrats held a one-vote advantage in the Senate, the Whigs would hold a nine-vote margin in a joint session, assuring the latter of the senatorial plum. Democratic strategy was to delay the selection of a senator until after the next elections. Incumbent Senator Dodge advocated this maneuver but nevertheless accepted his party's support for reelection in the face of the heavy odds against him. Though his chances of success were indeed slim, with the proper skill in management and procrastination he might still conceivably score a victory. Ben Samuels, of Dubuque, a loyal Dodge supporter and a prominent party figure there, believed that the Democrats might be able to pull through if everyone in the party could be held firmly in line. Party leaders, moreover, were encouraged by the evidence of dissension which existed within the ranks of their opposition.[1]

A large number of Whigs sought the position of United States senator, among them John P. Cook, Stephen B. Shelladay, Fitz Henry Warren, Ebenezer Cook, Milton D. Browning, and Joseph D. H. Street. James Harlan, the eventual winner, seems not to have been an early candidate. Ebenezer Cook and Milton D. Browning tried to secure Democratic support in order to carry the election. This in no way endeared these office seekers to the more militant antislavery elements of their own party. Split into the Silver Greys or National Whigs, who held moderate to conservative views on the slavery issue, and the radical faction, whose antislavery impulse was exceedingly strong, the Whigs could not easily unite behind a candidate. The Democrats hoped to widen this cleavage and profit from it, and thereby either secure the election of their own candidate or in accordance with the Dodge plan prevent an election entirely. Meeting in caucus, the Whigs

---

[1] Louis Pelzer, *Augustus Caesar Dodge*, 196, 324–25; Ben M. Samuels to Laurel Summers, December 7, 1854, in the Laurel Summers Correspondence at the Iowa State Department of History and Archives in Des Moines; Amos Witten to Laurel Summers, December 7, 1854, *ibid.*

closed ranks behind James Harlan, discarding all other candidates in a serious effort to unite all factions against the Democrats.[2]

Not all the Whigs in the Iowa General Assembly were willing, however, to accept the action of their caucus. Consequently, the legislative balloting continued with no results. On the third ballot Dodge withdrew from the race, discouraged that his long service as an elected public official was apparently about to end. With the deadlock still unresolved, the joint session decided to discontinue voting for senator until the three judges for the supreme court had been elected. Two of the candidates, both Whigs, won without difficulty—George G. Wright and William G. Woodward. But a stalemate developed over the third judicial position. The joint meeting of the legislature then decided to resume the balloting for senator.[3]

The Democrats resolved to back Milton Browning, a moderate Whig. The latter, however, failed to win enough votes from his own party, prompting some Democrats to withdraw their endorsement of his candidacy. When the scheme to support Browning fell through, the Democrats decided to adopt the Dodge strategy and prevent the election. On Saturday, January 6, 1855, the senate met briefly in its own chambers and immediately adjourned until the following Monday, refusing to go into joint session with the house. But the Whigs in the lower chamber, along with their counterparts in the senate, had different thoughts on the matter. Though the senate had adjourned for the ensuing week end, enough Whigs from the upper chamber appeared in the house to win recognition from officials there, and a joint session was formally convened. James Harlan and the Whig choice for the third judicial vacancy, Norman W. Isbell, a former Free-

---

[2] Dan E. Clark, *History of Senatorial Elections in Iowa: A Study in American Politics*, 68–70, 73, 81–82; Robert Robinson to Laurel Summers, October 28, 1854, in the Summers Correspondence.

[3] *Journal of the Senate*, 5th General Assembly of Iowa, 1854, 44–45, 75, 112–13.

Soiler, won without further difficulty. Governor Grimes immediately issued their commissions of election.[4]

As far as the Whigs were concerned, the election was now a *fait accompli*, but the Democrats had no intention of accepting in good grace the results of what they called "unusual" proceedings. Senator George W. Jones received formal notices of protest from Democrats of both branches of the assembly. They charged that Harlan had been improperly elected by an illegally constituted body of men calling themselves a joint convention, and they asked the United States Senate, now the sole judge of the legality of Harlan's election and of his qualifications and credentials, to declare his election void and his seat vacant.[5]

Curiously, Jones did not press for an immediate Senate investigation of Harlan's election but instead requested the Senate to recognize his new colleague and admit him to full membership by swearing him in. His motives behind this action have never been revealed. Perhaps he wanted and needed Harlan's support for the pending land-grant bill to aid Iowa's railroad-construction activities. Moreover, a spirited battle over the seating of Harlan could well have derailed the land-grant legislation, a donation of vast acreage dearly coveted by Iowans. It is doubtful that Jones believed that Harlan was truly entitled to his seat, in view of the irregularity of the proceedings in Iowa City. Whatever his motives, Jones did not raise the issue of Harlan's disputed election until August, 1856, when he formally requested the Senate to investigate its legality. The Committee of the Judiciary, to which Harlan's case was referred, reported back several months later, on January 5, 1857, and stated that Harlan's election was void and his seat vacant.[6]

[4] *Journal of the House of Representatives,* 5th General Assembly of Iowa, 1854, 183–88; James Grimes to ————, January 7, 1855, printed in William Salter, *The Life of James W. Grimes,* 64–65.

[5] Clark, *History of Senatorial Elections in Iowa,* 88; *Journal of the House of Representatives,* 5th General Assembly of Iowa, 1854, 189, 208–11; *Journal of the Senate,* 5th General Assembly of Iowa, 1854, 122–23.

[6] 34 Cong., 1 sess., *Congressional Globe,* 2, 2079; 34 Cong., 3 sess., *ibid.,* 221.

The Iowa legislature, by then completely controlled by the youthful Republican party, overwhelmingly endorsed Harlan, who immediately returned to Washington to resume his post, this time without any uncertainty about the legality of his status. He trounced his Democratic opponent, William F. Coolbaugh, by the substantial margin of 63 votes to 35.[7] Thus ended the somewhat complex struggle for Dodge's seat, a contest which originated late in 1854 and dragged on until early 1857. Despite the Senate decision, Harlan had nevertheless served virtually the entire six years of his term.

In the meantime, the Democrats faced the difficult task of repairing the serious rifts which beset their party. Iowa voters would cast ballots in April, 1855, to fill the posts of register and commissioner of the Des Moines River Improvement and register of the State Land Office, all sources of significant statewide patronage. More importantly, perhaps, socially as well as politically, the voters would also render their decisions on the question of adopting or rejecting prohibition in the state. On this major issue the Democrats were also badly divided; individual conscience often obstructed loyalty to party.

Consequently, when Democratic leaders announced that their party's convention would be held at Iowa City on January 24, 1855, editors loyal to the party greeted the call with a plea for the restoration of harmony and concord within the organization. The Democratic organ in Dubuque implored Democrats "to banish from their minds questions of local and personal difference" and rid themselves of the "animosities of the past" in a united stand on the serious issues confronting the state and the nation.[8] Though the offices to be filled in the coming election admittedly were not of major importance, nevertheless "the proper organization of the Democratic party of Iowa is not unimportant" and the meeting of the state convention was the proper time to

[7] *Journal of the Senate*, 6th General Assembly of Iowa, 1856, 366.
[8] *Iowa Sentinel* (Fairfield), January 11, 1855.

achieve this goal.[9] County conventions which met to select delegates to the January assembly also expressed the desire for a
revitalized as well as harmonious party.[10]

At Iowa City the Democrats drew up a platform designed to
heal the party's lacerations. On the important question of prohibition, the platform was silent; presumably each Democrat would
vote according to the dictates of his conscience. The party also
failed to take a stand on internal improvements, the tariff, or
homestead legislation. The Democrats did reaffirm support of the
Compromise of 1850 and again pledged their faith in the national
Democratic platform of 1852. Concerning the young American,
or Know-Nothing, organization, the party, while not directly
condemning the principles of that secret order, nevertheless
wanted it clearly understood that it would resist "every attempt
to abridge the right [of foreign-born persons] of becoming citizens and owners of soil among us."[11] Thus, by trying to ignore the
disruptive problems which created the schisms in the party, by
drawing up what must at best be termed a vague and weak platform, the Iowa Democratic party sought to heal its wounds
through the agency of time.

Too shattered and splintered even to consider calling a state
convention, the Iowa Whigs instead held a caucus of their legislative members to select candidates for the three offices to be
filled at the April election. This action provoked one Democratic
paper to caustic editorial comment about the unusual procedure,
but such partisan baiting was minimal during the months preceding the day of balloting.[12] Whigs did endeavor to rally around
the time-tested issues of homesteads and slavery, paying par-

[9] Dubuque (Iowa) *Express and Herald* quoted in *Iowa Sentinel,* January
18, 1855.
[10] Davenport (Iowa) *Democratic Banner,* January 26, 1855; Charles J.
Fulton, *History of Jefferson County Iowa,* I, 300.
[11] Roy V. Sherman, "Political Party Platforms in Iowa," unpublished M.A.
thesis, State University of Iowa, 1926, 126–28.
[12] *Iowa Sentinel,* February 8, 1855.

ticular attention to the fugitive-slave question, but these paled beside the matter of prohibition. And in April the Whigs won the three offices at stake, each by margins of four thousand or more votes.[13]

While the loss of the three statewide offices did not especially surprise them, Democratic leaders were thoroughly stunned and genuinely alarmed by the success of the infant Know-Nothing organization, which made serious inroads in areas of traditional Democratic strength in the southern and southeastern portions of the state. The Know-Nothings captured the town elections in Keokuk, Davenport, and Muscatine. In Appanoose County they won apparently with the aid of local Whigs, while from Des Moines County came word that their victory was "not an unexpected one."[14]

Although the Know-Nothings championed a vigorous brand of home-grown Americanism, coupled with a strong anti-Catholic bias, they really sought to reap large dividends from the unsettled political situation in the state. The secret order sought to attract the various uncommitted elements which Grimes had fused during his gubernatorial campaign: the antislavery and anti-Nebraska Democrats, Free-Soilers, antislavery Whigs, abolitionists, homestead advocates, temperance supporters, and other special interest groups. The anti-German, anti-Irish stance of the Know-Nothings could only have been rather pleasing to advocates of

[13] *Dubuque Tribune*, February 18, 1855, quoted in Franklin T. Oldt (ed.), *History of Dubuque County Iowa*, 336; *Journal of the Senate*, 5th General Assembly of Iowa, 1854, 120, 134; Election Records, 1848–1860, in the Office of the Secretary of State of Iowa, Des Moines.

[14] Willard I. Toussaint, "The Know-Nothing Party in Iowa," unpublished M.A. thesis, State University of Iowa, 1956, 56–57; *Biographical and Historical Record of Wayne and Appanoose Counties Iowa*, 693; William Harper to Laurel Summers, September 5, 1855, in the Summers Correspondence; V.P. Van Antwerp to Laurel Summers, April 5, 1855, *ibid.* See also George A. Boeck, "An Early Iowa Community: Aspects of Economic, Social, and Political Development in Burlington, Iowa, 1833–1866," unpublished Ph.D. dissertation, University of Iowa, 1961, 248–50, 260–61; and Faye E. Harris, "A Frontier Community: The Economic, Social, and Political Development of Keokuk, Iowa, 1820–1866," unpublished Ph.D. dissertation, University of Iowa, 1965, 323–24.

temperance, for no native or foreign-born blocs were louder in their condemnation of prohibition than the Germans and the Irish.[15]

The results of the referendum on the question of prohibition underscored and furnished concrete evidence to the Iowa Democratic party that its sense of political insecurity was not without foundation. Indeed, popular approval of prohibition came despite the opposition of a majority of Democrats to the measure, as the fusionists again demonstrated their political strength.

Sentiment against alcohol had been a long-standing American phenomenon. Indeed, the tendency to blame spirituous beverages for the ailments of society meets a sympathetic response in certain quarters even today. The tendency was present in Iowa during the 1850's. When a special committee of the Iowa assembly blamed alcohol for much of the poverty and misery in the state, a preponderant segment of private opinion supported the findings of the committee.[16]

During the winter of 1850–51 the advocates of temperance began to demand total prohibition, and petitions asking for prohibition began flooding the state legislature. Neal Dow's success in bringing prohibition to Maine in 1851 had encouraged temperance forces in Iowa. Each year the number of petitions reaching the assembly on the subject of prohibition increased, as temperance adherents achieved a greater degree of unity than ever before.[17] Many state and county temperance conventions adopted

15 Toussaint, "The Know-Nothing Party in Iowa," 44–45.

16 *Journal of the House of Representatives*, 3rd General Assembly of Iowa, 1850, 196–97; John Todd, *Early Settlement and Growth of Western Iowa or Reminiscences*, 177–78.

17 Dan E. Clark, "Recent Liquor Legislation in Iowa," *Iowa Journal of History and Politics*, Vol. XV (1917), 43; *Journal of the House of Representatives*, 3rd General Assembly of Iowa, 1850, 36–37, 77, 106, 160; *ibid.*, 4th General Assembly of Iowa, 1852, 231; *ibid.*, 5th General Assembly of Iowa, 1854, 81, 125, 178, 221; *Journal of the Senate*, 3rd General Assembly of Iowa, 1850, 119–20, 145, *ibid.*, 4th General Assembly of Iowa, 1852, 54, 65, 68–70, 85; Dan E. Clark, "The History of Liquor Legislation in Iowa, 1846–1861," *Iowa Journal of History and Politics*, Vol. VI (1908), 62–64.

resolutions seeking to persuade Iowa's lawmakers to enact prohibition legislation, and a giant state temperance meeting convened in Iowa City in December, 1853, to make plans to attain
their goal.[18]

Actually, some regulations governing the buying and selling of
alcoholic beverages did exist in Iowa. In 1851 the legislature,
perhaps in response to the temperance petitions, prohibited the
sale of "intoxicating liquors . . . by the glass or dram." Further
legislation designed to halt completely the flow of alcohol ran into
strong Democratic opposition.[19] In his first biennial message,
Governor Hempstead conceded the need of regulatory legislation
but doubted that prohibition was the remedy for the abuses connected with alcohol. Certainly the Democratic party was not
unanimous in its temperance convictions, as the election in 1854
had already attested. With the Germans and Irish so opposed to
prohibition, the party could not afford to sponsor or support any
such measure. But individual Democrats could, and did, favor
temperance.[20]

Until 1854 the advocates of temperance opposed the introduction of the question into politics. They favored the election
of lawmakers who would pass proper legislation on the issue, but
they resisted "any attempt to make such an organization [temper-
ance] pander to the necessities of any political party whatever."
Nevertheless, in the summer of 1853 the *Burlington Daily Telegraph* predicted that temperance would become a political issue
before long.[21] The temperance meeting in Iowa City on Decem-

[18] *The Iowa Weekly Republican* (Iowa City), September 11, 1850; Todd,
Early Settlement of Western Iowa, 98; *Burlington* (Iowa) *Daily Telegraph*,
January 1, 1853; *Iowa State Gazette* (Burlington), December 21, 1853.

[19] *Journal of the House of Representatives*, 3rd General Assembly of Iowa,
1850, 196; Clark, "The History of Liquor Legislation in Iowa, 1846–1861," 61–62.

[20] Benjamin F. Shambaugh (ed.), *The Messages and Proclamations of the
Governors of Iowa*, I, 438–39; Louis Pelzer, "The History and Principles of the
Democratic Party of Iowa, 1846–1857," *Iowa Journal of History and Politics*,
Vol. VI (1908), 199–200.

[21] *Burlington Daily Telegraph*, August 31 and September 9, 1853.

ber 21, 1853, demonstrated the accuracy of the *Telegraph's* prognostication. One of the resolutions adopted by the convention announced the future intention of the temperance advocates:

> *Resolved,* That . . . we do not contemplate the organization of any third or separate party, but only and simply the enactment and enforcement of stringent prohibitory liquor laws; but if the political organizations of the day turn a deaf ear to our petitions and remonstrances and attempt to force upon us rulers and lawmakers who are opposed to the legal enactments and enforcements before referred to, we will, relying on the justice of our cause, rally round the standard of the truth, and do battle for the right in a separate and distinct organization.[22]

So packed with political dynamite was this threat to form another party that in 1854 the Whigs adopted a plank favoring prohibition to curry the favor of the temperance forces. Grimes himself publicized his temperance sympathies. The temperance issue also became a factor of no little importance in the election of Thorington to Congress from the Second District. He received the support not only of the regular Whigs but also of the temperance men and nativists.

Before the formal enactment of the prohibition legislation, two Iowa towns strove to adopt prohibition by unique measures. These towns, incidentally, contained large numbers of settlers of native origin, especially from New England. In Mount Pleasant all the liquor in town was placed in the hands of one or two of the doctors in the town, who were to dispense the spirits only for medicinal purposes. In Fairfield one of the liquor retailers, caught up in the contagion of the temperance crusade, voluntarily destroyed his stock. Other liquor establishments in the town, however, were not disposed to be so generous, but the Sons of Temperance of Fairfield were nonetheless elated by their progress.[23]

---

[22] Clark, "The History of Liquor Legislation in Iowa, 1846–1861," 68.
[23] *Burlington Daily Telegraph,* January 28, 1854; *Fairfield* (Iowa) *Ledger* quoted in *Iowa State Gazette,* February 8, 1854.

Following his victory and subsequent inauguration, Governor Grimes called upon the new assembly to pass a prohibitory measure which, free from constitutional objections, would meet the approval of the majority of the citizens. On January 22, 1855, Grimes signed an act providing for prohibition and promptly submitted it to a popular referendum.[24]

The prohibition measure, which included beer and wine, received support from a powerful quarter when the bishop of Dubuque, Mathias Loras, "invited the members of the Catholic Church in Town to vote in favor of the contemplated Iowa Liquor Law." Although anti-Catholic and antitemperance forces attacked this pronouncement as an unnecessary interference of religion in secular matters, the fact remained that the leading figure of the Catholic church in Iowa backed the law.[25]

Newspaper support for prohibition came from both parties. The *Weekly Observer* of Mount Pleasant was certain that the future development and prosperity of Iowa depended upon the passage of the law. The Democrats denied that theirs was an antitemperance ticket in 1855, claiming only that they opposed the introduction of the question into politics. Other papers predicted the elimination of the maladies of society through the successful reception of the measure. The *Fairfield Ledger* was convinced that the eyes of the nation were upon Iowa, waiting to learn the outcome of the campaign.[26]

Despite protestations to the contrary, most of the opposition to prohibition did emanate from the Democratic camp. The enactment of the law, declared one party organ, would not result in

[24] Shambaugh, *The Messages and Proclamations of the Governors of Iowa*, II, 73; Clark, "The History of Liquor Legislation in Iowa, 1846–1861," 73.

[25] *Dubuque Tribune* quoted in *Burlington Daily Telegraph*, March 27, 1855.

[26] *Des Moines Valley Whig* (Keokuk, Iowa), May 20, 1852; *Iowa Capital Reporter* (Iowa City), September 28, 1853; *Iowa State Gazette*, October 16, 1850; Mount Pleasant (Iowa) *Weekly Observer*, March 1, 1855; *Democratic Banner*, August 3, 1855; *Burlington Daily Telegraph*, February 10, 1852; *Wapello* (Iowa) *Intelligencer*, March 28, 1854; *Eddyville* (Iowa) *Free Press*, February 23, 1855; *Fairfield* (Iowa) *Ledger*, March 29, 1855.

reform but rather would advance the interests of certain politicians who had staked everything upon its outcome. Moreover, the measure posed a definite threat to the liberties of the people, an ominous precedent for the future. There was undoubtedly a great deal of truth to the charge that certain politicians were using prohibition to advance their own careers. Thorington, especially, seemed vulnerable to this accusation.[27]

The voters who went to the polls in April to record their views on the prohibition question gave the temperance cause a decisive 25,555 to 22,445 victory.[28] The measure received 53.24 per cent of the ballots. Heaviest support for the act came from the eastern counties, where advocates of prohibition cast 60 per cent or more of their ballots in favor of its adoption. In this area of the state only Dubuque strongly opposed its enactment, despite the appeal by Bishop Loras, while Jackson, Allamakee, and Clayton counties were about evenly divided. In the southern and western portions of the state, where pro-Democratic sentiment was normally expressed, the voters condemned prohibition in no uncertain terms. The central portion of the state exhibited mixed feelings toward the measure.

The strong prohibition vote of the eastern counties indicated that the temperance forces had little cause to fear the foreign vote, at least in 1855. (It will be recalled that the foreign vote was largely concentrated in these counties.) The heavy prohibition sentiment may be interpreted in part, perhaps, as a reflection of the antiforeign feeling in this area. Advocates of prohibition, of course, hailed its passage. Iowa, they exclaimed, was worthy of national imitation. Indeed, they insisted, the troubles of humanity would begin to disappear, in Iowa at least.[29]

Reviewing the results, Congressman Henn concluded that the Democrats could have defeated prohibition by making a stronger

[27] *Morning Glory* (Keokuk, Iowa), March 28, 1855; *Iowa Sentinel*, March 1, 1855.
[28] Election Records, 1848–1860.
[29] *Weekly Observer*, April 19, 1855.

appeal to the voters in the eastern and central counties. Yet the voting indicated that many Democrats must have supported prohibition, for the percentages in favor of the measure would not have been so strong in the eastern counties without Democratic votes. Two consistently Democratic counties, Lee and Des Moines, also backed the measure by substantial margins, no doubt because of nativist sentiment there.[30]

In addition to the successful approval of prohibition, the Iowa Democrats had many other justifiable reasons for harboring feelings of gloom and dejection. They had lost several major political offices during the past two years, including the gubernatorial chair and a seat in the United States Senate. The schism within the party continued to plague the organization; the party not only was threatened by the Know-Nothings but also would face the challenge of contesting in the coming important political year of 1856 a new and dynamic opposition, the Republican party, which Grimes and his fusionist allies had constructed in time for the election. Nevertheless, despite these serious problems, Democrats could still find cause for pleasure and no little pride in the success of a long and hard-fought struggle to persuade Congress to appropriate lands to aid in the construction of railroads in Iowa. In late spring, 1856, Congress passed the measure which Iowans had long desired.

The demand for railroads was strong among Iowans. Western Iowa during the middle years of the 1850's maintained communication with the eastern portion of the state by means of the stagecoach, which scarcely could equal the railroad car in comfort and speed. Produce was usually transported down navigable streams to the larger towns and cities for shipment to the South or East. Rapids just above Keokuk, however, impeded traffic on the Mississippi River. Railroads were the practical solution.

[30] Bernhart Henn to George W. Jones, April 14, 1855, in the George W. Jones Correspondence at the Iowa State Department of History and Archives in Des Moines.

By 1856 towns and counties in Iowa had built up a debt of over $7 million to aid the construction of myriad railroad projects.[31]

The chief means to ensure the construction of railroads in a state where capital was limited and traffic scanty was to secure a grant of land from Congress. The state could then offer the land to railroad companies for sale to the general public, the proceeds or money borrowed on the security of the grants financing the construction of the rail lines. Iowans flooded the assembly with petitions seeking land grants, and the legislature dutifully passed land-grant memorials and shipped them off to Congress. Many meetings were held to demonstrate the feasibility of this or that railroad route.[32]

Members of Iowa's delegation to Congress, both Democratic and Whig, had labored indefatigably for years to obtain the land grant. In 1850, both Senators Jones and Dodge introduced bills to accomplish this purpose. Although the Senate did react favorably to Jones's proposal, the lower house never acted upon the bill. In 1852 and again in 1854 land-grant legislation on behalf of Iowa won Senate approval but failed to make much headway in the House. Jones and his new colleague, Harlan, kept up the pressure in the Senate in 1855 and 1856, while Hall and Thorington worked with equal diligence in the House.[33]

In 1856 the House of Representatives initiated and approved a land-grant bill for Iowa by a vote of 79 to 59 and sent the measure to the Senate. There Jones and Harlan joined to ensure Senate passage of the bill. They urged immediate approval without reference to the usual committee and without amendment. After

[31] Todd, *Early Settlement of Western Iowa*, 107; George W. Van Vleck, *The Panic of 1857*, 11; George R. Taylor, *The Transportation Revolution, 1815–1860*, 94.

[32] *Iowa Sentinel*, April 20, 1854; *Journal of the House of Representatives*, 5th General Assembly of Iowa, 1854, 76–77, 86; *ibid.*, 6th General Assembly of Iowa, 1856, 89; *Journal of the Senate*, 5th General Assembly of Iowa, 1854, 40, 50; *ibid.*, 6th General Assembly of Iowa, 1856, 39.

[33] 33 Cong., 1 sess., *Congressional Globe*, 486, 1806; 34 Cong., 1 sess., *ibid.*, 8, 350, 488.

brushing aside some minor opposition, the Iowans carried the day, and the Senate passed the bill by a vote of 31 to 9.[34]

The reason for the about-face of the House is difficult to determine. Jones furnished a possible clue. Speaking before the Senate in support of the House bill, he mentioned that on previous occasions Robert C. Shenck, president of the Philadelphia, Fort Wayne, and Platte River Air-Line Railroad Company, had helped kill Iowa land-grant measures by exerting influence upon congressmen from Indiana and Ohio. Shenck's motives were never revealed. Apparently, however, his influence had waned by 1856.[35]

The Iowa land grant, which received presidential sanction on May 15, provided for four railroad lines running across the state from the Mississippi to the Missouri River. One line would extend from Davenport, via Iowa City and Des Moines, to Council Bluffs; the second, from Lyons City via Maquoketa to the Missouri; the third, from Burlington west to a point near the mouth of the Platte River; and the last, from Dubuque via Fort Dodge to Sioux City. To assist in the construction of these lines, Iowa would receive a grant of land, totaling approximately four and a half million acres, in alternate sections six sections wide on each side of each road. The act further stipulated that the state could dispose of these lands only for the purpose of aiding railroad construction along the lines enumerated and for no other projects. If any of the lands granted to the state had already been sold or pre-empted, the state could have an amount equal to that which had been taken for public use.[36]

Governor Grimes called a special session of the Iowa General

[34] *Ibid.*, 1161–62, 1166–68; James Harlan to Samuel R. Curtis, June 7, 1856, in the Samuel R. Curtis Papers at the Iowa State Department of History and Archives in Des Moines.

[35] 34 Cong., 1 sess., *Congressional Globe*, 1187.

[36] *Ibid.*, 3–4; document entitled "Iowa Rail Road Grants" in Jones Correspondence; *Iowa State Gazette* quoted in *Des Moines Valley Whig*, May 14, 1856.

Assembly to consider the land grant. After about two weeks of oratory the Republican-controlled legislature accepted the congressional grant and drew up regulations to govern its disposal among the railroad companies. Unless the designated companies marked out their routes by April 1, 1857, constructed at least seventy-five miles of line by December 31, 1859, and completed the entire routes by December 1, 1865, the lands from the grant not yet transferred to the defaulting company would revert to the state.[37]

Construction crews had already begun work on some railroad lines before Congress approved the Iowa grant. The money for this construction came largely from the bonds voted by the towns and counties of the state. The Mississippi and Missouri Railroad, soon to become part of the Rock Island System, commenced construction in Davenport on September 1, 1853, but as late as June, 1855, not a single rail had been laid. Spurred by the offer of a bonus from Iowa City if the line could be completed to that point by the end of the year, the construction crews began to make better progress. The road had reached Muscatine by November and, with barely minutes to spare, reached Iowa City in time to meet the imposed deadline and collect the bonus. Even as late as 1860 the M & M road extended only thirty miles west of Iowa City to Marengo. It would not reach the Missouri River until well after the end of the Civil War. Some grading had been started on a few other lines by 1856, but little, if any, track had been laid.[38]

On April 21, 1856, with much popular enthusiasm and fanfare, a locomotive crossed the Mississippi River at Davenport over the first bridge to span the river. With the barrier of the great river now overcome, could a transcontinental railroad, asked one

[37] W. E. Alexander, *History of Chickasaw and Howard Counties Iowa*, 93–94.
[38] Dwight L. Agnew, "Iowa's First Railroad," *Iowa Journal of History*, Vol. XLVIII (1950), 2–3, 10, 12, 21 ff.; Cyrenus Cole, *A History of the People of Iowa*, 281; *Des Moines Valley Whig*, December 5, 1855; Dwight L. Agnew, "The Mississippi and Missouri Railroad," *Iowa Journal of History*, Vol. LI (1953), 230 ff.

paper, be far from realization?[39] Clearly the year 1856 marked a significant watershed in Iowa's transportation revolution.

The newborn Republican party, needing a broad base on which to appeal to the voters of the state once the slavery issue had faded, tied its future increasingly to the railroad. In effect, it became the railroad party. Republicans championed railroad construction throughout the state and reiterated Western desires for a line to the Pacific. Some of the leading figures in the Republican organization were intimately associated with one railroad line or another. Such outstanding party leaders as James W. Grimes, Samuel Curtis, H. M. Hoxie, James Harlan, Josiah Grinnell, William Penn Clarke, Hiram Price, Grenville Dodge, and John Kasson were closely connected with railroading in one capacity or another. Many lesser figures in the party also had railroad interests. The locomotive became the main vehicle of the Republican party's success in Iowa.[40]

[39] Dwight L. Agnew, "Jefferson Davis and the Rock Island Bridge," *Iowa Journal of History*, Vol. XLVII (1949), 13.

[40] David S. Sparks, "Iowa Republicans and the Railroads 1856–1860," *Iowa Journal of History*, Vol. LIII (1955), 276–78.

A Triumphant Beginning

Noteworthy on the Iowa political scene during the middle years of the 1850's were several groups of political dissidents who were unaffiliated with any of the organized political parties in the state. Free-Soilers, opponents of the Kansas-Nebraska Act, temperance advocates, abolitionists, disenchanted Democrats, disgruntled Whigs—all provided fertile ground for political ferment. Regular Democrats and Old-Line Whigs, as well as the antiforeign, anti-Catholic Know-Nothing party, sought to enlist these splinter elements behind their respective platforms. Since the Whig organization, though ostensibly triumphant over the Democrats in the vitally important gubernatorial election of 1854, had largely disintegrated, the Democrats might have looked forward to future political campaigns with renewed optimism. The union of the diverse splinter groups into an effective political organization could, however, augur the end of Democratic political power in Iowa. Indeed, the election of 1854 had provided the one individual who possessed the necessary skill, tact, and diplomacy to fuse the various opposition groups, together with the main body of the Old-Line Whigs, into a compact and efficient political machine. Such a person was Governor Grimes, who had won a bitter, uphill battle for the gubernatorial office against a solidly entrenched but sharply divided Democratic opposition.

Grass-roots support for a new political party manifested itself as early as the summer of 1854, when a Republican organization was formed in Fayette County with a strong antislavery base as its *raison d'être*. Later, on November 29, the *Burlington Daily Telegraph*, a self-proclaimed political neutral, suggested that a Republican party should be established on a statewide basis. In April of the following year, Grimes indicated to Salmon P. Chase of Ohio that "it is time to thoroughly organize the Republican party," which, he believed, would draw support from the state's sizable foreign-born population as well as from the outspoken nativists.[1]

Word of an impending Republican state convention began to circulate in December, 1855, even before publication of the official announcement. To persuade the Know-Nothings to join in a common cause with them, some Republicans-to-be suggested that their convention should coincide with the Know-Nothing meeting. All that would be necessary to unite the two groups would be an agreement on the basic issues; they could ignore minor questions and differences.[2] Indeed, that is what occurred, even though the two groups met separately. The Dubuque *Weekly Times* boasted that thousands of Know-Nothings had joined the Republican party, while at the same time "desiring

[1] George W. Fitch, *Past and Present of Fayette County Iowa*, I, 549–59; David S. Sparks, "The Birth of the Republican Party in Iowa, 1848 to 1860," unpublished Ph.D. dissertation, University of Chicago, 1951, 117; James Grimes to Salmon P. Chase, April 8, 1855, printed in William Salter, *The Life of James W. Grimes*, 69.

[2] N. M. Hubbard to William Penn Clarke, December 24, 1855, in the William Penn Clarke Correspondence at the State Historical Society of Iowa in Iowa City.

... that the purity of the elective franchise should be preserved, and that Jesuitism and political Romanism should not combine to endanger the peace and safety of our institutions."[3] Grimes himself was convinced that the Know-Nothings, whose principles he personally abhorred, were serving the useful function of destroying the old party alignments.[4]

On January 3, 1856, the official call went out for a convention to gather in Iowa City on February 22 for the purpose of organizing a Republican party. Believing that many persons had joined the Know-Nothing party merely on a temporary basis for want of any other desirable organization, Republican leaders were confident that a sizable number from the nativist group would join the new party. Although it was not known for certain at the time, it appeared probable that Governor Grimes had written the call and would be the leading figure at the Iowa City convention.[5]

When the convention assembled on the appointed date, it not only proceeded with the contemplated organization but also nominated a full slate of candidates for the state offices to be filled later in the year and selected delegates to attend the party's national convention. In addition, it drew up a platform and published an address to the people of Iowa which more or less restated the party's principles as expressed in its platform.[6]

Since representatives from virtually all the splinter groups attended the meeting, it was essential that nothing be adopted which might give offense, lest the entire effort to effect a unified party should end in failure. Thus the platform was essentially a

[3] Quoted in *Vinton* (Iowa) *Eagle*, October 9, 1858.
[4] James Grimes to Salmon P. Chase, May 12, 1855, printed in Salter, *The Life of James W. Grimes*, 70.
[5] John W. Gannaway, "The Development of Party Organization in Iowa," *Iowa Journal of History and Politics*, Vol. I (1903), 517–18; J. W. Cattrell to William Penn Clarke, January 8, 1856, in the Clarke Correspondence; Charles Roll, "Political Trends in Iowa History," *Iowa Journal of History and Politics*, Vol. XXVI (1928), 504–505; David S. Sparks, "The Birth of the Republican Party in Iowa, 1854–1856," *ibid.*, Vol. LIV (1956), 24–25.
[6] Gannaway, "The Development of Party Organization in Iowa," 519–20.

statement of the party's antislavery sentiments. The Republican party, according to one plank, had a "mission . . . to maintain the Liberties of the People, the Sovereignty of the States, and the Perpetuity of the Union." Slavery was a local institution "beyond our reach and above our authority," but with regard to the territories "we will oppose its spread." Other planks condemned the South and denounced the national Democratic administration and declared that the federal government was one of limited powers.[7] The last clause probably was inserted to satisfy both the Old-Line Whigs and the former Democrats who were present.

On the more controversial local issues which could have divided the convention, such as temperance and nativism, the Republican platform remained discreetly silent. Since prohibition had already been approved by Iowa voters the previous year, a strong stand on this question would have provoked needless strife with those who had opposed the measure. Silence might disappoint temperance groups but would not offend them.

But failure to condemn the Know-Nothings, a deliberate attempt to avoid alienating former members of the nativist party, aroused a good deal of anger and chagrin among the foreign groups in the state, particularly among the Germans, who were especially sensitive to antiforeign sentiment. Moreover, since they had already been angrily stirred by the successful enactment of prohibition, the presence of temperance men at the Republican convention could not have been very pleasing to them. Governor Grimes commented that the Germans resented the failure of the convention to state categorically that it abided by the existing federal naturalization laws. The reason for this, Grimes explained, stemmed from opposition from Know-Nothings and others who preferred merely an antislavery platform and nothing more.[8]

---

[7] *Des Moines Valley Whig* (Keokuk, Iowa), February 27, 1856.

[8] James Grimes to Salmon P. Chase, March 28, 1856, printed in Salter, *The Life of James W. Grimes*, 79–80.

The editors of three of the leading German-language newspapers in Iowa—*Die Freie Presse* of Burlington, *Der Demokrat* of Davenport, and *Die Staats Zeitung* of Dubuque—declared that they were not satisfied with the position taken by the Republican party on the question of nativism and naturalization laws. A group of Germans meeting in Dubuque adopted a number of resolutions echoing this disappointment.[9]

In the meantime, county Republican organizations continued to spring up, both before and after the state convention of the new party. In most cases they merely replaced the old Whig groups, but on a broadened base which included the splinter elements. The county platforms generally repeated the pronouncements of the state organization on the main issue of slavery.[10]

The Democratic press, of course, greeted the call for and formation of a new party with scorn and derision. According to the *Iowa State Gazette* of Burlington, "The Africanized organ of republicanism has boldly raised the standard of Seward niggerology and urges abolitionists, amalgamationists, and the scum of all isms to rally round free love and the free negro platform." The same journal insisted that the aims of the new party were "to distract the country and imperil the Union," for it could prevent the admission of any new state into the Union which might adopt a slavery constitution. The *Iowa Capital Reporter* of Iowa City charged that "Republicanism is . . . [synonymous with] Abolitionism." The new organization had merely changed names but had not abandoned its old characteristics. The Pella *Gazette* suggested that the new party should be called "Black" because sympathy with the black race was its major tenet.[11] Most anti-

9 Sparks, "The Birth of the Republican Party in Iowa, 1848 to 1860," 139–40; *Des Moines Valley Whig*, March 19, 1856.

10 Franklin T. Oldt (ed.), *History of Dubuque County Iowa*, 337–38; *The History of Warren County Iowa*, 355–56; *The History of Mahaska County Iowa*, 340–41.

11 Quoted in Louis Pelzer, "The Origin and Organization of the Republican Party in Iowa," *Iowa Journal of History and Politics*, Vol. IV (1906), 501–502,

Republican newspapers did, in fact, call their rivals "Black Republicans" as a matter of course. Nor did Republicans shirk from employing a few choice epithets of their own when referring to the Democrats.

In the elections of 1856 the Democrats of Iowa would face a series of contests against a party substantially united, embracing the various splinter groups of the state. The Democratic party, however, continued to suffer from the schism over the Nebraska issue, railroads, temperance, nativism, and other local and national questions. The outcome of the 1856 campaign would attest just how well Grimes and his allies had done their work of political reconstruction.

In order to reunite their quarreling elements and mold them into a smoothly functioning, harmonious party, the leaders of the Iowa Democrats needed to exhibit a spirit of conciliation. Ruffled sensibilities called for soothing balm. Yet the men who ran the party, principally Senator Jones and his supporters, refused to compromise with their disaffected brethren and instead insisted that only loyal supporters of the national administration be permitted to attend the party's state convention of January 8, 1856, to select delegates to the national convention and to nominate candidates for the local ticket.[12] Loyalty to the national administration and its policies was the essential test of party orthodoxy.

The Democratic state platform clearly reflected the predominance of administration supporters in the convention. After paying the usual lip service to the Constitution and to equal justice

---

518–19; see also George A. Boeck, "An Early Iowa Community: Aspects of Economic, Social and Political Development in Burlington, Iowa, 1833–1866," unpublished Ph.D. dissertation, University of Iowa, 1961, 263.

[12] Copy of circular letter written by George W. Jones, November 17, 1855, in the George W. Jones Correspondence at the Iowa State Department of History and Archives in Des Moines; Louis Pelzer, "The History and Principles of the Democratic Party of Iowa, 1846–1857," *Iowa Journal of History and Politics*, Vol. VI (1908), 223.

for all states regardless of section, the platform strongly supported the Kansas-Nebraska Act and excoriated all those, Democrats included, who had raised their voices in opposition to it. President Pierce and his official family received a ringing endorsement, while the state administration of Governor Grimes and his circle was severely rebuked. Another plank condemned the Know-Nothings by name and read out of the party any Democrat who belonged to that group. On the other issues vital to the interests of Iowans, such as homesteads, banking, internal improvements, and railroad grants, the party solons remained silent.[13]

The most charitable thing that can be said of the Democratic platform is that it was inept. At least one interested observer forecast a probable defeat for the Iowa Democrats because of their uncompromising stand on the Nebraska question as a test of party fidelity.[14]

The state convention weighted its delegation to the national Democratic convention at Cincinnati with administration men and chose "trusted" men as candidates for the local offices. If the renegade Democrats had expected to be conciliated at Iowa City, they must have been sorely disappointed.

At Cincinnati the Democrats adopted a platform designed to preserve the unity of the national organization. In various introductory planks the Democrats reaffirmed their opposition to a national bank and internal improvements, reiterated their belief in the principle of states' rights, and called for a strict interpretation of the Constitution. The crucial portions of the platform, however, concerned slavery. Not only did the Democrats pledge to resist the renewal of the slavery controversy, but they went on record as endorsing the principle of "non-interference by Con-

[13] Roy V. Sherman, "Political Party Platforms in Iowa," unpublished M.A. thesis, State University of Iowa, 1926, 130–36.

[14] Manuscript diary of Charles M. Mason, entry of January 20, 1856, in the Charles M. Mason Papers at the Iowa State Department of History and Archives in Des Moines.

gress with Slavery in State and Territory, or in the District of Columbia." Closing portions of the platform condemned the Republican and Know-Nothing parties and gave hearty support to the Pierce administration.[15]

Although some individuals, such as Charles M. Mason, viewed the action of the Democrats with a critical eye and were especially hostile to the platform, administration partisans, blinding themselves to the discontent which ripped the party, expressed optimistic hope of victory in the coming political struggle. Thus P. M. Casady could assure Senator Jones, leader of the administration group, that the party in the Polk County area "will certainly succeed." Another Democrat confidently believed his party would carry the state.[16]

Most portents, however, forecast a stunning disaster for the Democratic party unless the leadership cured its ills. From various corners of the state messages and newspaper editorials warned that the Germans were beginning to desert the Democrats and join the Republicans. (The latter, it should be remembered, had adopted a strict antislavery plank in response to the Democratic Nebraska endorsement.) While the Germans received the platform of the new party lukewarmly and with reservations, they could and did accept its pronouncements on slavery. In Keokuk, however, German dissatisfaction stemmed not so much from slavery as from a more personal issue, intimately connected with the pocketbook: wages for labor. Apparently they believed they were victims of wage discrimination. Indeed, the Republican party there, which came to embrace most of the local Know-Nothings, worked indefatigably to attract the German voters to its banner. As long as the Germans remained ardent Democrats, hostility to them was evident, but such ani-

[15] Kirk Porter (comp.), National Party Platforms, 41–47.
[16] P. M. Casady to George W. Jones, March 22, 1856, in the Jones Correspondence; N. T. Wynkoop to George W. Jones, March 10, 1856, ibid.

mosity quickly disappeared when their support became desirable.[17]

Dissension within the ranks, unified opposition under a new party label, the possibility of having alienated some of its foreign-born adherents—these were not the only difficulties confronting the Iowa Democratic party in 1856. The Know-Nothings (now officially known as the American party) had blossomed into a potentially strong group, with county and state organizations and a press of its own. The national convention of the American party met in Philadelphia on February 22 and chose Millard Fillmore for president and Andrew J. Donelson for vice-president. Their national platform reasserted the basic nativist tenets of the party and condemned the national Democratic administration for passing the Kansas-Nebraska measure, thereby reopening the slavery controversy.

Know-Nothing supporters in Iowa greeted the action of their national convention somewhat unenthusiastically. The backers of Fillmore and Donelson tried to drum up interest in the state convention, scheduled to meet in Iowa City on March 5, but when the date for the meeting arrived, attendance was disappointing. The forty-five delegates who did attend endorsed the national nomination, chose a slate of presidential electors, and adopted a prohibition resolution in addition to the usual nativist planks. Another sparsely attended Know-Nothing meeting convened at Chariton, Lucas County, in May. Delegates endorsed the Fillmore-Donelson ticket and the Philadelphia resolutions and nominated John J. Selman for Congress from the First District. In the Second Congressional District, however, the Know-Nothings failed to nominate a candidate. At a meeting at Oskaloosa, also in May, Know-Nothings refused to go along with the

[17] *Des Moines Valley Whig*, January 30, 1856; manuscript diary of Charles M. Mason, entry of July 8, 1856, in the Mason Papers; Boeck, "An Early Iowa Community," 281.

Philadelphia platform or the party ticket and condemned both. In June the Know-Nothings of Des Moines County assembled at Burlington, where they endorsed Millard Fillmore as the sole presidential candidate able to restore national harmony and generally sought to restrict voting by the foreign-born, largely through more stringent legislation. By and large, the Know-Nothings were themselves weakened by factionalism, caused partly, no doubt, by the formation of the Republican party which former Know-Nothing adherents could join without necessarily compromising their nativist attachments or antislavery principles.[18]

Notwithstanding the evidence of Know-Nothing weakness in Iowa, a few of the party newspapers strove valiantly to popularize their candidates. Fillmore received praise as the one man not pledged to either of the warring sections of the country. His two opponents—John C. Frémont, Republican, and James Buchanan, Democrat—were called sectional candidates; the former was too friendly to the North, while the latter was a captive of the South. In addition, Frémont was accused of being a Catholic. Thus did Know-Nothing editorials rant until election day.[19]

The Republicans were determined to take from the Democrats both congressional seats in addition to the other offices at stake in the coming elections. In the Second District, the northern portion of Iowa, they chose Timothy Davis to run against the Democratic nominee, Shepherd Leffler. Leffler, a Pennsylvanian, an alumnus of Washington College, and a resident of Burlington since 1835, had served in Congress from 1846 to 1850. He had defeated Davis in the congressional election of 1848. Davis, a New Jersey native, could also boast of long residence in the state, having gone to Dubuque in 1837 by way of Kentucky and Mis-

18 Willard I. Toussaint, "The Know-Nothing Party in Iowa," unpublished M.A. thesis, State University of Iowa, 1956, 84–85; *True Flag* (Bloomfield, Iowa), May 31, 1856; *Washington* (Iowa) *Press*, September 10, 1856; Boeck, "An Early Iowa Community," 270.

19 *Iowa Flag* (Bloomfield), August 9 and 23 and October 25, 1856; Bloomfield *True Flag*, April 26, 1856.

souri. Democrats had not controlled the Second District since 1852, and now the Republicans appeared able to claim it as their own private bailiwick.[20]

In the First District, the southern part of Iowa, the Democrats renominated the incumbent Augustus Hall, a staunch supporter of the administration and the Kansas-Nebraska Act. This strategy seemed wise, for Hall had demonstrated his vote-getting ability two years earlier, when he had won with a pro-Nebraska platform. The Republicans, however, introduced a sure-fire issue that would defeat their opponents. In addition to the usual condemnations of slavery, the passage of the Kansas-Nebraska Act, and the repeal of the Missouri Compromise, they adopted a plank in which they condemned Hall for "negligence and inefficiency" owing to his failure to secure federal grants of land to aid in the construction of other railroads in the district apart from the grant which Congress had approved for Iowa in 1856. To run against Hall the Republicans selected Samuel R. Curtis, a graduate of West Point and former railroad surveyor and engineer.[21] The railroad issue had earlier unseated one Democratic congressman; perhaps it could defeat another.

In many ways the Republican party of Iowa was born under a lucky star. The Iowa land grant of 1856, for example, had come at an opportune moment politically, and the Republicans in the state sought—successfully, as it turned out—to obscure the role of the Democrats in securing the land grant.[22] Also fortuitous for the Republicans was the creation of a new political issue which dropped into their laps during the 1856 campaign. Within the space of a single week national passions again became heated as Preston Brooks played the role of avenger against Charles Sumner, and John Brown acted as the self-appointed agent of the

[20] *Washington Press*, June 18 and 25, 1856; *Biographical Directory of the American Congress 1774–1949*, 1064, 1451; Gue, *History of Iowa*, IV, 167.

[21] *Des Moines Valley Whig*, June 14, 1856; *Biographical Directory of Congress*, 1046.

[22] 34 Cong., 1 sess., *Congressional Globe*, 1161–62, 1166–68.

Lord at Ossawattamie following the Southern attack on Lawrence, Kansas, a Free-Soil town. Kansas and the troubles there became the chief—indeed, almost the only—issue of the election campaign in the Hawkeye State. Kansas became the focus of a veritable crusade, charged with enough moral explosives to arouse the entire nation.[23]

In Congress the members of the Iowa delegation carried on running battles with one another over the Kansas question. While Democrat Hall in the House defended popular sovereignty and denied that the national government could interfere in any way with the proceedings in Kansas, Whig-turned-Republican Harlan in the Senate insisted that the federal government had the power to regulate slavery in the territories and hence in Kansas. He demanded the admission of Kansas into the Union under its Topeka Constitution. Democratic Senator Jones replied to his Republican colleague three weeks later. He held steadfastly to the administration line on the Kansas problem, denying the right of the federal government to interfere in Kansas and backing popular sovereignty. "The people of Kansas," Jones declared, had the right to decide "for themselves this question of admitting slavery within their borders, and to be admitted into the Union with or without it, as they may elect."[24]

In Iowa the Democrats charged their foes with deliberately stirring up emotions over the Kansas situation to improve the chances of success for their ticket. Iowa, wrote United States Marshal Laurel Summers, "is literally overrun with '*interlopers*' haranguing the people in favor of '*free Kansas*' as they say. Fanaticism is the order of the day and among a certain class of people all love for the Union and Constitution seems to have fled."[25] Even some Republicans conceded that much of the ex-

<hr>

23 W. E. Alexander, *History of Chickasaw and Howard Counties Iowa*, 93–94.

24 34 Cong., 1 sess., *Congressional Globe*, Appendix, 177–79, 271–77, 406–409.

25 *Iowa Capital Reporter* (Iowa City), July 30, 1856; Laurel Summers to George W. Jones, June 14, 1856, in the Jones Correspondence.

citement over Kansas was "made for electioneering purposes."[26]

Perhaps one of the reasons why the Republicans, and many other Iowans, felt so keenly about Kansas was that they were not discussing an abstract issue but had long been engaged in playing positive roles in the bitter conflict which raged in that territory between free-state and slave-state proponents. Many Iowans were active in the operation of the Underground Railway, which spirited runaway slaves through the North into Canada. One of the routes extended across Iowa from Tabor, in the southwest corner, through Des Moines and Iowa City, up to Clinton, and across the Mississippi River into Illinois. Fugitive slaves were also taken through Appanoose County, one of the Democratic party's strongholds along the southern tier of counties.[27] Many of the operators of the Underground brought back a different cargo along the same routes, carrying guns and munitions to be used against the proslavery forces in Kansas. The little town of Tabor became the headquarters of the northern Kansas forces. Free-state men made little or no effort to conceal their trips through Iowa, backed as they were by a Kansas Committee operating in the Hawkeye State. Iowa City became the eastern focal point in the state for the free-state adherents.[28]

Responsible leaders of the Republican party were among those who actively and energetically supported and encouraged the movements of men and munitions to and from troubled Kansas. William Penn Clarke, a former fiery Free-Soil party leader, was chairman of the Kansas Committee in Iowa. He assisted John

[26] A. J. Sears to C. C. Carpenter, June 15, 1856, in the Cyrus C. Carpenter Letters at the State Historical Society of Iowa in Iowa City.

[27] Louis Pelzer, "The Negro and Slavery in Early Iowa," *Iowa Journal of History and Politics*, Vol. II (1904), 480; Leola N. Bergmann, "The Negro in Iowa," *ibid.*, Vol. XLVI (1948), 24–25; L. I. Taylor (ed.), *Past and Present of Appanoose County Iowa*, I, 253.

[28] John Todd to William Salter, September 17, 1856, in the William Salter Collection at the Iowa State Department of History and Archives in Des Moines; R. H. Sylvester to Laurel Summers, September 5, 1856, in the Laurel Summers Correspondence, also at the Historical Department in Des Moines.

Brown on more than one occasion.[29] A member of the Republican State Central Committee, Henry O'Connor, spent considerable time in Kansas in behalf of the free-staters. Governor Grimes, as chief executive of Iowa, wrote to President Pierce demanding federal protection for Iowans who migrated to Kansas. Unless the federal government acted promptly to protect the lives and property of Iowans in Kansas, Grimes threatened to take state action to achieve this end. Later in the year he asked the Iowa General Assembly to support his statements. He also suffered an astonishing lapse of memory to aid the antislavery cause in Kansas. He carelessly left the key to the Iowa arsenal on his desk one day, where it was found by the "proper" Kansas man, who then appropriated about fifteen hundred muskets from the stock available for use in Kansas. Josiah B. Grinnell was another prominent Republican who more than once entertained John Brown in his home and supplied him with whatever supplies he could collect.[30]

Still, despite the Kansas crisis, some Republicans were pessimistic about their party's ability to carry Iowa. Clarke wrote to Senator Harlan asking him to obtain outside speakers to stump the state. Harlan replied that national Republican leaders considered Iowa safe for the party and that local speechmaking efforts would have to turn the trick. The senator admitted, nevertheless, that he was not as confident about Iowa as the national party spokesmen were. Republican campaign speakers, such as Charles C. Nourse, who attempted to stump for the party in areas of Democratic preponderance faced hostile crowds armed with rotten eggs. He and his supporters were called "damn black republicans."[31]

[29] Erik M. Eriksson, "William Penn Clarke," *Iowa Journal of History and Politics*, Vol. XXV (1927), 42.

[30] Salter, *The Life of James W. Grimes*, 84–86; *The Washington Press*, October 22, 1856; Benjamin F. Shambaugh (ed.), *The Messages and Proclamations of the Governors of Iowa*, II, 38–39; Charles E. Payne, *Josiah Bushnell Grinnell*, 102.

Meanwhile, Democratic campaign tactics were weak and ineffectual. The Republicans, the Democrats charged, were merely a sectional group, while the Democratic party was a national organization and had the best interests of the Union at heart. At the same time the Democrats assailed the antiforeign, anti-Catholic bias of the Know-Nothings and promised to strive "for the free, unrestrained, unlimited, and unqualified right of Catholics as well as others to worship God according to the suggestions and dictates of their consciences and without subjecting them to any political disabilities whatever therefor." Moreover, continued a staunch Democratic journal, the party "will insist upon the unrestrained right of slaveholders, as of others, to migrate with their goods and chattels to the Territories of the United States."[32] So far as the Democratic party was concerned, it did not intend to bother itself with any moral pronouncements on the subject of slavery pro or con. Hence it was able to do little or nothing to counter the emotional appeal and moral attractiveness of the Republican position with regard to the Kansas issue. To be sure, Kansas was bleeding a bit; but the Republicans transformed the rivulets of blood into a flood of gore for public consumption throughout Iowa.

On August 4, 1856, the voters of Iowa went to the polls to cast their ballots for the congressional seats and the state offices. The results of the election stunned the Democrats. In their very first campaign in the Hawkeye State as an organized political party, the Republicans swept the election with ridiculous ease. They captured every state office by a margin of 7,500 votes or better. They secured control of the Iowa General Assembly by a two-to-one majority in each branch.[33]

[31] James Harlan to William Penn Clarke, September 13, 1856, in the Clarke Correspondence; *Autobiography of Charles Clinton Nourse*, 36–37.

[32] *Iowa State Gazette* (Burlington), August 19, 1856; Dubuque *Express and Herald*, June 19, 1856, quoted in Pelzer, "The History and Principles of the Democratic Party of Iowa, 1846–1857," 231.

[33] Election Records, 1848–1860, in the office of the secretary of state of Iowa, Des Moines.

In the congressional races Democrats relinquished their control of the First District for the first time in the state's brief history, while the party defeat in the Second District was even more decisive. There Davis defeated Leffler by a vote of 21,885 to 15,870. The former received 57.89 per cent of the total vote, the largest percentage won by any victorious candidate during the 1850's. Democrat Leffler carried only six of the forty-three counties in his district, including the Democrats' Dubuque stronghold. Four of the Democratic counties—Boone, Greene, Story, and Woodbury—were located in the western portion of the district, attesting to the overwhelming Republican superiority in eastern Iowa.[34]

In the First District the incumbent, Hall, succumbed to his Republican rival, Curtis, in a close contest complicated somewhat by the presence of the third-party candidate, John J. Selman of the Know-Nothings. Hall received 17,110 votes in contrast to Curtis' 18,065 votes. In percentage figures Curtis won 50.17 per cent of the vote, while Hall received 47.52 per cent, and Selman, with 826 votes, received 2.29 per cent. Hall's figures represent a decline of 2.75 percentage points over the totals he had received in 1854. Selman gained most of his support from the southern counties—Appanoose, Davis, Henry, Lee, and Lucas—all of which, with the exception of Henry, went Democratic by comfortable margins.[35]

Whether the German vote was a significant factor in the Republican sweep of the congressional races is open to question. In the First District, 4,194 persons, not all of whom were of German origin, were naturalized and entitled to cast ballots.[36] Of this number, 3,018 lived in counties carried by the Democrats or in counties where Hall's percentage change from his 1854 figures was negligible. Another 422 citizens of foreign birth lived in

[34] *Ibid.*
[35] *Ibid.*
[36] *The Census Returns of the Different Counties of the State of Iowa for 1856*, insert between pages 414 and 415.

Henry, Mahaska, Jasper, and Warren counties, where Curtis compiled majorities totaling more than 2,000 votes. An additional 422 naturalized voters lived in ten counties which switched to the Republican column. In two of these counties, Keokuk and Monroe, where Curtis' margin of victory was slender, the German vote may have been a significant factor in his victory. His pluralities in the other eight counties combined were more than triple the number of naturalized persons living there. The remainder of the naturalized voters made their homes in counties which gave Curtis thumping majorities, far exceeding the number of foreign-born voters. One can only conclude that in the First Congressional District as a whole the German vote was not a decisive factor in the defeat of the Democrats. Although the German vote may have been significant in certain counties, such as Keokuk and Monroe, even this possibility cannot be demonstrated with certainty. It should be noted here that more than 1,500 immigrants from the Netherlands lived in Marion County, where their leader, the Reverend Henry P. Scholte, angered by prohibition and nativism, worked hard to ensure a Democratic victory. On election day, Dutch-born voters cast their ballots overwhelmingly for Democrats and thereby helped to keep Marion County in the Democratic column.[37]

The same conclusion must apply, also, to the Second District, which contained 10,295 naturalized voters.[38] The German vote may have been responsible in part for the defection of four counties—Bremer, Des Moines, Jackson, and Johnson—to the Republican column. Davis' margin of victory in these counties, with 1,708 naturalized voters, was 397 votes. Elsewhere in the district the Democrats carried six counties with 2,268 foreign-born voters and scored gains in eight Republican counties having 3,028 naturalized voters. Twelve counties cast ballots for the first time

[37] Robert P. Swierenga, "The Ethnic Voter and the First Lincoln Election," *Civil War History*, Vol. XI (1965), 36.
[38] *Ibid.*

in a congressional election. They went overwhelmingly to Davis, but only 353 citizens of foreign birth resided in these newer counties. Twelve other counties where the Democrats suffered percentage losses numbered 2,919 naturalized citizens, but Davis' margin of victory exceeded this amount by more than five hundred. Thus, except for the four counties enumerated above, it is doubtful whether the German vote in the Second District did little more than add a few hundred votes to Davis' already imposing margin of victory.

In November the voters of Iowa again journeyed to the polls, this time to register their preference for president. Once more the Democrats were soundly trounced. Of Iowa's 101,300 eligible voters more than 92,400 cast their ballots, giving Frémont 45,174 votes, Buchanan 37,568 votes, and Fillmore 9,669 votes. Frémont won 48.88 per cent of the total vote, Buchanan a mere 40.65 per cent, and Fillmore a surprising 10.46 per cent.[39]

Democratic strength, as usual, was concentrated along the southern tier of counties, in Dubuque County, and in a cluster of five counties in central Iowa. Pottawattamie and Woodbury counties, in the western part of the state, also returned heavy Democratic majorities.

The Republicans dominated northern and eastern Iowa for the most part and scored victories in two groups of counties in the southwestern sector of the state. The northern and eastern portions of the state had long ceased to furnish the Democrats with any reason for political joy.

Fillmore attracted his largest following from the southern counties, but his appeal elsewhere was also considerable. Fillmore's popularity ran deeper than his association with the American party. His association with the Compromise of 1850 undoubtedly contributed not a little to his appeal to Iowans.

Despite the universality of the Democratic defeat in the state, party leaders nevertheless found something to celebrate in the

[39] Election Records, 1848–1860.

triumph of the Buchanan ticket in the nation. A gala victory celebration took place in Dubuque to the accompaniment of speeches and bonfires.[40] But the Democrats could not alter the fact that the Republicans had carried the state overwhelmingly. Still, the *Express and Herald* of Dubuque crowed that "the most dangerous political organization this country has ever seen" had been beaten nationally. The Republicans, the *Express* insisted, sought only spoils and power, not principles and Union.[41]

Thus the infant Republican party of Iowa, expertly led by Grimes, Harlan, Clarke, and other capable political figures, brilliantly parlayed a series of fortunate circumstances into a great victory in its first encounter with the Democratic party. The splintered, dissident elements had been effectively molded into a powerful force which, acting with the regular Whigs, would enable it to continue to hold the reins of political power in the state during the waning years of the antebellum decade.

The new party, as noted earlier, needing in addition to the slavery question a broad base upon which to appeal to Iowa voters, tied its future in large measure to the railroad, as Curtis' victory partly attests. Republicans continued to champion railroad construction throughout the state and a line to the Pacific.[42] While the Republican party grew out of the slavery controversy, it employed the railroad question, together with several other key local and national issues, to maintain itself in power in Iowa. The results of the elections of 1856 certainly testify to the effectiveness of the policy.

[40] Warner Lewis and C. C. Hewitt to George W. Jones, November 18, 1856, in the Jones Correspondence.

[41] November 26, 1856, quoted in Oldt, *History of Dubuque County Iowa*, 339.

[42] David S. Sparks, "Iowa Republicans and the Railroads 1856–1860," *Iowa Journal of History*, Vol. LIII (1955), 276–78.

The Consolidation of Power

Having scored an impressive victory in the state elections of 1856, the triumphant Republicans moved swiftly to consolidate and fortify their political posture throughout the state. They now held all the important elective offices, and, with the Iowa General Assembly in their control, they had a rather free hand in directing the operations of the government. The Democrats were virtually powerless before the Republican tide.

The first action which the Republicans took to solidify their position was to alter the boundaries of both the congressional and the local districts. Curtis' surprising victory in the First District, an area heretofore normally Democratic, indicated to Republicans that his grip upon the congressional seat was at best tenuous. In the Second District, however, where the Democrats had been out of office since 1852, the Republicans could rely on receiving heavy majorities in almost any given election.

With both branches of the assembly firmly in their control,

146

the Republicans, much to the dismay of the Democrats, proceeded to ensure that the First Congressional District would remain "safe." On January 24, 1857, the Senate Committee on Apportionment introduced a bill to modify the boundaries of the congressional districts by detaching Des Moines, Louisa, and Washington counties from the Second District and adding them to the First. Four days later, having passed the legislature with ease and having received the governor's signature, the measure became law.[1]

It was claimed that the slight alteration would equalize the congressional districts; the population of the Second District had outstripped that of the First, and the reapportionment would restore the balance. The real aim of the act, however, was strictly a political one. Both Louisa and Washington counties were Republican strongholds, as they had long been Whig centers before 1856. Des Moines County, while still voting in the Democratic column, was beginning to lean toward the new party.[2] Assuming that the Republicans could hold their own in the original counties in the First District, the heavy Republican votes from Louisa and Washington counties would virtually assure them of victory in future congressional races. Nor would the changes in any way endanger the Republican position in the Second District.

The second goal of the Republican consolidation program was the enactment of a measure which provided for a referendum on the question of holding a constitutional convention to revise or replace the state constitution. In the past both Whigs and Democrats had backed proposals for a referendum on the question of revising the Constitution of 1846. The movement resulted primarily from a need to approve the establishment of banks. Iowa continued to be inundated by paper money from other states, and this abundance of depreciated currency had the effect of

[1] Paul S. Pierce, "Congressional Districting in Iowa," *Iowa Journal of History and Politics*, Vol. I (1903), 337–39.
[2] Election Records, 1848–1860.

making gold and silver extremely scarce. Additional factors also made change desirable.[3]

The Democratic executive rather than the Democratic General Assembly had blocked bills providing for a referendum. Twice the legislature had enacted measures to secure this goal, and twice Governor Hempstead had vetoed them. The first veto, on January 13, 1853, was based primarily on a minor technicality.[4] But Hempstead's inaugural address should have given members of the legislature a clue to his attitude on the question:

> The principles by which I shall be governed in the administration of your affairs are distinctly marked out in the Constitution of this State, a Constitution which in my judgment is eminently calculated to secure to us the enjoyment of life, liberty, equality, and the pursuit of happiness, or in other words, to secure the great objects for which governments should be established among men; and the prosperity of the State from its organization to the present time is a forcible commentary of the justice and wisdom of the policy thus adopted.[5]

Hempstead's message should have convinced Iowa's lawmakers that a measure providing for a change in the state constitution or even for a referendum on the subject would not receive his approval.

Nevertheless, the legislature made one more attempt. Modifying the measure to overcome Hempstead's veto objections, the assembly again passed the bill, but again it was vetoed. The vote in both chambers had been strongly in favor of passage: 40 to 22

[3] Russell M. Ross, "The Development of the Iowa Constitution of 1857," *Iowa Journal of History*, Vol. LV (1957), 102.

[4] *Journal of the House of Representatives*, 4th General Assembly of Iowa, 1852, 125, 209, 320–21, 344; Benjamin F. Shambaugh (ed.), *The Messages and Proclamations of the Governors of Iowa*, I, 475–76; Louis Pelzer, "The History and Principles of the Democratic Party of Iowa, 1846–1857," *Iowa Journal of History and Politics*, VI (1908), 203.

[5] Shambaugh, *Messages and Proclamations*, I, 425–26.

in the house and 18 to 12 in the senate. Democrats controlled the lower chamber 40 to 23 and the upper chamber 20 to 11.[6]

Though Hempstead's second veto was also based upon technical grounds, he voiced his disapproval of a revision of the constitution. In his second veto message he expressed "a deep concern at the opinion entertained by some portion of the people in favor of . . . the establishment of banks, of special acts of incorporation for pecuniary profit, and of contracting debts without limitation by the General Assembly." These views, rock-ribbed Jacksonian declarations, had "undergone no change" during his years as governor. Furthermore, Hempstead insisted, most of the people were satisfied with the state constitution as it stood. The petitions flowing into the legislature, however, contradicted his claim.[7]

Following Grimes's surprising gubernatorial victory in 1854, the Iowa legislature passed another measure calling for a referendum on the question of revising the constitution. The senate, Democratic by a single vote, approved the bill 29 to 2. This time the governor affixed his signature to the constitutional referendum bill, and the voters later approved the proposed constitutional convention by a vote of 32,790 to 14,162.[8]

The meeting to revise the Constitution of 1846 assembled at the capitol building in Iowa City on January 19, 1857. Of the thirty-five delegates elected in November, the Republicans outnumbered the Democrats 21 to 14. Since the Republicans were numerically superior, Democrat Jonathan C. Hall lost the presidency of the convention to his Republican rival, Francis L. Springer. Hall was the only delegate who had served in both the

[6] *Journal of the House of Representatives*, 4th General Assembly of Iowa, 1852, 344, 412–14; *Journal of the Senate*, 4th General Assembly of Iowa, 1852, 291.

[7] Shambaugh, *Messages and Proclamations*, I, 476–78; *Burlington* (Iowa) *Daily Telegraph*, January 28, 1853; *Journal of the Senate*, 4th General Assembly of Iowa, 1852, 69, 81, 117, 191.

[8] *Ibid.*, 5th General Assembly of Iowa, 1854, 196; Election Records, 1848–1860.

earlier constitutional conventions in the state. His defeat was not a personal rejection but rather a rebuke to the party leadership which had sponsored, maintained, and defended the old constitution.[9]

Though the members of the convention retained much of the Constitution of 1846, they enacted several new provisions in the new document. In keeping with long-standing Whig demands, their political heirs, the Republicans, sponsored an article to permit the establishment of public banking and succeeded in securing its approval by a vote of 29 to 6. Five of the negative votes were Democratic; the lone Republican dissenter was William Penn Clarke. Other new clauses provided for an increase in the state debt limit from $100,000 to $250,000, the election of a lieutenant governor, the popular election of judges, biennial elections for all state offices, the removal of the state capital to Des Moines, and the permanent location of the University of Iowa in Iowa City.[10]

The article on suffrage provoked considerable debate when the question of permitting Negroes to vote was raised. In Article 1, which became the state's Bill of Rights, Negroes received legal rights in the state along with a measure of personal security.[11] They could, for example, testify in court. The effort to give them the vote, however, met with strong opposition. Not wishing to take upon themselves the responsibility of deciding for or against the granting of voting privileges to Negroes, the members of the convention agreed to permit the voters to decide this point when they voted to accept or reject the new constitution. As

[9] Ross, "The Development of the Iowa Constitution of 1857," 102; Erik M. Eriksson, "The Framers of the Constitution of 1857," *Iowa Journal of History and Politics*, Vol. XXII (1924), 60–61; Irving B. Richman (ed.), *History of Muscatine County Iowa*, I, 38.

[10] Eriksson, "The Framers of the Constitution of 1857," 71–74; John E. Briggs, "The Removal of the Capital from Iowa City to Des Moines," *Iowa Journal of History and Politics*, Vol. XIV (1916), 92–93.

[11] Leola N. Bergmann, "The Negro in Iowa," *Iowa Journal of History and Politics*, Vol. XLVI (1948), 21; Benjamin F. Shambaugh, *The Constitutions of Iowa*, 299–351.

it read, the article on suffrage extended the franchise to every white male citizen of the United States living in the state at least six months and in a given county at least twenty days. The voters were to determine whether or not the word "white" should be retained in the article on suffrage.[12] Concerning this point, the state House of Representatives adopted a resolution against striking out the word "white" from the suffrage provisions by the decisive vote of 51 to 6.[13] Clearly, despite their emotional and practical solicitations on behalf of Negroes in bondage, as well as Democratic accusations that they wanted to enact a pro-Negro constitution, Republicans were as unwilling as their partisan opponents to accept Negroes as political equals. Indeed, William Penn Clarke declared that his party was primarily committed to opposition to the extension of slavery, not to the granting of suffrage to Negroes. Having added a partly new superstructure to an older foundation, the convention adjourned after stipulating that a vote on the acceptance or rejection of the new constitution would be held in August, 1857.[14]

The new document received a mixed response from the press. Republican papers generally greeted it with enthusiasm and insisted that it was strictly a Republican creation, despite the course of action of the Democratic members of the convention who also strongly sustained it. The *Washington* (Iowa) *Press*, noted, however, that "there has been a studied effort on the part of certain Journals recently to make the Constitutional question a party issue, and to array the Democratic party in open hostility to the New Constitution." That was a most unfortunate pro-

[12] Eriksson, "The Framers of the Constitution of 1857," 70; Carl H. Erbe, "Constitutional Provisions for the Suffrage in Iowa," *Iowa Journal of History and Politics*, Vol. XXII (1924), 204.

[13] *Journal of the House of Representatives*, 6th General Assembly of Iowa, 1856, 466.

[14] Eugene H. Berwanger, *The Frontier Against Slavery: Western Anti-Negro Prejudice and the Slavery Extension Controversy*, 41–42; George A. Boeck, "An Early Iowa Community: Aspects of Economic, Social, and Political Development in Burlington, Iowa, 1833–1866," unpublished Ph.D. dissertation, University of Iowa, 1961, 272–73.

cedure, for "some of the ablest members of that party were in the Convention that framed it, and are still its warm advocates." Most Republican papers, however friendly they were to the constitution, sought to convince their readers of their opposition to Negro suffrage, which generated most of the controversy over ratification of the document.[15]

Democratic newspapers critical of the constitution raised objections primarily to the Negro suffrage referendum and to the new articles covering banking, incorporation, and state indebtedness. In true Jacksonian fashion the *North Iowa Times* of McGregor expressed concern that a chartered bank, in reality, would be a "*chartered* monopoly" with "its fangs . . . buried in the flesh of business."[16] In some instances Democrats sought to link Negro suffrage with Republicanism and racial amalgamation, but one editor confessed that "there is no man of our acquaintance, be his politics Republican or Democratic, who desires to have negroes come among us." Because Republican papers sought to denigrate the role of the Democrats in the formulation of the constitution, the issue of ratification became, to some extent at least, a test of political partisanship.[17]

In the meantime, political activity in 1857 continued as usual. Three minor state offices were to be contested in the spring elections. Accordingly, both major parties held state conventions in January to select candidates for the posts of superintendent of public instruction, register of the State Land Office, and commissioner of the Des Moines River Improvement. The Democrats nominated Maturin L. Fisher, superintendent of public instruction; Theodore S. Parvin, register of the State Land Office;

---

[15] *Montezuma* (Iowa) *Weekly Republican*, July 18, 1857; *Washington* (Iowa) *Press*, July 1, 1857; *Iowa Weekly Citizen* (Des Moines), September 2, 1857, quoted in Louis Pelzer, "History of Political Parties in Iowa 1857–1860," *Iowa Journal of History and Politics*, Vol. VII (1909), 183.

[16] Quoted in Mildred Throne, "Contemporary Editorial Opinion of the 1857 Constitution," *Iowa Journal of History*, Vol. LV (1957), 116–17.

[17] Berwanger, *The Frontier Against Slavery*, 41–42.

and Gideon S. Bailey, commissioner of the Des Moines River Improvement.[18]

The long Democratic platform restated the party's belief in the supremacy of the United States Constitution and reaffirmed the Democratic national platforms of 1852 and 1856. Another plank indicted the Republicans for creating and fostering sectional strife designed to destroy the Union. Democrats castigated Republicans on a variety of state issues. They criticized the Republicans for extending civil liberties to Negroes and Indians and accused them of attempting to elevate the Negro above the white man. In addition, they attacked the prohibition law, asked Democratic members of the constitutional convention to oppose extension of the franchise to nonwhites, and again defended popular sovereignty. On the problems of Kansas the Democrats remained silent.[19]

The Republicans met in state convention a few days after the Democratic gathering had adjourned. For the offices at stake they chose L. H. Bugbee, superintendent of public instruction; William Holmes, register of the State Land Office; and Edwin Manning, commissioner of the Des Moines River Improvement.

The Republican state platform pledged that the party would continue its efforts on behalf of liberty and freedom and reaffirmed the principles of the party's national platform of 1856. It labeled Frémont's defeat a moral victory. On the state level, the Republicans approved the extension of civil liberties to Negroes and Indians, asked for a continuation of the prevailing naturalization laws, and demanded an investigation of certain state officers. The last, undoubtedly, was a reference to the departing superintendent of public instruction, James D. Eads, a Democrat, whose mismanagement of certain school funds was just beginning to come under fire, causing considerable embarrassment to the

[18] *Iowa Weekly Republican* (Iowa City), January 17, 1857.
[19] Roy V. Sherman, "Political Party Platforms in Iowa," unpublished M.A. thesis, State University of Iowa, 1956, 142–45.

Republican administration despite the superintendent's political affiliation.[20]

The April elections were extremely heartening to the Democrats. Maturin L. Fisher and Theodore S. Parvin defeated their Republican adversaries, while Gideon S. Bailey lost an extremely close contest to his Republican opponent. A probable factor in the success of Fisher and Parvin was that these men were better known to Iowa voters than Bugbee and Holmes. Fisher, for example, had recently served as president of the Iowa senate.[21]

Four months later Iowa voters again went to the polls, this time to cast ballots in the constitutional referendum. They ratified the new state constitution by the close count of 40,311 to 38,701. The percentage in favor of the new constitution was 51.02 per cent. In contrast, by the overwhelming vote of 49,387 to 8,484, Iowans refused to strike the word "white" from the article on suffrage.[22]

Forty-eight counties returned majorities of 50 per cent or more in favor of the new constitution, while thirty-three counties cast majorities against ratification. Four counties—Lee, Polk, Henry, and Warren—gave the constitution a combined majority of 4,947 votes.[23] If Lee and Polk counties had been as equally divided on the issue as most of the other counties, the constitution might well have been rejected. Polk County ratified by an overwhelming margin undoubtedly because of the constitutional provision to relocate the capital at the county seat, Des Moines. The business interests in the larger eastern Iowa towns—Davenport, Keokuk, Muscatine, and Burlington—also played key roles in securing the ratification of the new constitution. Though they might not have

[20] *Ibid.*, 149–51; see Thomas Teakle, "The Defalcation of Superintendent James D. Eads," *Iowa Journal of History and Politics*, Vol. XII (1914), 205–44.

[21] Election Records, 1848–1860.

[22] *Ibid.*; Erbe, "Constitutional Provisions for the Suffrage in Iowa," 206; Bergmann, "The Negro in Iowa," 20–21.

[23] Election Records, 1848–1860.

favored the removal of the capital, they approved the clauses on banking, incorporations, and the increased ceiling on state debts.

In general, opposition to the constitution was centered in the strongly Democratic areas of the state: the city and county of Dubuque, along the southern tier of counties directly north of Missouri, and the region of the Missouri River slope. Some of the older counties, which had lately voted Republican, also cast majorities against ratification; Jacksonian suspicion of banks was deeply ingrained among a sizable element of the electorate.

Ratification of the new state constitution was politically significant because it meant, among other things, that a third election would take place during this busy political year of 1857. In anticipation of this possibility, both Republicans and Democrats scheduled second state conventions to meet in Iowa City to choose candidates for governor and lieutenant governor. The election itself would take place in October and would include the election of members of the assembly. To the new legislature would fall the important responsibility of picking a successor to George W. Jones, whose term in the United States Senate would expire in March, 1859.

The second Republican state convention of 1857 met in Iowa City on August 21, one week before the scheduled meeting of the Democratic party. As early as March 24 incumbent Governor Grimes had indicated that he would not be a candidate for reelection, because "I am satisfied that I have not the physical ability to canvass the state. The truth is I used myself up for all such purposes the year I was a candidate before." He believed that his successor should come from "the central part of the state which has never yet had a governor nor a candidate for the office. . . . The Lieut. Gov. should be taken from the North or Northwest."[24] Competition, therefore, among Republicans for the

[24] James W. Grimes to Samuel J. Kirkwood, March 24, 1857, in "Letters of James W. Grimes," *Annals of Iowa*, 3rd ser., Vol. XXII (1940), 478–80; *Montezuma Weekly Republican*, July 4, 1857.

important nominations was keen. Eventually the convention endorsed a moderate and former Whig, Ralph P. Lowe, for governor and Oran Faville for lieutenant governor. Lowe was born, reared, and educated in Ohio, graduating from Miami University in 1829. Moving to Iowa in 1840, he shortly afterward took up permanent residence in Keokuk. In 1844 he served as a member of the constitutional convention. Thus Lowe was one of Iowa's "old-time" residents. Faville, a native of New York, moved to Mitchell County, Iowa, in 1855. A graduate of Wesleyan University in Connecticut, he was a professor of languages at Lebanon College in Illinois before moving to Iowa.[25]

The new Republican state platform of 1857 asserted that the federal government was one of limited powers, condemned the repeal of the Missouri Compromise, opposed the spread of slavery into the territories, and blamed the Democrats for raising the slavery issue again. The Republicans also condemned the Mormons of Utah, deplored the maintenance of federal troops in Kansas, and took issue with the decision of the Supreme Court in the Dred Scott case, claiming that the Court was biased in favor of the South. Finally, the Republicans congratulated Iowans for adopting the new constitution and lauded the Grimes administration.[26]

The Democratic convention, which assembled in Iowa City on August 28, was the scene of lively political scrambling, for, with Dodge absent as United States ambassador to Spain, there was no logical candidate for any of the major elective posts at stake. The *Daily Crescent* of Iowa City listed as gubernatorial possibilities such men as Henn, of Fairfield; Ben M. Samuels, of

[25] Ralph P. Lowe to William Penn Clarke, August 7, 1857, in the William Penn Clarke Correspondence at the Iowa State Department of History and Archives in Des Moines; James W. Grimes to Samuel J. Kirkwood, March 9, 1857, in William Salter (ed.), "Old Letters," *Annals of Iowa*, 3rd ser., Vol. VIII (1908), 508–509; Shambaugh, *Messages and Proclamations*, II, 115; Gue, *History of Iowa*, IV, 89–90.
[26] Sherman, "Political Party Platforms in Iowa," 151–55.

Dubuque; George Green, of Cedar Rapids; and William Thompson, of Des Moines. Aspirants for the second place on the Democratic ticket included P. Gad Bryan, of Warren County; D. H. Solomon, of Mills; D. O. Finch, of Polk; Austin Corbin, of Scott; and William F. Leffingwell, of Clinton. Encouraged by the results of the April election, Iowa's Democrats confidently expected to win the state's major elective offices.[27]

When the balloting for the Democratic gubernatorial nomination ended on the eighth roll call, Samuels emerged with the coveted prize. George Gillaspie of Wapello County secured his party's endorsement for lieutenant governor on the tenth ballot. Born in Virginia in 1823, Samuels, the son of an eminent attorney, also chose law for his profession and moved to Dubuque in 1848. By 1850 he was a member of the Democratic Central Committee for Dubuque County. Winning election to the Iowa House of Representatives in 1854, Samuels helped his party carry Dubuque against Grimes the same year. Gillaspie, a Kentuckian, had been a prominent leader in Ottumwa since 1850 and had served in the constitutional convention just ended.[28]

The Democratic platform praised the Buchanan administration and condemned the extremists of the South along with the Republicans of the North. The party pledged, in addition, to maintain the federal Constitution. The major portion of the Democratic platform was devoted to the new state constitution. Democrats rebuked Republicans for extending civil rights to Negroes and Indians and demanded an immediate amendment to eliminate these liberal provisions. They attacked their political rivals for reapportioning the state's representative districts, both congressional and local, charging that a minority of the voters se-

[27] August 13 and 18, 1857.
[28] Pelzer, "History of Political Parties in Iowa 1857–1860," 181–82; Leland L. Sage, "The Early Life of William Boyd Allison," *Iowa Journal of History*, Vol. XLVIII (1950), 331–32; Iowa City *Daily Crescent*, September 1, 1857; Edward H. Stiles, *Recollections and Sketches of Notable Lawyers and Public Men of Early Iowa*, 659–60.

lected a majority of the members of the assembly. Finally, the Democrats lauded Jones and outgoing First District Congressman Hall.[29]

The Democratic platform made no reference to the problems distressing Kansas, nor did the party mention such other divisive issues as homesteads and internal improvements. These were deliberate omissions designed to minimize party discord.

The Know-Nothing party also proposed a slate of candidates for the major offices. The party, however, had suffered a sharp decline in membership after its rather good showing in 1856, and the organization of the Republican party had sounded the death knell for the Know-Nothings. Only four counties—Davis, Muscatine, Johnson, and Washington—sent delegates to what had been intended to be a state convention at Iowa City on September 2. The gubernatorial nomination went to J. F. Henry, of Des Moines County, while Eastin Morris was nominated for lieutenant governor.[30]

The platform adopted by this last Know-Nothing convention in Iowa contained twelve planks. The usual antiforeign sentiments of the group were expressed in demands that only native Americans should hold state and national offices. The Know-Nothings also requested an extension of the residence requirements for citizenship to twenty-one years, insisted upon separation of church and state, and reaffirmed their faith in the federal Constitution. In addition, they renounced all secrecy at meetings and at other party proceedings. Finally, they denounced the Democrats for opposing the new state constitution and at the same time declared that the residents of the territories possessed the right to frame their own laws.[31] But it was a shadow party which entered candidates for this election.

[29] Sherman, "Political Party Platforms in Iowa," 146–49.
[30] Willard I. Toussaint, "The Know-Nothing Party in Iowa," unpublished M.A. thesis, State University of Iowa, 1956, 96; Pelzer, "History of Political Parties in Iowa, 1857–1860," 180.

Immediately after he received the Democratic gubernatorial nomination, Samuels wrote to Lowe, the Republican nominee, inviting him to participate in a joint speaking tour of Iowa. Lowe replied that he had already drawn up his schedule of speeches and invited Samuels to join him instead. The tone of Lowe's letter indicated that he did not care to debate the issues with Samuels, who had the reputation of being one of the ablest speakers in the state. Nothing developed from this exchange of letters.[32]

The campaigns of all the parties lacked the fervor and excitement that had characterized Iowa's previous gubernatorial campaigns. Missing were the great emotional issues of past elections. The main point of controversy was the new constitution. Following the Jacksonian pattern, Samuels condemned the new constitution primarily because of the clause permitting the establishment of public banks. For his part, Lowe asserted that since the Democrats were opposing the constitution they were incapable of conducting the state government under it.[33]

Some partisan newspapers, for want of better political fodder, began to smear the major party candidates. Lowe, one Democratic paper charged, was a "Spiritualist." Another declared that Faville was incompetent to preside over the Iowa senate. The Republican *Daily Hawk-Eye* of Burlington accused Samuels of being too aristocratic to merit the support of the voters. It branded his Virginia birthplace as "the chivalrous land of political abstractions and niggers." Moreover, it cautioned, "if Samuels is elected it will be a victory for the fire-eaters and approval of their infernal doings in Kansas." The Democratic *Iowa State Gazette*, also of Burlington, retorted that Samuels' election

---

[31] Sherman, "Political Party Platforms in Iowa," 139–42.

[32] Ben M. Samuels to Ralph P. Lowe, August 28, 1857, in the Clarke Correspondence; Ralph P. Lowe to Ben M. Samuels, August 28, 1857, *ibid.*

[33] James Thorington to William Penn Clarke, August 25, 1857, in the Clarke Correspondence; Pelzer, "History of Political Parties in Iowa 1857–1860," 185.

was necessary to combat Republican plans to integrate the public schools in the state.[34]

Responding to the Democratic accusations, the *Hamilton Freeman* of Webster City conceded that while Lowe might have been interested in spiritualism it had been strictly from an intellectual standpoint. The *Montezuma Weekly Republican* declared that Lowe's membership in the Presbyterian Church in Keokuk precluded the notion that he was or could be a believer in spiritualism.[35]

The Republicans did attempt to raise the Supreme Court's Dred Scott decision to the level of a campaign issue. Either Iowans were tired of the slavery controversy or they accepted the verdict of the Court. A number of newspapers did contain editorials attacking the Republicans for their opposition to the decision.[36]

In October, for the third time in 1857, the voters went to the polls. About 15,000 fewer voters participated in the gubernatorial elections than in the presidential balloting a year earlier. There were more than 6,600 fewer Republican votes, but the decrease in the Democratic totals amounted to about 1,500. The Know-Nothings received about 8,600 fewer ballots. Lowe edged past Samuels by a vote of 38,508 to 36,092. The former attracted a scant 50.93 per cent of the total votes cast, or a smaller part of the whole than Grimes had obtained in 1854. Faville defeated Gillaspie 36,667 to 34,635. Republicans also won strong majorities in both branches of the legislature.[37]

[34] Quoted in Boeck, "An Early Iowa Community," 387–89; *State Democrat* and *Dubuque Northwest* quoted in *Daily Crescent*, August 27, 1857; Edward Younger, "The Rise of John A. Kasson in Iowa Politics, 1857–1859," *Iowa Journal of History*, Vol. L (1952), 295.

[35] *Hamilton Freeman* (Webster City, Iowa), September 17, 1857; *Montezuma Weekly Republican*, September 12, 1857.

[36] *Iowa Sentinel* (Fairfield), May 14, 1857.

[37] Election Records, 1848–1860; *Montezuma Weekly Republican*, October 24, 1857; Robert E. Lee, "Politics and Society in Sioux City, 1859," *Iowa Journal of History*, Vol. LIV (1956), 124.

The Democratic party continued to appeal strongly to the voters in Dubuque, along the southern tier, and in the southwestern quarter of the state. Moreover, the party registered significant gains in several Republican counties, including Clayton, Floyd, Mitchell, Mahaska, Tama, and Iowa. But the southwestern corner revealed unmistakable evidence of a decline in Democratic popularity, caused in part by the constitutional issue. Four counties there—Adair, Adams, Montgomery, and Taylor—switched to the Republicans; three of them—Adair, Adams, and Taylor—had given the constitution strong majorities.

Many voters loyal to each of Iowa's major parties failed to vote. Three elections in one year may simply have been too much for the electorate, whose zest for politics had manifestly declined by mid-autumn. The Democrats apparently were more derelict than their opponents. Henry Clay Dean, writing in late winter, 1858, blamed the slavery controversy for his party's recent defeats:

> The negro question, with which we have legitimately nothing under the Heavens to do, has cost us two Governors, two United States Senators, four Congressmen, the whole of the Supreme Bench, and both Houses of the Legislature. . . . We have nothing left us but our party platform and our political integrity.[38]

Nevertheless, having taken two of the minor state offices in April and having come within an eyelash of succeeding in the October contests, the Iowa Democrats could look to the future with renewed confidence.

[38] Louis Pelzer, "The Disintegration and Organization of Political Parties in Iowa 1852–1860," Mississippi Valley Historical Association *Proceedings* for 1911–1912, 163–64; James W. Grimes to Samuel J. Kirkwood, October 16, 1857, in "Letters of James W. Grimes," 491–92; Edward Younger, *John A. Kasson: Politics and Diplomacy from Lincoln to McKinley*, 79.

Kansas Explodes Again

THE REPUBLICAN party's tenuous, though complete, control of state politics was seriously threatened almost as soon as Lowe assumed the responsibilities of office. His administration opened on a rather unpleasant note as a series of scandals reached public attention. Moreover, Iowans began to experience the unfortunate effects of the Panic of 1857, as well as hardships brought on by severe weather conditions during the year.

The scandals which seriously compromised and embarrassed the Republicans involved the bribery of at least one of the five commissioners appointed to select the exact site of the new capitol building, the defalcation of the superintendent of public instruction, whose office showed an arrearage of more than seventy thousand dollars, and the chaotic disarray of the records and accounts in the various state offices. Indeed, no systematic procedure of record keeping existed from the highest to the lowest levels. Many town, city, and county records were also confused and disorganized. Governor Lowe appointed a committee, headed by John A. Kasson, to ascertain the extent of the disorder and to make recommendations to remedy the situation. At best, only a promising beginning was made.[1]

Economic misfortunes, more than governmental scandals, however, concerned Iowans. Farmers suffered from the collapse of real-estate values, the declining prices for grain, and the scarcity of currency. In addition, poor weather conditions destroyed crops throughout the state. Business interests were also hard hit; bankruptcies in 1858 exceeded those for the previous year. All levels of state government suffered from the inability of Iowans to meet their tax obligations.[2]

Excessive speculation in land and railroad stocks brought countless investors economic grief along with some public disapproval. Seeking answers for the causes of the depression, a newspaper editor in Keokuk wrote:

> We might ask who have been the principal movers in the real estate speculations of the West? Eastern men. If Tom, Dick, and the Devil from New York, New England, and every place else towards sunrise, had not puffed and blowed at these bursted bubbles, the West would have been all right to-day.

In reality, however, the out-of-state investors poured large amounts of money into Iowa when it was most sorely needed. Nor were resident land speculators especially scorned by the voters at election time.[3]

The depression halted virtually all railroad construction throughout the state. Because the assembly had responded favorably to appeals from Iowans for the enactment of legislation to

---

[1] Edward Younger, "The Rise of John A. Kasson in Iowa Politics 1857–1859," *Iowa Journal of History*, Vol. L (1952), 300–302.

[2] Frank I. Herriott, "Republican Presidential Preliminaries in Iowa 1859–1860," *Annals of Iowa*, 3rd ser., Vol. IX (1910), 257.

[3] Quoted in Robert P. Swierenga, "Pioneers and Profits: Land Speculation on the Iowa Frontier," unpublished Ph.D. dissertation, University of Iowa, 1965, 325, 331, 336.

relieve their economic woes, railroad promoters also sought state aid. Platt Smith, president of the Dubuque and Pacific Railroad, endeavored to convince Governor Lowe that public opinion supported state aid for railroads. He insisted that only two newspapers in the state, the *Express and Herald* of Dubuque and the *Vinton Eagle,* opposed the scheme for the state to help the railroads. "I have no doubt," Smith wrote to the governor, "that every paper from here [Dubuque] to the Missouri River, and for thirty miles on each side, will be in favor of the measure in less than two months if the subject is agitated."[4] Lowe favored Smith's proposals, but other Republican leaders were more cautious. Although many Republican officials were intimately associated with railroads in one capacity or another, they did not believe that the times were politically propitious for the state to favor the railroads legislatively. Prominent party figures, including Senator Harlan, urged Lowe not to involve the state or the Republican party in plans to aid the railroads with state funds. One Republican genuinely feared that the railroads would soon become the strongest political and economic force in the state. In the end, Lowe reluctantly heeded the advice of party leaders and refused to call a special session of the assembly to consider relief measures for railroads.[5]

Events on the national scene now conspired to save the Republicans from reaping the bitter harvest of governmental scandals and economic depression and drove a new wedge into the split but reuniting Democratic party. News of political skull-

[4] Platt Smith to Ralph P. Lowe, September 3 and November 24, 1858, in the Governors' Papers: Correspondence at the Iowa State Department of History and Archives in Des Moines; Platt Smith to Cyrus C. Carpenter, November 2, 1858, in the Cyrus C. Carpenter Letters at the State Historical Society of Iowa in Iowa City.

[5] John Bertram to Ralph P. Lowe, March 15, 1858, in the Governors' Papers: Correspondence; Thomas F. Withrow to Cyrus C. Carpenter, November 8 and December 23, 1858, in the Carpenter Letters; James Harlan to Ralph P. Lowe, November 11, 1858, in the James Harlan Papers at the State Historical Society of Iowa in Iowa City; *Vinton* (Iowa) *Eagle,* December 25, 1858; *Weekly Iowa State Reporter* (Des Moines), December 22, 1858.

duggery on the part of the proslavery forces in Kansas reached Iowa early in 1858. Their machinations ultimately played a significant role in rescuing the Republicans from what so astute a politician as Grimes believed would be certain defeat in the fall elections. He hoped that Congress would sustain the activities of the Southern element in Kansas, because "the passage of the Lecompton bill will be the only thing that can save our party. If I believed, therefore, that the end justified the means, I think I should pray for its adoption."[6]

On September 7, 1857, forty-four delegates with Southern proslavery sympathies appeared at Lecompton, Kansas, to draft a constitution for a state government with the goal of securing the admission of Kansas into the Union.[7] Owing to the efforts of the president of the convention, John Calhoun, the delegates agreed to adjourn until October 9, after the territorial elections. The results of the elections satisfied few, for evidence of fraud was uncovered.

When the delegates reassembled, it was evident that they did not intend to submit their completed document to the voters of Kansas for acceptance or rejection. The pro-Southern delegates preferred to submit their constitution directly to Washington. But Calhoun persuaded them to offer two versions of the constitution to Kansans. One would permit the admission of slaves into Kansas; the other would prohibit it. On November 6 the assembled delegates affixed their signatures to the Lecompton constitution.

Among other clauses, the Lecompton constitution provided for the protection of slaveholders already in Kansas. Voters would decide whether additional slaves and their masters would be

[6] James W. Grimes to S. J. Kirkwood, March 11, 1858, "Letters of James W. Grimes," *Annals of Iowa*, 3rd ser., Vol. XXII (1940), 494.

[7] Numerous excellent works have discussed the critical situation in Kansas following the passage of the Kansas-Nebraska Act. For two examples, see Roy F. Nichols, *The Disruption of American Democracy*, and James W. Rawley, *Race and Politics: Bleeding Kansas and the Coming of the Civil War*.

admitted in the future. Free Negroes were barred from the area. Other articles confined voting to male citizens, specified that the governor had to be a citizen of at least twenty years' duration, decreed that only one bank with a maximum of two branches could be incorporated by the state legislature, and provided for a grant of land to two railroad lines. Ambiguous wording implied that the constitution could not be amended for at least seven years.

The chief objections to the constitution centered on the slavery clause, as well as the composition of the constitutional convention. Fifteen of the thirty-four counties in Kansas had not been represented. Moreover, the general character of the delegates was far from desirable.

Unfortunately for the state and national Democratic party, President Buchanan, having promised Southern leaders his support, determined to accept the Lecompton constitution in the face of opposition from Stephen A. Douglas and other Northern Democrats, and made acceptance of the document a test of party fidelity. Douglas' refusal to bend to Buchanan split the national organization as well as many state groups.

In Kansas the referendum sponsored by the proslavery constitutional convention was held on December 21, 1857. Proslavery voters ratified the constitution by a one-sided vote of 6,143 to 569. On January 4, 1858, another referendum was held, this one endorsed by the free-state legislature. Antislavery voters turned down the Lecompton constitution by the substantial margin of 10,226 to 162. Nevertheless, John Calhoun certified the first referendum and notified Washington that the Lecompton constitution had been accepted. Obviously, however, the majority in Kansas had rejected the slavery constitution.

Despite the evidence that most Kansans had opposed the Lecompton constitution, Buchanan accepted it, ignoring the entreaties of Douglas and the anti-Lecompton Democrats in Congress. He submitted the constitution to Congress and recommended the admission of Kansas under it. Eventually, Congress decided to resubmit the constitution to the voters of Kansas, but the damage had already been done: the national Democratic party was irrevocably split.

Iowa Democrats generally recoiled at the action of the Lecompton convention. Early in January, 1858, a meeting of Democrats at Mount Pleasant, led by Henry Clay Dean and B. J. Hall, resolved: "We now repudiate the base-born abortion of fraud and perjury—the Lecompton Constitution."[8] Another Democratic gathering in Keokuk on January 9, 1858, commended Douglas, the Cincinnati platform, and even Buchanan, but demanded a free and honest application of the principles of self-government. Democrats of Des Moines County, desirous of preventing a split in the organization, adopted resolutions upholding the Kansas-Nebraska Act as the final arbiter of policy for the territories, deploring a party schism over the affairs in Kansas, and pointing out that the Kansas problem was not the only one upon which the parties differed.[9] Except for the Dubuque *Northwest*, every Democratic newspaper in the state was said to support Douglas against Buchanan. No Republican journal was more critical of the Lecompton constitution than the anti-Jones Democratic paper at Dubuque, the *Express and Herald*. This organ assailed that constitution, as well as administration supporters in Congress, as

> a triumph of corruption, fraud, and treachery. . . . It is a triumph of the Administration over the advocates of pure, sound Democratic principles, but it is a barren triumph—a triumph that will bring down upon the head of the Administration the curses, deep and fervent, of sound national Democrats every-

[8] Quoted in Louis Pelzer, "History of Political Parties in Iowa 1857–1860," *Iowa Journal of History and Politics*, Vol. VII (1909), 191.

[9] *Ibid.*; George A. Boeck, "An Early Iowa Community: Aspects of Economic, Social, and Political Development in Burlington, Iowa, 1833–1866," unpublished Ph.D. dissertation, University of Iowa, 1961, 391.

where—curses for the ruin and division of the party, curses for the suicidal and obstinate policy of the President.[10]

Republicans, of course, sought to employ the Lecompton fraud to further their own purposes. In his biennial address to the Iowa General Assembly, outgoing Governor Grimes made it a special point to denounce the action at Lecompton. On January 19, 1858, Republican John W. Rankin of Lee County introduced resolutions in the legislature condemning the Lecompton duplicity, instructing Iowa's senators to oppose the admission of Kansas under the Lecompton constitution, denouncing the President and all others who supported that document, and demanding the resignation of any Iowa senator who refused to comply with the instructions of the legislature. The last resolution was obviously directed at George W. Jones, who supported Buchanan's policy in Kansas.[11]

In the Senate Harlan condemned the administration for accepting what was an obvious and palpable fraud. Senator Jones, however, presented the Iowa resolutions to the upper house "as a matter of respect to the State Legislature of Iowa" but announced that he had no intention whatever of obeying the instructions they contained. He informed his colleagues that he would "vote for the admission of Kansas under the Lecompton Constitution."[12]

Smarting from the sting of the Republican resolutions, the Douglas Democrats in the assembly, led by Lincoln Clark of Dubuque, drew up a protest against the action of the Republican-controlled legislature. Clark and his group protested "because this General Assembly had no jurisdiction in Law over the Presi-

---

[10] Quoted in Pelzer, "History of Political Parties in Iowa 1857–1860," 196; Mildred Throne, "C. C. Carpenter in the 1858 Iowa Legislature," *Iowa Journal of History,* Vol. LII (1954), 48–49.

[11] Benjamin F. Shambaugh (ed.), *Messages and Proclamations of the Governors of Iowa,* II, 65–66; Throne, "C. C. Carpenter in the 1858 Iowa Legislature," 46–47; *Journal of the Senate,* 7th General Assembly of Iowa, 1858, 82–83.

[12] 35 Cong., 1 sess., *Congressional Globe,* 383–86, 566.

dent of the United States, to arraign and condemn" and no power or right to condemn senators of the United States. Nevertheless, the Douglas wing declared that Congress could and should investigate the facts behind the ratification of the Lecompton constitution. Moreover, Clark and his followers agreed with their Republican opponents that the people of Kansas had not had a fair opportunity to pass judgment on the constitution.[13]

The protest of the Douglas Democrats drew fire from the small but powerful administration faction of the party. Senator Jones bitterly wrote to Iowa United States Marshal Laurel Summers:

> I rejoice to think that Lincoln Clark, the Wilson's, Hall, Coolbaugh & the other fools of that ilk went off at a tangent against us on the Lecompton Kansas question. I hope they will follow Douglas into the ranks of the Black Republicans, for like him they are corrupt, ambitious, and cowardly liars & disorganizers.

Administration Democrat Robert Robinson, a regular Summers correspondent, believed that Clark and his group could have saved themselves the trouble of drawing up their protest "by voting with the Black Republicans on the same subject."[14]

Dennis Mahoney and four other Buchanan Democrats in the legislature—Samuel H. Casady, Theopolis Crawford, Squire Ayers, and E. R. Guiberson—issued a protest against both the Republican resolutions and the Douglas faction. Mahoney declared that the Republicans had no right to instruct senators about their course of action concerning the admission of new states into the Union. As for the statements of the antiadministration Democrats, Mahoney denied that Congress had the right or authority to "go behind" the Lecompton constitution. Thus the split in the national Democratic organization was reflected in a further

---

[13] *Journal of the House of Representatives,* 7th General Assembly of Iowa, 1858, 311–13.

[14] George W. Jones to Laurel Summers, March 6, 1858, in the Laurel Summers Correspondence at the Iowa State Department of History and Archives in Des Moines; Robert Robinson to Laurel Summers, March 5, 1858, *ibid.*

schism of the state party. The long-standing anti-Jones animosity reappeared, as anti-Jones Democrats supplied the leadership for Iowa's pro-Douglas partisans.[15]

In the meantime, the Iowa legislature had turned to the task of selecting a United States senator to replace Jones. Although most Republicans favored Grimes for the position, opposition to his candidacy developed because of a geographical factor. Since Senator Harlan came from the southern part of Iowa, some preferred the election of a senator from northern Iowa to maintain the traditional geographical balance.[16] Moreover, a number of individuals who were personally at odds with Grimes, led by William Penn Clarke, labored to secure his defeat at the Republican caucus. Clarke, hoping to gain Harlan's support, tried to convince him that the geographical factor would operate against his reelection should Grimes be successful, for then both of Iowa's senators would come from southern Iowa. Harlan suggested that Clarke should strive to drive a wedge into the Grimes-Kirkwood coalition. To gain more time to unite the anti-Grimes forces, Clarke strove to prevent a first-ballot victory for his political enemy.[17] Cyrus C. Carpenter, newly elected to the lower chamber from Fort Dodge, wrote his future wife, "My very heart sickens at the name of politics" owing to the designs of a few "to defeat the man who has done more for the Republican party and our state than any other man living." Carpenter had received a note from Grimes before the opening of the assembly:

I do not know how you feel on this question. If you can con-

[15] *Journal of the House of Representatives*, 7th General Assembly of Iowa, 1858, 322–25.

[16] *Montezuma* (Iowa) *Weekly Republican*, November 28, 1857; *Iowa State Journal* (Des Moines), January 16, 1858; David S. Wilson to Mrs. Wilson, January 8, 1858, in the David S. Wilson Papers at the Iowa State Department of History and Archives in Des Moines; William Vandever to William Penn Clarke, December 20, 1857, in the William Penn Clarke Correspondence, also at the Historical Department in Des Moines.

[17] James Harlan to William Penn Clarke, December 21, 1857, in the Clarke Correspondence.

scientiously give me your support I shall surely always feel very grateful for it, but I wish also to say, that your failure to do so will in no degree lessen my respect & esteem for you.

Elijah Sells, soon to be Iowa's secretary of state, wrote letters in support of Grimes's candidacy. Grimes then asked Samuel J. Kirkwood of Iowa City to perform a similar service on his behalf.[18]

The anti-Grimes faction, together with the Dubuque and Pacific Railroad, supported Frederick E. Bissell, of Dubuque, an attorney for that line. Grimes saw Bissell as his chief threat:

I have no fears about my election. The principal opposition to me . . . will be from DuBuque. That ambitious city insists that one Senator must always be from DuBuque & will present Mr. Bissell of that ilk. Bissell is a man I never saw—is represented to be a good lawyer & a good man, but as far as I know, he has never been particularly identified with the Republican party or done any thing to promote its success except perhaps to vote. I understand from a friend at DuBuque that the members of the DuBuque & Pacific R.R. Co. are particularly anxious on his behalf.[19]

Nevertheless, Grimes was confident of succeeding in the Republican caucus and of carrying the election. Nor was he disappointed. At the Republican caucus, Grimes received 39 of the 63 ballots cast to win his party's senatorial nomination. With Republicans in control of the legislature, Grimes's election was certain.[20]

[18] Cyrus C. Carpenter to Kate Burkholder, January 15, 1858, in the Carpenter Letters; James W. Grimes to Cyrus C. Carpenter, November 11, 1857, *ibid.*; Elijah Sells to Cyrus C. Carpenter, November 17, 1857, *ibid.*; James W. Grimes to Samuel J. Kirkwood, October 24, November 17, and December 15, 1857, "Letters of James W. Grimes," 483–84, 487–88, 490–91.

[19] James W. Grimes to Samuel J. Kirkwood, November 5, 1857, "Letters of James W. Grimes," 484–85; W. H. Farner to William Penn Clarke, December 10, 1857, in the Clarke Correspondence; Dan E. Clark, *History of Senatorial Elections in Iowa: A Study in American Politics*, 114.

[20] Copy of a letter from James W. Grimes to Edward C. David, November 11,

171

Still, Democrats fought for the honor of opposing the Republican nominee. The split within the Iowa Democratic party over the Lecompton fraud pitted the Douglas, anti-Jones wing of the organization against Jones, who sought renomination. Thomas S. Wilson, like Jones a citizen of Dubuque, and Jones's long-standing foe, also coveted the Democratic nomination. Though most Iowa Democrats were Douglasites, Jones was not without friends and allies. The *Iowa State Journal* of Des Moines promoted his candidacy, as did other proadministration Democrats. The pro-Jones faction, however, reluctantly conceded that Douglas Democrats controlled the party in the legislature.[21] Robert Robinson informed Laurel Summers that "the prospect to nominate Gen'l Jones is rather discouraging." Moreover, the Keokuk delegation intended to oppose Jones on the ground that he had sacrificed the interests of that city during his service in the Senate.[22]

In the Democratic caucus the contenders ultimately narrowed down to Jones and Ben M. Samuels, also of Dubuque and a leader, with Lincoln Clark and Thomas S. Wilson, of the anti-administration wing of the party. William F. Coolbaugh, a Burlington leader, joined forces with Samuels to engineer Jones's defeat by a vote of 26 to 10. It was said that Jones's pro-Lecompton stand was chiefly responsible for his downfall. Keeping Laurel Summers informed of the proceedings, Robert Robinson remarked that he was sorry Samuels had received the nomination: "It will keep up the war in the northern part of the state."[23]

1857, in the William Salter Collection at the Iowa State Department of History and Archives in Des Moines; Des Moines *Session Citizen*, January 28, 1858.

[21] Clark, *History of Senatorial Elections in Iowa*, 104–105; *Iowa State Journal*, December 26, 1857.

[22] Robert Robinson to Laurel Summers, January 14, 1858, in the Summers Correspondence; Jonathan R. Allen to George W. Jones, November 3, 1857, in the George W. Jones Correspondence at the Iowa State Department of History and Archives in Des Moines.

[23] Robert Robinson to Laurel Summers, January 28, 1858, in the Summers Correspondence.

At the joint session of the assembly everything went according to form. Grimes defeated Samuels on a straight party vote of 64 to 41. The last Democrat in Congress from Iowa before the Civil War was Jones, and he would leave office in March, 1859.[24]

At stake in the fall elections of 1858 were state offices and the two congressional seats. With the Kansas troubles reverberating throughout the state and nation, both parties mapped plans to summon state conventions before launching their campaigns.

The Republican state convention met in Iowa City on June 17, one week before the Democratic meeting. To run for the state positions the party chose Elijah Sells, secretary of state; J. W. Cattell, auditor; John W. Jones, treasurer; and Samuel A. Rice, attorney general.

The Republican state platform of thirteen planks opened with the usual reaffirmation of the national party platform of 1856. In succeeding planks the Republicans accused the Democratic party of seeking to extend slavery into the territories, condemned the Lecompton constitution and the Dred Scott decision, and berated the national government for its extravagance. Republicans also called for additional land grants to aid railroad construction in Iowa, requested legislation for river and harbor improvements, and pledged to administer the state government with strict economy. Finally, the party applauded Iowa's Republican delegation in Congress for opposing the Lecompton fraud.[25]

Before the meeting of the Democratic state convention, the party press issued a plea for harmony in the face of the intraparty warfare. The *Iowa State Journal* warned:

> The present is a crisis in the life of the Democratic party, and it behooves every member of the party, be he high or low, great or humble, to act calmly, honestly, mildly yet firmly, at

[24] *Journal of the Senate*, 7th General Assembly of Iowa, 1858, 119–20.
[25] Roy V. Sherman, "Political Party Platforms in Iowa," unpublished M.A. thesis, State University of Iowa, 1926, 158–62.

this time. There is no need for crimination or recrimination between Democrats in this state at this time.[26]

The paper also warned Democrats that only the Republicans would benefit from a split in the Democracy. The *Weekly State Reporter* of Iowa City advised the party to stop fuming about Negroes and "reassert its true dignity . . . upon the broad platform of Popular Rights."[27]

Democratic delegates assembled in Iowa City on June 24. They nominated Samuel Douglas and Theodore S. Parvin for secretary of state and auditor, respectively. Samuel L. Lorah was the party's choice for treasurer, and James M. Ellwood won convention approval for attorney general.

The state platform of the Democratic party betrayed the schism in the organization. After reaffirming the national Democratic platform of 1856, the party deplored the efforts of some to promote sectional strife and called upon all Americans to oppose these plots. In other planks the Democrats reiterated their support of nonintervention by the federal government in the local affairs of states and declared that all decisions of the Supreme Court merited respect and obedience. Concerning the administration of the state government, the Democrats accused the Republicans of wanton extravagance and corruption.[28] Conspicuously absent from the platform was any mention of the Lecompton issue. Nor did the party endorse the Buchanan administration. The platform was a generalized collection of vague statements, attesting to the rift in the organization.

Dissatisfied with the platform of the state party, a group of forty-six proadministration Democrats held a rump convention in Iowa City on June 24. These anti-Douglas Democrats elected Ver Planck Van Antwerp as their president and adopted a resolution which was highly laudatory of the Buchanan administra-

26 Des Moines *Session Journal*, March 8, 1858.
27 *Weekly Iowa State Reporter*, April 21, 1858.
28 Sherman, "Political Party Platforms in Iowa," 155–58.

tion. The division within the party apparently had become a wide gulf.[29]

The congressional conventions of both parties met to nominate candidates for the congressional races. In the First District the Republicans renominated Curtis, a reward for his successful campaign two years earlier and for his acceptable record in Congress. To oppose him the Democrats picked Henry H. Trimble, a Douglas Democrat. Trimble was a native of Indiana, an alumnus of Asbury University, and a veteran of the Mexican War. He had come to Iowa in 1849 and had served in the state senate in the Sixth General Assembly.[30]

In the Second Congressional District the Democrats nominated William E. Leffingwell, a Douglas sympathizer. An early settler in Clinton County, Leffingwell had served in the Iowa legislature from 1846 to 1852. During the next two years he was judge of the Eighth Judicial District. To run against him the Republicans tapped William Vandever, a native of Maryland. Vandever had come to Iowa in 1851 via Illinois and established a law practice in Dubuque. Since incumbent Congressman Davis had earlier announced that he would not seek reelection from his district, Grimes tried to persuade his ally, Kirkwood, to become a candidate. But the latter had set his sights on a loftier office. Leffingwell and Vandever agreed to engage in a series of debates throughout the district from August 5 to September 25.[31]

A major stumbling block to Leffingwell's chances of success was the schism within his party. Apparently the Jones faction had considered Leffingwell a "safe" choice. But during his tour

---

[29] Pelzer, "History of Political Parties in Iowa 1857–1860," 199.

[30] Robert Robinson to Laurel Summers, April 17, 1858, in the Summers Correspondence; Benjamin F. Gue, *History of Iowa*, IV, 267.

[31] Edward H. Stiles, *Recollections and Sketches of Notable Lawyers and Public Men of Early Iowa*, 939; *Biographical Directory of the American Congress 1774–1949*, 1948–49; *Weekly Iowa State Reporter*, July 28, August 4, and September 8, 1858; *Vinton Eagle*, August 14, 1858; James W. Grimes to Samuel J. Kirkwood, February 27, 1858, "Letters of James W. Grimes," 493.

of his district, the proadministration group began to have misgivings about him. Thomas Sargent, a Jones Democrat from Fort Dodge, informed the senator that Leffingwell's speeches were not at all satisfactory: "In that part of his speech having reference to the Lecompton Constitution . . . he exhibited a considerable degree of defiant feeling." A few days later Sargent again wrote Jones: "The proof is positive, that if we elect Judge Leffingwell to represent us in Congress, we may expect all his efforts and influence with Judge Douglas and coadjutors." Sargent believed that "the election of a professed & heretofore confessed Democrat, whom I know will not act in harmony with the policy of the Universal Democracy is really far more to be feared than an open and avowed Republican."[32]

On September 2, Jones and several others of his faction met with Leffingwell, who protested that "he had never differed with Mr. Buchanan on any save the Lecompton issue—that if elected he would go to Congress as the friend & supporter of Mr. Buchanan's administration." Relating the details of the conference to Laurel Summers, Jones wrote, "We then by formal resolution pledged our hearty support of the Judge & I sincerely hope he may be elected, tho I would not have voted for him but for his pledges as above."[33] In Fort Dodge the proadministration Democrats were pacified by Leffingwell's promises: "Otherwise we were determined not to support him."[34] Toward the end of the month, Augustus C. Dodge wrote Jones from his ambassador's post in Madrid and expressed "hope that no difference touching the vexed question of Kansas may have operated to prevent you & all of our friends from giving Leffingwell & Trimble a cordial support for Congress. I trust you will act upon the principle that

[32] Thomas Sargent to George W. Jones, August 28, 30, 1858, in the Jones Correspondence.

[33] George W. Jones to Laurel Summers, September 2, 1858, in the Summers Correspondence.

[34] W. W. Williams to George W. Jones, September 8, 1858, in the Jones Correspondence.

the meanest Democrat is better than the best Black Republican."[35]

Republicans, of course, sought to profit from both the Lecompton issue and the cleavage in the Democratic party. The *Hamilton Freeman* denounced the Buchanan administration for championing the Lecompton fraud. The editor of *Ward's Own* of Bloomfield insisted that the only issue before the voters of Iowa was the Lecompton question. The *Vinton Eagle* claimed that the Lecompton constitution demonstrated the "complete failure of Popular Sovereignty as a rule of territorial government." Other Republican papers hailed Douglas for his courageous opposition to the attempted swindle by the administration and published letters from Douglas Democrats criticizing the Lecompton treachery and the Buchanan administration.[36]

The Republicans again tried to promote the Dred Scott decision as a campaign issue, but oddly enough, the case once more failed to capture the imagination of Iowa voters. The *Vinton Eagle* was diligent in its denunciation of the Supreme Court verdict, and both Governors Grimes and Lowe took pains to condemn the decision in their official messages to the Iowa legislature. To popularize Lowe's anti–Dred Scott statements, the Republican-controlled assembly voted to publish seven thousand copies of his address, a move which prompted an immediate Democratic protest. Still, despite Republican efforts, Iowans did not become greatly excited about the case.[37]

About a week before the October 12 election the Iowa Democratic party published an *Address to the Voters of Iowa*, which

[35] A. C. Dodge to George W. Jones, September 30, 1858, *ibid.*

[36] *Hamilton Freeman* (Webster City, Iowa), April 15, 1858; *Ward's Own* (Bloomfield, Iowa), August 7, 1858; *Vinton Eagle*, March 26, 1858; Charles E. Payne, *Josiah Bushnell Grinnell*, 103; Boeck, "An Early Iowa Community," 394–95; David S. Sparks, "The Birth of the Republican Party in Iowa, 1848 to 1860," unpublished Ph.D. dissertation, University of Chicago, 1951, 167.

[37] *Vinton Eagle*, May 22, 1858; Shambaugh, *Messages and Proclamations*, II, 64, 132–33; *Journal of the House of Representatives*, 7th General Assembly of Iowa, 1858, 803–805.

summarized the party's grievances against the Republicans. The Democrats depicted the Republican party as the direct political heir of the outmoded Whig and Federalist organizations. They accused the Republicans of sustaining themselves solely through slavery agitation and of subverting the federal Constitution. They charged, moreover, that the Republicans were overpaying state officers and were depleting the state treasury, and they urged the election of their entire slate of candidates as the only means by which Iowans could save themselves from the evils of Republicanism.[38]

But when Iowans went to the polls, they gave the Republican party another vote of confidence. All the Republican aspirants for the state offices defeated their Democratic rivals by margins of 2,700 to 3,600 votes. Republicans also triumphed in both congressional races. In the First District, Curtis edged past Trimble by a count of 23,529 to 22,929, winning a mere 50.65 per cent of the total vote. Had not the Republicans added Des Moines, Louisa, and Washington counties to the First District, Curtis' margin over Trimble would have been a scant 81 votes of a total of more than 46,000 ballots. The three counties added 3,456 votes to Curtis' column, while Trimble received only 2,937 additional votes. The Republican maneuver to "equalize the districts" had proved efficacious.[39]

In the Second District, where William E. Leffingwell had to overcome opposition from the Jones faction, Vandever defeated his Democratic opponent by a vote of 25,503 to 22,784. Nevertheless, Leffingwell's percentage of the vote, 47.18 per cent, represented a gain of 5.20 percentage points over the Democratic record in the 1856 contest there.[40]

The October elections revealed that Iowans were very nearly equally divided in their political sentiments. The hard times ex-

[38] *Weekly Iowa State Reporter*, October 6, 1858.
[39] Election Records, 1848–1860.
[40] *Ibid.*

perienced by farmers, businessmen, merchants, railroad entrepreneurs, and investors, together with the revelations of the scandals in the state government, might well have cost the Republicans dearly. But the Lecompton constitution and the trickery which accompanied its "ratification" drove a deeper wedge into the already split Iowa Democratic party. Still, rapprochement between the contending factions was not impossible, as Jones's support of Leffingwell demonstrated. Democrats might yet discover a candidate who could unite all elements of their party in time to offer an effective challenge to the Republicans in the approaching gubernatorial contest.

The Democrats Counterattack

DESPITE THEIR string of victories in Iowa after the success of the original fusion ticket in 1854, the Republicans could not be certain of political success in 1859 or during the important presidential year 1860. To be sure, the party controlled the statewide patronage and therefore had a core of reliable workers in all the counties. Still, many problems confronted the organization. The only election-tested, popular vote getter was Grimes. Except for the state's congressmen, all other Republicans were largely untried. Widespread criticism existed among Iowans concerning high taxes, administrative scandals, and financial difficulties which, to the popular mind, were chargeable to the party in power. The emotional outbursts over events in Kansas were beginning to lose their effectiveness, as signs of public apathy became discernible. Religious and commercial elements opposed extremist arguments about slavery and its expansion. The nativist faction of the Republican party brought considerable embarrassment to its leadership. Prohibition, narrowly approved in 1855, caused increasing resentment. Indeed, antiprohibition forces had won recent concessions permitting retail sales of state-produced beer and wine.[1]

Moreover, all was not completely harmonious within Republican ranks. William Penn Clarke, the ardent Free-Soiler who had been unsuccessful in his candidacy for the Republican senatorial nomination, was at odds with several leading Republicans, including such stalwarts as Grimes and Kirkwood, Grimes's choice for the governorship in 1859. Grimes, in fact, cautioned Kirkwood that Clarke intended to "stir up all the strife that may be possible."[2]

Meanwhile, the break in the Democratic party did not appear to be beyond repair. Facing an uphill struggle in the approaching election, the Buchanan and Douglas wings of the party tried to terminate their quarrel. Henry Clay Dean, the dynamic minister-orator of the party, implored outgoing Senator Jones to make his peace with the Douglas faction for the good of the organization. Jones agreed "to support heartily . . . the nominees of our party whether my personal friends shall be of the number or not."[3] The *Anamosa Gazette*, a Buchanan organ, reprinted an editorial from the Davenport *Democrat* which urged Democratic harmony:

[1] Cyrenus Cole, *Iowa Through the Years*, 268; Frank I. Herriott, "The Germans in the Gubernatorial Campaign of Iowa in 1859," *Deutsch-Amerikanische Geschichtsblätter: Jahrbuch der Deutsch-Amerikanischen Historischen Gesellschaft von Illinois*, Vol. XIV (1914), 495–96; Edward Younger, "The Rise of John A. Kasson in Iowa Politics 1857–1859," *Iowa Journal of History*, Vol. L (1952), 304; Charles W. Emery, "The Iowa Germans in the Election of 1860," *Annals of Iowa*, 3rd ser., Vol. XXII (1940), 433–34.

[2] James W. Grimes to Samuel J. Kirkwood, April 28, 1859, in the Samuel J. Kirkwood Correspondence at the Iowa State Department of History and Archives in Des Moines; William Penn Clarke to Ralph P. Lowe, May 17, 1859, in the William Penn Clarke Letterbook at the State Historical Society of Iowa in Iowa City.

[3] Henry Clay Dean to George W. Jones, February 2, 1859, in the George W. Jones Correspondence at the Iowa State Department of History and Archives in Des Moines; copy of letter from Jones to Dean, February 12, 1859, *ibid*.

The coming fall election is one of the most important that ever took place since Iowa has been a State, and it is of the greatest importance to *all* Democrats that there should be a perfect harmony of feeling and a unity of action in all matters which pertain either to the nominations or to the convention. One thing is sure; if there is any factious feelings introduced into the State Convention, all our hopes of carrying *any* portion of the election in October will come to nought.[4]

Individual defections, nevertheless, continued to plague the Iowa Democrats. Of more than minor consequence was the departure from the party of Enoch W. Eastman and the Reverend Henry P. Scholte. Eastman, former state Democratic chairman, had been mentioned as a possible candidate in the fall elections. He left the party because of the slavery issue; specifically, he deplored the extension of slavery into the territories and the new nationwide agitation to acquire Cuba from Spain. Scholte, a leader of the Dutch community of Pella since its establishment in the 1840's, was believed to be able to deliver the vote of his fellow countrymen to whichever party he endorsed. He switched party allegiance largely because of his aversion to the Lecompton constitution. Delighted Republicans welcomed his affiliation by making him vice-president of their state convention, and Grimes optimistically reported:

> I just saw an intelligent man from Marion County. He says the Hollanders are nearly all going with Scholte and that we shall carry the county by as large a maj. as the democrats have usually done it, viz 200. As evidence that the democrats surrender the county, they are going in for a peoples ticket.[5]

Others who bolted the Democratic party were a number of news-

---

[4] *Anamosa* (Iowa) *Gazette*, April 22, 1859.

[5] James W. Grimes to Samuel J. Kirkwood, July 29, 1859, "Letters of James W. Grimes," *Annals of Iowa*, 3rd ser., Vol. XXII (1940), 556–57; Robert P. Swierenga, "The Ethnic Voter and the First Lincoln Election," *Civil War History*, Vol. XI (1965), 38–39; Frank I. Herriott, "Republican Presidential Preliminaries in Iowa 1859–1860," *Annals of Iowa*, 3rd ser., Vol. IX (1910), 253.

paper editors. "One by one," gloated a Republican editor, "the old veterans are jumping from the leaky old Democratic ship and seeking a safe voyage under the steamer of Republicanism."[6]

In March, 1859, however, an event in distant New England bolstered Democratic prospects in Iowa. The Republican-controlled legislature of Massachusetts approved an amendment to the state constitution which required all naturalized citizens to reside in the state for two years before they were eligible to vote. Undoubtedly the amendment was directed against the large numbers of Irish immigrants arriving in the Bay State.[7]

When the public learned about the Massachusetts bill, no group in Iowa denounced the measure more strongly than the Germans, who feared that the Iowa Republicans might someday follow Massachusetts' example. Republican leaders were well aware of German hostility to the Massachusetts amendment. Shortly after the publication of the amendment, the Republican State Central Committee, as if in anticipation of a German protest, adopted resolutions condemning the action as "an unjust and offensive discrimination between citizens on account of their birth," expressed the fear that the foundations upon which the Republican party had been formed might be undermined, and called upon the people of Massachusetts to reject the proposed amendment.[8]

The resolutions of the Republican State Central Committee did not wholly allay German suspicions about the state Republican party. Nicholas J. Rusch, a prominent German-born citizen of Davenport, a state senator, and a member of the Republican State Central Committee, reported to Kirkwood that many Germans were incensed at the Republican organization. Rusch em-

[6] Albia (Iowa) *Weekly Republican*, February 9 and March 16, 1859; Robert E. Lee, "Politics and Society in Sioux City, 1859," *Iowa Journal of History*, Vol. LIV (1956), 124–25.

[7] *Anamosa Gazette*, March 25, 1859; Iowa *Weekly Republican* (Iowa City), April 6, 1859; Albia *Weekly Republican*, June 1, 1859.

[8] Albia *Weekly Republican*, May 4, 1859.

phasized that Massachusetts had passed the amendment despite
a plank in the national Republican platform which specifically
condemned discrimination among Americans on account of place
of birth. "Of what use or weight is a national party platform,"
queried Rusch, "if the party in the several states do not feel
themselves bound by it, but think themselves justified to violate
the same whenever they choose?" For his own part, Rusch insisted, he still had confidence in the party, but many Germans
had lost theirs. Several German-language papers, he warned,
were concerned about the matter. Indeed, one German-language
journal published in Muscatine with a large circulation both in
the town and in neighboring counties, had already defected to
the Democrats as a result of the Massachusetts amendment.[9]

The Germans' anxiety was further underscored by a letter from
an influential group of Germans addressed to the Iowa congressional delegation, which demanded direct and immediate answers to three questions:

> Are you in favor of the naturalization laws as they now
> stand and particularly against all and every extension of the
> probation time?
> Do you regard it as a duty of the Republican party as the
> party of equal rights to oppose and war upon each and every
> discrimination that may be attempted to be made between
> native born and adopted citizens as to the right of suffrage?
> Do you condemn the late action of the Republicans in the
> Massachusetts Legislature for attempting to exclude the
> adopted citizens for two years from the ballot box as unjust and
> uncalled for?[10]

Senator Grimes was the first of Iowa's congressmen to reply
to the Germans. Writing from Burlington on April 30, 1859,
Grimes unhesitatingly responded in the affirmative to all the
questions. Concerning the third query, he added:

[9] Nicholas J. Rusch to Samuel J. Kirkwood, in the Kirkwood Correspondence.
[10] Albia *Weekly Republican*, May 18, 1859.

While I admit that the regulation sought to be adopted is purely of a local character, with which we of Iowa have nothing whatsoever directly to do, and whilst I would be one of the last men in the world to interfere in the local affairs of a sovereign state upon local matters, yet I claim the right to approve or condemn, as my judgment may indicate, such State or party action, when in my conviction it is based upon a false and dangerous principle. I believe the action of the Massachusetts legislature alluded to to be frought [sic] with evil and only evil continually to the whole country and not to Massachusetts alone.[11]

Not so concise and unequivocal was Senator Harlan's reply. In a lengthy letter he discussed the various facets of the controversy in detail and avoided outright commitment. He summed up by affirming that

I am compelled as a Republican to say in reply to your first interrogatory that I am not an advocate for any material change in the naturalization laws; to the second, I do not approve any discrimination whatever against the rights of naturalized citizens; to the third, I would not, if I were a citizen of Massachusetts, advocate the adoption of the proposed amendment to the constitution.[12]

Harlan's vacillation may be explained, in part at least, by the fact that he was in a delicate political position. Since he would be a candidate for reelection to the Senate in 1860, he did not want to antagonize those Republicans who were not especially friendly to the Germans, prohibition supporters and former Know-Nothings, for example. Furthermore, Harlan himself may not have been genuinely opposed to the Massachusetts amend-

[11] *Ibid.*
[12] Frank I. Herriott, "The Germans of Iowa and the 'Two-Year' Amendment of Massachusetts," *Deutsch-Amerikanische Geschichtsblätter: Jahrbuch der Deutsch-Amerikanischen Historischen Gesellschaft von Illinois,* Vol. XIII (1913), 244.

ment. Only three years earlier he had viewed the influx of foreigners into Iowa with deep concern.[13]

After delaying about a month, Congressman Curtis answered the Germans' queries. Curtis declared that he opposed an extension of the probation period, as well as the existing naturalization laws. He agreed that the Republican party should oppose all attempts to discriminate between native-born and naturalized citizens in order to perpetuate the "fundamental principles of the founders of our Republic who made their platform wide enough for all the world." Finally, he unconditionally condemned the action of the Massachusetts General Assembly.[14]

Meanwhile, W. W. Hamilton, who aspired to be Iowa's next lieutenant governor, had informed Kirkwood that the Massachusetts amendment had disturbed the Germans in his region of the state. Hamilton pointed out that Democratic criticism of the Republican action in the Bay State was making a deep impression upon the Germans. He continued:

> The Germans in Winneshiek, Allamakee, Clayton, Dubuque, etc. are just now like a hive of bees just swarmed—very threatening to outsiders. The Masstts. resolutions are very inopportune for us. And in fact we cannot endorse any such policy as they are based upon. . . . See the constant appeals to them on this point in the *Herald* and other Democratic papers. They look upon an attack upon their naturalization rights as a revival of Know-Nothingism; and they will bolt any ticket in a moment that squints at that. I commend this to your serious consideration. I have just left some influential Germans after a long talk; and am sure of the truth of what I say.[15]

Democrats assailed the Massachusetts amendment as an "in-

13 *Ibid.*, 239–40; James Harlan to William Penn Clarke, December 1, 1856, in the William Penn Clarke Correspondence at the Iowa State Department of History and Archives in Des Moines.

14 Albia *Weekly Republican*, May 25, 1859.

15 W. W. Hamilton to Samuel J. Kirkwood, April 29 and May 17, 1859, in the Kirkwood Correspondence.

sult" and a "disgrace" and as "treacherous" and sought to paint the Republican party with Know-Nothing tar, for similar amendments had received Republican sponsorship elsewhere in the East.[16] The latter, of course, worriedly labored to refute these statements. One Republican editor even blamed the Democrats for passage of the amendment. Although admitting that Republicans controlled the Massachusetts legislature, he insisted that "there was but a slim turnout at the election, yet we are satisfied that the majority was not all Republicans. The Democrats, thinking they could see an opportunity for making political capital, have heralded it from one part of the world to the other, but it falls upon their own heads, and their capital they find is all pure counterfeit." Another Republican paper accused the Democrats of placing restrictions upon naturalized Americans long before Massachusetts took similar action. Democrats hotly denied the accusation and insisted that, although South Carolina had enacted a discriminatory law back in 1784, the measure had long since been repealed.[17]

Republicans would have found it extremely difficult to explain or justify the Massachusetts law, had not a blunder by the national Democratic administration turned the tide of criticism from them. On May 17 Democratic Secretary of State Lewis Cass, wrote a letter to Felix Le Clerc, of Memphis, Tennessee. Cass told Le Clerc that "it is understood that the French government claims military service from all nationals of France who may be found within its jurisdiction. Your naturalization in this country will not exempt you from that claim if you should voluntarily repair thither."[18] Many persons had come to the United States to

[16] *Anamosa Gazette*, March 25, 1859; George H. Daniels, "The Immigrant Vote in the 1860 Election: The Case of Iowa," *Mid-America*, Vol. XLIV (1962), 156.

[17] Albia *Weekly Republican*, June 1, 1859; *Fayette County Public Review* (West Union, Iowa), August 11, 1859; *Iowa State Journal* (Des Moines), June 11, 1859.

[18] Dubuque *Express and Herald* quoted in *Iowa Weekly Republican*, June 22, 1859.

avoid military service in their homelands. The obvious implication to be drawn from Cass's letter was that the American government would not protect any naturalized citizen who voluntarily returned to his place of birth for a visit.

Perhaps alarmed by the storm of protest he had unleashed, Cass elaborated a month later in a published communication to a Mr. Hofer of Cincinnati. The secretary of state explained that, according to an agreement reached between the United States and Prussia, naturalized citizens who returned to their homelands were not

> liable to any duties or penalties, except such as were existing at the period of their emigration. If at that time they were in the army or actually called into it, such emigration and naturalization do not exempt them from the legal penalty which they incurred by their desertion, but this penalty may be enforced against them whenever they voluntarily place themselves within the local jurisdiction of their native country.[19]

Legal explications, however, did not satisfy irate Iowans. Cass's first letter was condemned by all sides—by native and naturalized citizens, by Republicans and Democrats. The Dubuque *Express and Herald*, an antiadministration Democratic paper, denounced the letter as "anti-national, anti-American, and entirely anti-Democratic." The *Weekly Times* of Dubuque, a Republican paper, declared that "no political party, whatever might have been its professions, ever made so odious a distinction between native and foreign-born citizens as made in Cass' communication."[20] The *Daily Hawk-Eye* of Burlington, another Republican organ, charged that Cass was a tool of the South and had written his letter at the behest of that section:

> It is the interest of the South to discourage immigration from Europe, but to open the African slave trade. The Democratic

19 *Iowa State Journal*, July 2, 1859.
20 Quoted in *Iowa Weekly Republican*, June 22, 1859.

party is the slave of the South and proud to do its bidding; hence, General Cass, speaking for the government, has informed naturalized citizens, in effect, that when they voluntarily sail from our shores, they must take care of themselves.[21]

Republican condemnation of both Cass letters was politically more effective than Democratic criticism of the Massachusetts amendment. Cass's letters embodied an official pronouncement of national policy, while the Massachusetts amendment was merely the act of a single state and not binding upon the other states. Although Republicans faced a difficult campaign in the coming election in Iowa, their prospects for success began to brighten considerably, thanks to Lewis Cass.

In the midst of the excitement generated by the Massachusetts amendment and the Cass letters, the contending parties made plans for their state conventions. Announcements of candidates came thick and fast. Among the Democrats the man who received the earliest consideration and the strongest support for the gubernatorial office was Augustus C. Dodge. A former United States senator, Dodge was ending four years of service as American ambassador to Spain. A tested vote getter and sympathetic to the Douglasites, he was popular with both wings of the Iowa Democratic party, his service in Spain having removed him from the intramural squabbles of his party. As early as January 15, 1859, his name was mentioned for the gubernatorial nomination. Henry Clay Dean told Senator Jones that if Dodge "will be a candidate he will have my hearty support for that or any other office." Dean believed that "Gen. Dodge will unite all the elements of the party for success." But Dodge refused, at least so early in the year, to declare himself a candidate for governor. He confided to Henn, the former Democratic congressman from Iowa's First Congressional District, that he would not seek the position because of "want of time and on account of the ill health of Mrs.

---

[21] Quoted in Herriott, "The Germans of Iowa and the 'Two-Year' Amendment of Massachusetts," 272.

Dodge." Nor would Senator Jones, whose term of office expired in March, consent to be a candidate. Despite the urging of many friends, Jones informed Dean that he would not permit his name to be offered in nomination for any state office.[22]

With Dodge ostensibly out of the running and Jones definitely eliminated, several prominent Democratic stalwarts became gubernatorial possibilities. These included such men as Henn, Van Antwerp, Leffingwell, Gillaspie, Maturin L. Fisher, Gilbert C. R. Mitchell, and Dean. The last-named drew Republican fire for mingling religion and politics.[23]

Competition among Democrats for the nomination for lieutenant governor was also sharp. Most prominently mentioned for the post were Lysander W. Babbitt, James Baker, John F. Duncombe, James D. Test, D. H. Solomon, J. M. Ellwood, and H. Dunlavy.[24]

The preconvention rivalry for the three vacancies on the state supreme court was also keen. The Fort Madison *Plain Dealer*, however, counseled the party to select its judicial candidates with extreme care, for "no man should be nominated for Supreme Judge unless he is a good lawyer in the broadest sense of the term." Moreover, added the *Plain Dealer*, "mere party consideration should be laid aside and the very best jurists in the party nominated." Among the aspirants for the supreme court were Joseph C. Knapp, Charles M. Mason, Thomas S. Wilson, Jonathan C. Hall, C. C. Cole, Curtis Bates, P. M. Casady, and H. B. Hendershott.[25]

[22] Henry Clay Dean to George W. Jones, January 15 and February 2, 1859, in the Jones Correspondence; Bernhart Henn to Laurel Summers, May 5, 1859, in the Laurel Summers Correspondence at the Iowa State Department of History and Archives in Des Moines; copy of letter from George W. Jones to Henry Clay Dean, February 12, 1859, in the Jones Correspondence.

[23] Louis Pelzer, *Augustus Caesar Dodge*, 236; *The Anamosa Gazette*, June 17, 1859.

[24] *Iowa State Journal*, June 18, 1859.

[25] Quoted in *Anamosa Gazette*, April 29, 1859; *Iowa Weekly Republican*, April 27, 1859.

Nor did the Republicans experience a shortage of office seekers. Although Republican leaders knew that incumbent Governor Lowe wanted a second term, they believed that he lacked the colorful, dynamic personality which would be necessary for success against Dodge, whom most persons expected would be the Democratic standard bearer, despite his disavowal. In April, W. W. Hamilton informed Kirkwood of the growing opposition among Republican leaders to a second term for Lowe. "He is said to be a very good man," wrote Hamilton, "but a man may be too good and too soft." John Bittman, a prominent German-born editor from Dubuque, confirmed Hamilton's opinion of Lowe. Bittman told Kirkwood that "Lowe has proven rather weak and lame without any energy whatever, aside of his deficiency as a leader and organizer."[26]

More significant than any ostensible flaw in his character or weakness in his leadership ability was Lowe's open and avowed support of state aid for railroad construction, which had made him a liability to his party. Such aid was not only unconstitutional but also exceedingly unpopular with Iowans. Writing to Kirkwood, who had become the principal aspirant for the gubernatorial office, Grimes reported, "There is no one talked of at all, save you & Lowe & our friends are pretty much all for you, so far as I can learn." Late in April, Grimes assured Kirkwood, "I do not think that Lowe can be nominated." Three weeks before the Republican state convention Grimes emphatically declared, "No man with a thimble full of brains if he desired the success of our party would seek to have our convention endorse in any way, directly or indirectly," a proposal for state aid to railroads. Democrats, he warned, "are all for Lowe, of course. They hope his nomination & then they will publish some of his foolish letters in favor of state aid written by him last autumn. In this way they

[26] Cyrenus Cole, A History of the People of Iowa, 320–21; W. W. Hamilton to Samuel J. Kirkwood, April 12, 1859, in the Kirkwood Correspondence; John Bittman to Samuel J. Kirkwood, May 22, 1859, ibid.

hope to get the question drawn into the canvass, by which they can lose nothing & may gain." But, he continued, "outside of Lee, Polk & DuBuque counties I do not know any body in favor of his nomination in our party."[27] Lowe's replacement was essential for the good of the Republican cause, but it had to be accomplished without forcing a split in the organization. John A. Kasson, chairman of the Republican State Central Committee, suggested that Lowe might be willing to accept a nomination to the supreme court as compensation for losing the governorship.[28]

Urged by his chief supporter, Grimes, Kirkwood wrote to Republican leaders throughout the state announcing his candidacy for governor and asking for their endorsement. Most replies were favorable. Among his backers, in addition to the powerful Grimes, were W. W. Hamilton, Kasson, John Edwards, and Rusch. If Lowe could be induced to withdraw voluntarily from the race, Kirkwood would have a clear road to his goal.[29]

When Faville declined to be a candidate for lieutenant governor again, Edwards and Hamilton offered themselves for the post. Party chairman Kasson indicated that he would gladly accept either aspirant for the office. But with the German voters thoroughly aroused by the Massachusetts amendment, a movement grew to place a German-born citizen on the Republican ticket, preferably in the number-two slot. The *Davenport Gazette* urged Rusch's nomination to the post of lieutenant governor. Rusch, however, questioned whether he should accept the nomination, since his "broken English and little experience are not

27 Leonard F. Ralston, "Governor Ralph P. Lowe and State Aid to Railroads: Iowa Politics in 1859," *Iowa Journal of History*, Vol. LVIII (1960), 207–18; James W. Grimes to Samuel J. Kirkwood, April 24 and May 29, 1859, "Letters of James W. Grimes," 496–97, 499–500, 563–64.

28 John A. Kasson to Samuel J. Kirkwood, May 1, 1859, in the Kirkwood Correspondence.

29 James W. Grimes to Samuel J. Kirkwood, April 28, 1859, "Letters of James W. Grimes," 497–98; W. W. Hamilton to Samuel J. Kirkwood, April 13, 1859, in the Kirkwood Correspondence; Alvin Saunders to Samuel J. Kirkwood, April 27, 1859, *ibid.*; John Edwards to Samuel J. Kirkwood, May 1, 1859, *ibid.*; Des Moines *Citizen* quoted in Albia *Weekly Republican*, April 27, 1859.

proper qualifications for an office of that nature." Other Republicans mentioned as prospects for the office included Josiah B. Grinnell, Charles Pomeroy, and Enoch Eastman.[30]

Many Republicans sought a seat on the state supreme court after Chief Justice George G. Wright declined another term. Cited as possibilities for the high court were William Penn Clarke, Kasson, C. C. Nourse, L. D. Stockton, William Smyth, and Samuel Miller.[31]

The Republican state convention opened its sessions on June 22, 1859, one day before the scheduled meeting of the Democrats. After settling the routine business of organization, the convention began the task of selecting the party's nominees amid unsolicited advice from friendly journals to choose men who possessed the highest principles of liberty. Governor Lowe sent word to the delegates of his intention to decline another nomination to the position he held; this news must have relieved the pro-Kirkwood delegates. Immediately, Kirkwood was nominated by acclamation for governor. He had come a long way since his arrival in Iowa. Born in Maryland, he moved to Ohio, where he taught school and later studied law. After moving to Iowa City in 1853, he worked successfully as a farmer, miller, and merchant. A former Democrat, he had taken part in the formation of the Iowa Republican party in 1856. In that year, too, he had been elected to the state senate.[32]

The selection of the remaining nominees on the Republican ticket proceeded without difficulty. On the first formal ballot for lieutenant governor Rusch received 225 votes, defeating Ed-

---

[30] Albia *Weekly Republican*, May 18, 1859; *Iowa Weekly Republican*, May 4, 1859; *Iowa State Journal*, June 18, 1859; *Anamosa* (Iowa) *Eureka*, June 17, 1859; W. W. Hamilton to Samuel J. Kirkwood, April 13, 1859, in the Kirkwood Correspondence; John A. Kasson to Samuel J. Kirkwood, May 1, 1859, *ibid.*; Nicholas J. Rusch to Samuel J. Kirkwood, April 20, 1859, *ibid.*

[31] Albia *Weekly Republican*, May 18 and 25, 1859.

[32] *Iowa Weekly Republican*, June 20, 1859; Cole, *A History of the People of Iowa*, 321–22.

wards and Hamilton. For the judicial posts the convention picked Lowe, Caleb Baldwin, and L. D. Stockton.[33]

The Republican state platform reaffirmed the principles of the national party platform of 1856 and assailed the Democratic administration for extravagance. Other planks condemned the Democrats for refusing to prohibit slavery in the territories, asked for a liberal naturalization law, opposed the revival of the African slave trade, and recommended the enactment of homestead legislation. In addition, the Republicans demanded protection for American citizens at home and abroad, regardless of place of birth or duration of residence in the United States. Concerning other local matters, the party advocated economy in state government and reform in county administration.[34]

The Republican press generally endorsed the party platform and nominees. The Council Bluffs *Nonpareil* praised the platform as a "broad and manly exposition of the cardinal points in the Republican faith." The *Davenport Gazette* expressed pleasure with Rusch's nomination because he was "one of the most talented and zealous Republicans in the State." The *Iowa Weekly Republican* of Iowa City described Rusch as being "an elegant and grammatical public speaker" despite his inability "to pronounce the *th*."[35]

But Rusch's nomination was unsatisfactory to some Republicans. The *Weekly Visitor*, the Republican organ in Indianola, ridiculed Rusch's speech and commented that it was "strange that such a man as John Edwards should be rejected by an intelligent convention and Rusch taken in his place." Hamilton, unhappy at his lack of success at the convention, complained to Charles Aldrich, editor of the *Hamilton Freeman* of Webster City, that the Republicans had erred in selecting Rusch and in

[33] *Iowa Weekly Republican*, June 29, 1859; Albia *Weekly Republican*, June 29, 1859.
[34] *Anamosa Eureka*, July 1, 1859.
[35] Quoted in Albia *Weekly Republican*, July 14 and 21 and September 22, 1859; *Iowa Weekly Republican*, September 21, 1859.

ignoring "the very existence of the northern half of the state. . . . It remains to be seen whether it is good policy not only thus to ignore us, but to place a Dutchman who cannot speak our language . . . to preside over the Senate."[36] Instead of adding strength to the Republican ticket, Rusch's nomination might well have driven a wedge into the party and also could have proved costly at the ballot box.

James A. Williamson, Democratic state chairman, had originally scheduled his party's convention to meet in Des Moines on June 1, three weeks before the Republican convention. Other Democrats, however, requested a postponement and persuaded Williamson to reschedule the convention for June 23. One Republican journal immediately accused the Democrats of deliberately delaying their meeting until the results of the Republican meeting were known.[37]

The Democratic gubernatorial nominee surprised few Iowans. Dodge changed his mind about running for office and secured the nomination for governor by acclamation. Lysander W. Babbitt, editor of the Council Bluffs *Bugle,* won a first-ballot victory to become Dodge's running mate. For the judicial vacancies on Iowa's high court the convention selected Thomas S. Wilson, Charles M. Mason, and C. C. Cole.[38]

The Democratic platform was a lengthy document divided into national and state sections. On the national level the party reaffirmed the Cincinnati platform and the doctrine of nonintervention in the internal affairs of states. Insisting that the territories were entitled to self-government, the platform reiterated the principle of popular sovereignty. Other planks recommended low, equitably administered tariffs; affirmed that both native and

[36] Cole, *A History of the People of Iowa,* 323–24; Herriott, "The Germans in the Gubernatorial Campaign of Iowa in 1859," 457; W. W. Hamilton to Charles Aldrich, June 29, 1859, in the Kirkwood Correspondence.

[37] *Iowa State Journal,* March 19, April 9, 1859; *Iowa Weekly Republican,* February 23 and April 13, 1859; *The Anamosa Gazette,* March 11, 1859.

[38] Gue, *History of Iowa,* IV, 9; *Anamosa Gazette,* July 1, 1859.

naturalized citizens possessed the same rights and deserved the same protection from the federal government regardless of place of residence; favored the acquisition of Cuba; requested passage of a homestead law; and disavowed responsibility for decisions of the United States Supreme Court. Concerning state matters, the Democrats called for the termination of the increases in state taxation and expenditures, opposed the immigration of free Negroes into Iowa, and assailed the end of segregation in the public schools of the state, going on to demand an overhaul of the entire structure of the public-school system. Other planks condemned the Maine liquor law and the Massachusetts franchise amendment.[39]

Conspicuously absent from the Democratic platform was any statement of support of the Buchanan administration, attesting to the strength of the Douglasites in the convention. The *Davenport News* later explained that an endorsement of Buchanan *"might distract the party."* Another Democrat, however, regretted that "the convention did not endorse the Administration. I have never seen a timid course of conduct win in politics." The *Chicago Times* nonetheless confidently predicted a Democratic victory in Iowa.[40]

Differences between the platforms of the contending parties were many. The Republican document neglected to mention prohibition, tariffs, and the school system, while the Democratic party was silent on the question of county government. On the issue of slavery the parties were, of course, poles apart. The Republicans seemed reluctant to mention certain state topics that would arouse controversy, but the Democrats did not hesitate to raise them. Their criticism of the prohibition act, for example, appealed to antitemperance groups in the state, while their con-

[39] Herbert S. Fairall, *Manual of Iowa Politics,* 31–36.
[40] Quoted in Albia *Weekly Republican,* May 4, 1859; James A. Buchanan to Laurel Summers, June 28, 1859, in the Summers Correspondence; quoted in *Anamosa Gazette,* July 15, 1859.

demnation of integration in the public schools was welcomed by the Iowans with anti-Negro prejudices.

Vituperation characterized the editorials of the party presses as they assailed the platform and the candidates of their rivals. *Life in the West* of Sigourney, Iowa, considered the Democratic platform of poor quality, commenting that the "Iowa Democracy are hard up for political capital." The Burlington *Hawk-Eye* accused the Democrats of stealing the Republican platform. The Iowa City *Republican* ridiculed the Democratic standard-bearer: "The politics of our opponents are indeed very *dodgy* just at present and seem to require a *Dodge* for a candidate." Babbitt had to defend himself against charges of Mormonism. And the Keokuk *Gate City* accused him of misappropriating fifteen thousand dollars while serving as register of the Land Office at Council Bluffs.[41]

Nor was the Democratic press slow in hurling derogatory epithets at the Republicans. The *Plain Dealer* of Fort Madison labeled Kirkwood a "dog fennel, polk weed, and stramonia politician." The Council Bluffs *Bugle* questioned Kirkwood's fitness for the gubernatorial office. The *Express and Herald* of Dubuque derided Rusch's nomination as but "a bait thrown out to catch the German vote." Furthermore, declared that paper, the Republicans had no intention of supporting Rusch's candidacy, for "that which was intolerant Iowa Know-Nothingism four short years ago is now known by the more specious title of Republicanism."[42]

When the Democratic Bloomfield *Clarion* christened the Republican slate the "Plow Handle Ticket," it set the tenor of the Republican campaign approach. Several Republican papers immediately published the names of the Republican candidates under a cut of a plow, while others began to contrast the simple,

[41] *Iowa Weekly Republican*, April 13, July 20, and August 3, 1859; Albia *Weekly Republican*, July 28 and August 4, 1859; *Iowa State Journal*, July 30, 1859.

[42] Quoted in *Anamosa Gazette*, August 26, 1859.

homespun appearance of Kirkwood with the well-groomed, dignified, seemingly haughty demeanor of Dodge.[43]

The state central committees of both parties mapped extensive speaking tours for their principal candidates. Kirkwood and Rusch launched the Republican campaign at an informal ratification meeting in Davenport on July 8. Two weeks later Kirkwood inaugurated his formal speaking tour of Iowa at Muscatine. He intended to remain on the stump until October 8, traversing the length and breadth of the state. Aware that Rusch might be the weak man on their ticket, Republican leaders advised Kirkwood to praise him whenever possible. Kasson urged Kirkwood "to allude to Rusch's fine education, interest in agriculture, and earnest support of a law to secure the purity of the ballot box," and Grimes agreed that Kirkwood should put "in a good word for Rusch" wherever he spoke, for "he must not be allowed to drop behind his ticket." Moreover, Republican leaders determined to keep Rusch out of the southern tier of counties adjacent to the Missouri border, the scene of strong Know-Nothing sentiment three years earlier, lest he injure his ticket. "Should he mingle with the people south of the Des Moines [River]," warned one party member, "he will do our whole ticket an essential injury." Grimes informed Kirkwood: "Kasson has written me that we shall be apt to lose votes in Davis, Appanoose, Monroe, Lucas, Clark, Decatur & Wayne on account of the nomination of Rusch for Lieut. Gov. . . . I do not doubt that in the counties named Rusch will run five to seven hundred votes behind his ticket," but, Grimes continued, "he can very well afford to lose them, considering what we gain elsewhere through his name." Moreover, with Rusch on the Republican ballot, Grimes was confident that much of the Democrats' political thunder about nativism and the Massachusetts' amendment had been silenced.[44]

[43] Pelzer, *Augustus Caesar Dodge*, 242; *Davenport Gazette* quoted in Albia *Weekly Republican*, August 18 and 25, 1859.

[44] *Iowa Weekly Republican*, July 13 and 27, 1859; Albia *Weekly Republican*, July 28, 1859; John A. Kasson to Samuel J. Kirkwood, July 18, 1859, in the

In addition to Kirkwood and Rusch, other men spoke in be-half of the Republican slate. Grenville M. Dodge, Frank W. Palmer, and William B. Allison, all destined to be leading Re-publican figures after the Civil War, won their political spurs in the 1859 election. Senator Harlan, well aware of the impor-tance of the campaign for his own ambitions, also toured Iowa in support of the Republican candidates, as did W. W. Hamilton and Congressman William Vandever. And Abraham Lincoln spoke at Council Bluffs in Kirkwood's behalf.[45]

The Iowa Democrats also decided to make a thorough can-vass of the state, but the Republicans gained an early advantage, owing to Dodge's failure to return to Iowa until July 9. The Dem-ocratic State Central Committee prepared an exhaustive speak-ing schedule for Dodge and arranged for other men to stump the state for the party. Ben M. Samuels, D. H. Solomon, D. O. Finch, C. C. Cole, and Henry Clay Dean, among others, worked long and hard for their ticket.[46]

Democrats also tried to persuade national party personalities to tour Iowa in behalf of the state ticket. A group of Democrats journeyed to Chicago in September to invite Senator Douglas to speak in several cities throughout the state. They were unsuc-cessful in their mission, however.[47]

Since both parties had planned extensive itineraries for their principal candidates, the party chairmen concluded an arrange-ment whereby Dodge and Kirkwood would engage one another

Kirkwood Correspondence; William M. Stone to Samuel J. Kirkwood, June 27, 1859, *ibid.*; James W. Grimes to Samuel J. Kirkwood, July 14 and 29, 1859, *ibid.*; James W. Grimes to Samuel J. Kirkwood, June 25, 1859, "Letters of James W. Grimes," 500–501.

[45] Edward Younger, *John A. Kasson: Politics and Diplomacy from Lincoln to McKinley*, 90; *Iowa Weekly Republican*, July 27, 1859; William Vandever to Charles Aldrich, October 24, 1859, in the Kirkwood Correspondence; Johnson Brigham, *James Harlan*, 130.

[46] Dan E. Clark, *Samuel Jordan Kirkwood*, 130; *Iowa Weekly Republican*, August 17, 1859; *Iowa State Journal*, August 13 and September 3, 1859.

[47] Robert Robinson to Laurel Summers, September 22, 1859, in the Summers Correspondence.

in a series of debates. Kasson had issued the Republican challenge to P. M. Casady, the new Democratic chairman, as early as June 24, but Dodge's absence from Iowa delayed definite Democratic acceptance. One month later, however, Casady notified Kasson that Dodge would inaugurate the joint tour with Kirkwood at Oskaloosa on July 29. The debates, which continued until September 17, aroused keen interest throughout the state and were generally well attended.[48] Throughout the campaign Kasson and Grimes frequently offered advice to the Republican standard-bearer with respect to the various topics to be discussed, points emphasized, and items ignored or played down. "Be sure," Grimes wrote, "to always get Dodge mad. Show him to be a fool, as he is." Early in August Grimes suggested that Kirkwood should keep Dodge "on the defensive, & see that he is well 'stirred up' all the time . . . and lead him to abuse Harlan & myself just as much as possible. The more he flounders about in his abuse of others the better." Grimes held Dodge in low esteem. "The real truth is," the former told his friend Cyrus C. Carpenter, "between us, he is a great vain pompous blockhead."[49]

Popular features of the Democratic campaign were barbecues, which became the occasions for campaign oratory as well as gala festivities. Several barbecues were held in September to climax the Democratic campaign. The barbecue at Des Moines on September 23 was a particularly grand affair, featuring beef, pork, mutton, wheat, corn bread, and "chicken fixins." One participant wrote that he "had a most glorious time. . . . General Dodge was here and made one of his finest effort[s]. There was [sic] more than four thousand people present. We had a procession more than one mile long. I have never seen the like in Iowa."[50]

[48] *Iowa Weekly Republican*, August 24 and September 14, 1859; Pelzer, *Augustus Caesar Dodge*, 240–41.

[49] James Grimes to Samuel J. Kirkwood, August 2 and 5, 1859, "Letters of James W. Grimes," 557–58; James Grimes to Cyrus C. Carpenter, July 15, 1859, *ibid.*, 503–504.

[50] *Iowa State Journal*, September 3, 1859; Louis Pelzer, "History of Political

Judging from the party platforms, editorials, and reports of the debates, the main issues of the campaign centered upon nativism, state expenditures and taxation, Cuba, and slavery, as well as personalities. In the main, the Democrats sought to confine the campaign to issues of state interest, while the Republicans preferred to concentrate on topics of national importance. The homestead issue did not stimulate much discussion in the press. Perhaps Dodge's favorable record on homesteads while in the Senate tended to minimize Republican agitation on that score. Iowa's German-born population was vitally interested in the homestead question, as were native-born Hawkeyes. In this connection, President Buchanan's efforts to acquire Cuba from Spain had disturbed some Iowans. Republicans endeavored to demonstrate that, while the Democrats were quite willing to spend thirty million dollars to purchase another area of slavery, they continually refused to distribute land from the vast public domain free of cost to the poor farmers of the West. Dodge, who had supported attempts to acquire Cuba, came in for his share of criticism on this issue.[51]

From time to time the county-judge system provoked discussion in the Iowa press. The Iowa Code of 1851 had abolished the old system of county commissioners and substituted the newly created office of county judge. This had the effect of lodging legislative, executive, and judicial functions in the hands of one individual. Iowans from New England and New York disliked the county-judge system by tradition and also, perhaps, because it was a Southern institution. Since the Democrats had been largely responsible for legislating the change in the system, the

Parties in Iowa 1857–1860," *Iowa Journal of History and Politics*, Vol. VII (1909), 209; Isaac W. Griffith to Laurel Summers, September 29, 1859, in the Summers Correspondence.

[51] Albia *Weekly Republican*, August 11, 1859; *Iowa Weekly Republican*, July 6, August 10, and September 7, 1859; *Anamosa Gazette*, September 9, 1859; *Iowa State Journal*, July 23, 1859; Herriott, "The Germans of Iowa and the 'Two-Year' Amendment of Massachusetts," 257–58; *Daily Hawk-Eye* (Burlington, Iowa) quoted in *Hamilton Freeman* (Webster City, Iowa), August 27, 1859.

Republicans sought to capitalize on its increasing unpopularity. The *Nonpareil* of Council Bluffs reported that the county-judge system was a failure in Polk and Pottawattamie counties. Because it established a petty despotism, the paper maintained, the office of county judge should be abolished. The Des Moines *Session Citizen* agreed. "We are led to infer that the whole system is vitally objectionable," declared an editorial. "The great evil consists in the fact that one man is vested with absolute power. Each county is a petty kingdom, of which the judge is sole ruler." Grimes told Kirkwood that "we must abolish our present county system and give the *people* a chance to govern themselves a little more than they do under the county judge system."[52]

Not all criticism of the system emanated from Republican sources, however. Democrats, too, urged modification or elimination of the county-judge system. A Democratic convention of the Thirty-sixth Representative District, embracing Harrison, Guthrie, Audubon, and Shelby counties in west-central Iowa, adopted a resolution calling for "the repeal of the law creating the office of County Judge," and requesting "a thorough reorganization of the system of managing county affairs."[53]

Republicans and Democrats also exchanged accusations concerning the expense of state administration. The *Iowa State Journal*, a Democratic paper in Des Moines, wanted to know what had happened to about $20,000 from a fund created to pay salaries to school commissioners. Other Democratic organs criticized the insane asylum, the blind asylum, the agricultural college, and the high salaries of public officials as needless extravagances. In addition, Democrats accused Republicans of exceeding the constitutional debt limit of $250,000 by at least $122,000.

52 *Hamilton Freeman*, March 11, 1859; Frank I. Herriott, "Whence Came the Pioneers of Iowa?" *Annals of Iowa*, 3rd ser., Vol. VII (1906), 462; quoted in *Fremont Herald* (Sidney, Iowa), April 23, 1859; James W. Grimes to Samuel J. Kirkwood, October 25, 1859, in William Salter (ed.), "Old Letters," *Annals of Iowa*, 3d ser., Vol. VIII (1908), 514.

53 *Iowa State Journal*, August 27, 1859.

Republicans countered by charging that various Democratic officials had enriched themselves with public funds. J. W. Cattell, Republican state auditor, published a statement which purported to demonstrate that the Democratic figures of Republican expenditures were incorrect and misleading. Instead of being in debt, the state, according to Cattell, actually had a surplus of $15,000.[54]

Five days before the election the *Fayette County Public Review* of West Union, cognizant of the vituperative bitterness engendered by the long and strenuous campaign, counseled Iowa voters to ignore the mudslinging and weigh carefully the merits of the issues involved before casting their ballots.[55]

On October 11 about 80 per cent of Iowa's eligible voters went to the polls. The Republicans scored close but sufficient triumphs in all the important contests. In the battle for the state legislature the Republicans won control of the house by sixteen votes and of the senate by eight votes. A joint ballot would give the victorious Republicans a decisive margin of 24 votes, thus assuring the election of another Republican United States senator from Iowa. The three Republican candidates for Iowa's supreme court defeated their Democratic opponents by margins of 2,100 votes or more.[56]

In the major contests Kirkwood and Rusch edged Dodge and Babbitt by votes of 56,502 and 55,789 to 53,332 and 52,722, respectively. Kirkwood obtained 51.44 per cent of the total vote. All told, Kirkwood carried 58 counties, while Dodge took only 34. Three counties—Calhoun, Carroll, and Monona—produced ties.

As it had done throughout the 1850's, the Democratic party showed well in a cluster of counties about Dubuque in east-

[54] *Ibid.*, May 10, August 27, and September 14, 1859; *Anamosa Gazette*, August 26, 1859; Pelzer, *Augustus Caesar Dodge*, 242–43; Albia *Weekly Republican*, February 9, 1859; *Iowa Weekly Republican*, September 14, 1859.

[55] October 6, 1859.

[56] *Iowa Weekly Republican*, November 2, 1859; Election Records, 1848–1860.

central Iowa—Dubuque, Delaware, and Jackson. Along the southern tier of counties and in west-central Iowa the Democrats also maintained their traditional strength.

The factors which produced the Republican victory in 1859 are somewhat obscure. The antislavery, anti-Cuba arguments of the Republicans no doubt appealed to Iowans in the eastern counties, where abolitionism and Free-Soilism had long been centered. Sentiment against the county-judge system was confined chiefly to western Iowa, but there both parties supported the elimination or modification of the system. The Democratic campaign against the end of segregation in the public schools may account for the party's strength in northeastern and west-central Iowa, where anti-Negro feeling may well have been stronger than antislavery emotions. In addition, the homestead question was neutralized as a partisan issue. The importance of such other issues as state expenditures, internal improvements, and nativism appears to have been minimal in the Republican victory.

The value to the Republicans of Nicholas Rusch as candidate for lieutenant governor is difficult to determine. Along the Mississippi and in the extreme western portion of the state Rusch ran ahead of Kirkwood. In western Iowa, Rusch led his party in Adair, Cass, Crawford, Harrison, Mills, Page, Plymouth, Taylor, and Woodbury counties, but there the number of Germans was very small. Rusch's good showing in the western part of the state may have stemmed in part from hostility to Babbitt, who hailed from Council Bluffs. Possibly the voters believed Republican accusations that Babbitt had been dishonest during his term as register of the Land Office in Council Bluffs.

In eastern Iowa, which contained large groups of Germans, Rusch led his ticket in Clayton, Dubuque, Jackson, and Clinton counties but fell behind Kirkwood in Scott, Muscatine, Lee, and Des Moines counties. In all, Rusch ran ahead of Kirkwood in twenty counties, tied him in twenty-two others, and trailed him in the remaining fifty-three counties. Thus the election statistics seem to show that Rusch did not appreciably aid his party. More probably he injured the Republican cause somewhat, for his nomination undoubtedly displeased nativists in his party, as well as several disappointed office seekers. Indeed, in Davis, Lee, Johnson, Muscatine, and Scott counties, where the Know-Nothings had obtained more than 2,300 of their 9,600 votes in 1856, Rusch did very poorly—and Scott County, it should be noted, was Rusch's home county. In other counties which had manifested Know-Nothing sympathy in 1856, such as Appanoose, Henry, Linn, Van Buren, and Washington, Rusch also lagged behind his ticket.

It is doubtful, therefore, that the German vote was a significant factor in the Republican triumph. Kirkwood carried Clayton, Clinton, Iowa, Johnson, Muscatine, and Scott counties, which contained sizable German settlements. Nevertheless, he lost Des Moines, Dubuque, Jackson, and Lee counties to Dodge. Large numbers of Germans also lived in those counties.

Moreover, Democratic fears about the possible ill effect of Scholte's defection proved unfounded. The Hollanders gave more than 71 per cent of their vote to the Democrats. Prohibition and nativism, both strongly identified with the Republicans, held the allegiance of the Dutch to their traditional voting patterns. One may infer that these factors were no less disturbing to Iowa's German-born residents.[57]

The Republican press was elated at the success of its party. The *Iowa Weekly Republican* observed that the Iowa congressional delegation was solidly Republican and boasted that "no western state presents so clean a record of Republicanism." The *Oskaloosa Herald* sarcastically suggested that Dodge, now without employment, be appointed a commissioner "endowed with special powers to personally run down, capture, try, and return into slavery every wandering African found on the soil of Iowa."

[57] Swierenga, "The Ethnic Voter and the First Lincoln Election," 40–41.

Because Dodge had announced that he would obey the Fugitive Slave Law and had declared in a campaign speech that slavery was a Christianizing institution, the editor of the *Herald* believed that "Gen. Dodge would be just the man to run down these poor sinners who are so depraved that they will not consent to go to heaven from the plantations of Missouri."[58]

The Republican victory in Iowa, although not overwhelming, was substantial. Kirkwood had defeated the Democratic party's ablest vote getter, Dodge, who had infused new life into the party by uniting the warring Buchanan and Douglas factions. And the Republicans had captured the legislature and all the important state offices. Credit for the results of the election must be given to Kasson, Grimes, and Kirkwood for their brilliant and meticulous organization of the campaign. Grimes and Kasson proved their adroitness as political leaders; Kirkwood demonstrated an uncommon amount of energy and ability as a stump orator. In an era when personalities counted heavily in an electoral contest, Kirkwood's homespun appearance and mannerisms, in a campaign cleverly managed and directed by Grimes and Kasson, had carried the day for his party. And with the shadow of the approaching presidential election year looming large, the failure of the resurging Iowa Democratic party could only have bitterly disappointed the national party.

[58] *Iowa Weekly Republican*, November 2, 1859, quoted in Albia *Weekly Republican*, December 8, 1859.

The Collapse of the Democratic Party

TㅎHE EXCITEMENT generated by the Kirkwood-Dodge guberna-torial battle had hardly begun to fade when the news of events at Harper's Ferry, Virginia, reached Iowa. John Brown, self-appointed avenger of the Lord against the sinful advocates and protectors of slavery, and personal friend of several Iowans, de-cided that the time had come to eradicate the "peculiar institu-tion." By seizing the federal arsenal at Harper's Ferry, however, Brown bared himself to treason charges. A unit of marines, com-manded by Colonel Robert E. Lee, soon destroyed his dreams and his band, killing or capturing all but a handful of his fol-lowers. Iowans had been intimately associated with Brown be-fore and during his raid into Virginia. Three residents of the Hawkeye State—Jeremiah Anderson, Barclay Coppoc, and Ed-win Coppoc, his brother—joined Brown for the venture, while others apparently contributed funds for the undertaking. Letters from William Penn Clarke and Josiah B. Grinnell appeared among Brown's papers after his arrest.[1]

Iowans received the news of the Brown-inspired incident with mixed feelings. Law-abiding citizens condemned the outrage against federal property. One Democratic paper interpreted Brown's act as a logical product of Republican agitation: "All these things have been encouraged and palliated by the press and orators of a great political party."[2] Most Republicans sympathized with the intent, if not the actual deed. Burlington's Republican organ observed, "His crime is against slavery, and he must atone for it with blood. We will hear nothing but *Brown* for weeks." A sympathetic physician in Fairfield best summed up local attitudes by noting that "Republicans in Iowa all condemn Brown's rash act but they do admire his bravery, truthfulness and fidelity to what he conscientiously deemed right."[3] In January, 1860, Governor Kirkwood, seeking to make political capital out of the affair for the benefit of his party, devoted a significant portion of his inaugural message to the Iowa General Assembly to Brown and events at Harper's Ferry. "The great mass of our northern people utterly condemn the act of John Brown," he declared in part. Yet "they feel and express admiration and sympathy for the disinterestedness of purpose by which they believe he was governed, and for the unflinching courage and calm cheerfulness with which he met the consequences of his failure." Believing that Kirkwood's statement should be widely distributed, the Republican-controlled legislature ordered the publication of 7,500 copies of the inaugural address. Democrats in the

---

[1] Frank I. Herriott, "Republican Presidential Preliminaries in Iowa 1859–1860," *Annals of Iowa*, 3rd ser., Vol. IX (1910), 259–60.

[2] *Iowa State Journal* (Des Moines), October 29, 1859, quoted in Louis Pelzer, "History of Political Parties in Iowa 1857–1860," *Iowa Journal of History and Politics*, Vol. VII (1909), 210.

[3] George A. Boeck, "An Early Iowa Community: Aspects of Economic, Social, and Political Development in Burlington, Iowa, 1833–1866," unpublished Ph.D. dissertation, University of Iowa, 1961, 402; Herriott, "Republican Presidential Preliminaries in Iowa," 280.

lower house bitterly but vainly protested that the speech was unnecessary, inflammatory, and divisive. Moreover, as Grimes observed in a note from Washington, D.C., several prominent Democrats in Congress were also extremely unhappy about the speech of Iowa's new governor.[4]

As if to rub salt into Democratic wounds, still stinging from their recent defeat, the General Assembly very rapidly and easily proceeded to reelect Harlan United States senator. Whatever opposition Harlan might have had from members of his own party was based largely either on his personality or on his place of residence in the state, close to that of Grimes. These minor objections quickly evaporated. Dodge permitted his name to be entered in opposition to Harlan, merely to accept an honor accorded to him by the Democrats.[5]

The political confrontations between the contending parties in the state legislature were at best interesting preliminary jousts compared to the more important activity to come during this most significant of antebellum presidential election years. The Republicans' eagerness to launch the presidential campaign manifested itself as early as December 5, 1859, when State Chairman Kasson issued a call for a state convention to assemble at Des Moines on January 18, 1860, to select delegates to the national Republican convention at Chicago in May. Apparently a number of individuals were unhappy at such an early meeting of the state party, for Kasson felt compelled to justify it by pointing out that the party's national convention "would be held at a much earlier date than is usually appointed for calling a state convention for the nomination of state officers." Moreover, he added, it was

---

[4] Benjamin F. Shambaugh, *Messages and Proclamations*, II, 241; Herriott, "Republican Presidential Preliminaries in Iowa," 260–61; James W. Grimes to Samuel J. Kirkwood, February 25, 1860, "Letters of James W. Grimes," *Annals of Iowa*, 3rd ser., Vol. XXII (1940), 565–66; *Journal of the Senate*, 8th General Assembly of Iowa 1860, 169–71; *Journal of the House of Representatives*, 8th General Assembly of Iowa 1860, 184–86.

[5] *Journal of the Senate*, 8th General Assembly of Iowa, 1860, 87–88; Herriott, "Republican Presidential Preliminaries in Iowa," 251.

"most convenient to procure a general representation of counties during the session of the legislature." From Washington, Senator Grimes wrote that the delegates should be neither instructed nor committed as a unit to any of the preconvention candidates of the party. He hoped, further, that the Republicans "would select a goodly number to cast the vote of Iowa."[6]

Eventually the Republican state convention elected thirty-three delegates to cast Iowa's eight votes at the party's national convention. The uninstructed delegates divided their support among several contenders for the presidential nomination: William H. Seward, Abraham Lincoln, Edward Bates, Salmon P. Chase, Simon Cameron, and John McLean. This sentiment was to be reflected during the first two presidential ballots at the national convention, but on the third and final ballot Iowa's eight votes went to Lincoln. Hannibal Hamlin of Maine became his running mate.[7]

The Republican national platform was designed to attract Westerners, Easterners, conservatives, moderates, and radicals. The party reaffirmed its faith in the Declaration of Independence and the Union and reiterated its support of states' rights. Republicans condemned the Democratic administration for attempting to force the Lecompton constitution upon Kansas and for extrava-

[6] *South-Tier Democrat* (Corydon, Iowa), January 4, 1860; Albia (Iowa) *Weekly Republican*, December 29, 1859; *Iowa Weekly Republican* (Iowa City), December 14, 1859; Herriott, "Republican Presidential Preliminaries in Iowa," 250; James W. Grimes to Samuel J. Kirkwood, December 26, 1859, "Letters of James W. Grimes," 562–63.

[7] *Page County Herald* (Clarinda, Iowa), January 27, 1860; Mildred Throne (ed.), "Iowa Newspapers Report the 1860 Nomination of Lincoln," *Iowa Journal of History*, Vol. LVIII (1960), 229–30; Eliphalet Price to Samuel J. Kirkwood, May 13, 1860, in the Samuel J. Kirkwood Correspondence at the Iowa State Department of History and Archives in Des Moines; William Penn Clarke to Will Cumbuck, February 6, 1860, in the William Penn Clarke Letterbook at the State Historical Society of Iowa in Iowa City; William Penn Clarke to Henry P. Scholte, April 22, 1860, *ibid.*; Charles W. Emery, "The Iowa Germans in the Election of 1860," *Annals of Iowa*, 3rd ser., Vol. XXII (1940), 446–48; Marvin R. Cain, "Edward Bates and the Decision of 1860," *Mid-America*, Vol. XLIV (1962), 118–19, 122.

gance and corruption. In addition, the party advocated homestead legislation, a transcontinental railroad, a tariff, and internal improvements.[8]

Meanwhile, the Democrats were not idle. Dennis A. Mahoney published the announcement that the Democratic state convention would meet on Washington's Birthday in Des Moines to choose the delegates to the national convention at Charleston. Several counties, including Buchanan, Davis, Des Moines, Johnson, Linn, Lucas, and Woodbury, instructed their delegates to the state meeting to work for the election of pro-Douglas delegates. Some county leaders, however, hoped that "our delegation may go to Charleston untrammeled by instructions." Early indications pointed to a straight Douglas delegation headed by Dodge and Samuels, and these men did lead Iowa's eight-man contingent to Charleston.[9]

Not all of Iowa's Democrats, however, supported Douglas for president. The dissenters were proadministration supporters, partisans of George W. Jones, to whom Douglas was anathema because of his break with Buchanan. They would reluctantly vote for him, if he was nominated, but they preferred that someone else head the party ticket. Moreover, they believed that the Democrats could select a stronger man than Douglas. Key figures of the small anti-Douglas group included Laurel Summers, Ver Planck Van Antwerp, and P. M. Casady, the party's state chairman in 1859. One proadministration advocate was convinced that "there would be more apathy in our party with Douglas as a candidate than almost any other man." Apparently contributing to the notion that Douglas would be a weak candidate was the

[8] Kirk Porter (comp.), *National Party Platforms*, 55–58.

[9] *Iowa State Journal*, December 17, 1859; *South-Tier Democrat*, January 11, February 15 and 22, and March 7, 1860; W. W. White to Charles M. Mason, January 23, 1860, in the Charles M. Mason Papers at the Iowa State Department of History and Archives in Des Moines; F. M. Irish to Charles M. Mason, February 5, 1860, *ibid.*; D. A. Mahoney to Charles M. Mason, February 9, 1860, *ibid.*; C. C. Cole to Laurel Summers, February 11, 1860, in the Laurel Summers Correspondence, also at the State Historical Department in Des Moines.

opinion "that his pet, popular sovereignty, is a humbug: it is quite common now to hear *that* expression from Democratic lips —from intelligent farmers and the rank and file."[10]

At Charleston the political atmosphere was anything but serene.[11] Eastern Democrats hoped to strike the best bargain possible with either Westerners or Southerners. Western delegates, fearful of losing their remaining power at home, looked to Douglas as their only hope. Southerners were determined to maintain their honor as well as their unique way of life. Hence the delegates from Alabama, Arkansas, Florida, Georgia, Louisiana, Mississippi, and Texas insisted that the party endorse the principle of federal protection of slavery in the territories. Unless the organization embodied their demand in the national platform, they would withdraw from the convention. In a showdown, other Southern delegations could be expected to follow suit.

When the Democrats attempted to draw up a platform before the nomination of candidates, the convention split over the slavery clause. A majority of the resolutions committee adopted a plank favorable to the Southerners, while a minority of the committee reaffirmed the slavery provisions of the Cincinnati platform.

Ultimately the Douglas supporters were able to marshal enough votes on the convention floor to secure the passage of the minority report. In addition to reiterating the Cincinnati platform, the Democrats recommended construction of a transcontinental railroad, denounced the personal-liberty laws of certain states designed to contravene the Fugitive Slave Act, favored the acquisition of Cuba, and pledged protection to naturalized citizens. Southern delegates refused to accept the verdict of the convention and withdrew amid cheers from the gallery.

[10] W. W. White to Charles M. Mason, March 1 and 6 and April 22, 1860, in the Mason Papers; P. M. Casady to Laurel Summers, February 10 and 27, 1860, in the Summers Correspondence.

[11] An excellent discussion of the events at Charleston, Baltimore, and Richmond appears in Roy F. Nichols, *The Disruption of American Democracy.*

In an attempt to reunite the party and elect Douglas, the Western Democrats decided to adjourn the convention for six weeks and reassemble at Baltimore on June 18. The Douglasites hoped that the Southerners would choose Union Democrats to replace the delegates who had withdrawn. The latter also adjourned and agreed to reconvene at Richmond on June 11.

On the appointed day at Baltimore many of the bolters appeared and sought to be seated in place of pro-Douglas delegations from the South. Although the pro-Douglas convention voted to admit the bolters from Delaware, Mississippi, and Texas, it recognized the new men as well as the bolters from Arkansas and Georgia and excluded the bolters from Alabama and Louisiana. When the Douglas men proposed to begin the balloting, many delegates from Arkansas, Kentucky, Missouri, North Carolina, Tennessee, and Virginia, as well as those from California and Oregon, angered at Douglas and dissatisfied with the platform and the formula for seating the delegates, stalked out of the convention. Nevertheless, the balloting commenced. The remaining delegates selected Douglas on the second ballot. Benjamin Fitzpatrick of Alabama became his running mate, but Robert Toombs of Georgia persuaded him to withdraw. Herschel V. Johnson of Georgia replaced him.

Meanwhile, the Southern bolters, joined by men from Minnesota, New York, and Pennsylvania, reassembled and adopted a platform which pledged federal protection to slavery in the territories. They nominated John C. Breckinridge of Kentucky for president and Joseph Lane of Oregon for vice-president.

Another group, composed mostly of conservative Democrats and former Whigs, feared for the preservation of the Union. Styling themselves the Constitutional Union party, they offered a slate led by John Bell of Tennessee and Edward Everett of Massachusetts. Their platform embraced the Constitution and the Union.

A second state convention of the Iowa Democrats met in Des

Moines on July 12 to ratify the work of the national convention and to nominate candidates for the state's minor offices. The assembly selected J. M. Corse, secretary of state; G. W. Maxfield, auditor; John W. Ellis, treasurer; William McClintock, attorney general; and Patrick Robb, register of the State Land Office.[12]

Iowa's Democrats pledged to support the Douglas ticket, reaffirmed the principles of nonintervention of the federal government in the local affairs of the states and popular sovereignty, and advocated a homestead law. Concerning state matters, the Democrats accused the Republicans of needless extravagance and unnecessary taxation and called for a revision of the state constitution as well as safeguards to curb what they considered to be outrages of the banking system. The failure of the party to endorse the Buchanan administration dramatically emphasized the Douglasite character of the state convention.[13]

Earlier, a second Republican state convention, which assembled for purposes similar to those of the Democratic meeting, had offered a brief platform commending the national Republican platform to the voters. In addition, the party pledged to administer the state government efficiently and honestly. For the state offices the Republicans nominated Elijah Sells, secretary of state; J. W. Cattell, auditor; John W. Jones, treasurer; C. C. Nourse, attorney general; and A. B. Miller, register of the State Land Office.[14]

Supporters of the Breckinridge-Lane ticket held a mass meeting at Davenport on August 15 to pick a slate of presidential electors. Most of the delegates came from Davenport and Dubuque, while the remainder were from counties scattered throughout the state. The Lyons City *Advocate* was the lone

---

[12] *Iowa Valley Democrat* (Marengo), June 13, 1860.

[13] Roy V. Sherman, "Political Party Platforms in Iowa," unpublished M.A. thesis, State University of Iowa, 1926, 171–76.

[14] *Ibid.*, 176–77; Herriott, "Republican Presidential Preliminaries in Iowa," 242.

newspaper supporting this group. In their platform the partisans of the Southern ticket praised the Dred Scott decision, condemned the principle of congressional interference with the introduction of slavery into the territories, and lauded the Buchanan administration.[15]

Shortly afterward, those Iowans who were convinced that the only salvation of the Union was through the Constitutional Union party convened in Iowa City on August 31. Most of the forty to fifty delegates who attended the meeting came from Muscatine and Scott counties. Like the Breckinridge forces, they assembled primarily to choose a slate of presidential electors. In their platform the Constitutional Unionists deplored the sectional strife which threatened to divide the nation, commented on the ambiguity of both the Democratic and Republican platforms, expressed alarm at the growth of the power of the Executive, and invited the voters to support the Bell-Everett ticket, which ran on "the basis of the Constitution, the Union of the States and the enforcement of the laws."[16]

To add further to the discomfiture of the regular Democratic party, William Penn Clarke enticed the *Iowa State Reporter* of Iowa City from the Democratic fold. At one time this journal had been one of the two or three most influential Democratic papers in Iowa. On July 25, only one day after Clarke disclosed his intrigues to Fitz Henry Warren, a local Republican leader, the editor of the *Reporter* announced his intention to support the Republican ticket on the ground that neither wing of the Democratic party was acceptable to him. The switch of the *Reporter* to

[15] Louis Pelzer, "The Disintegration and Organization of Political Parties in Iowa 1852–1860," Mississippi Valley Historical Association *Proceedings* for 1911–1912, 165; Pelzer, "History of Political Parties in Iowa 1857–1860," 222; Kenneth F. Millsap, "The Election of 1860 in Iowa," *Iowa Journal of History,* Vol. XLVIII (1950), 109.

[16] *Hamilton Freeman* (Webster City, Iowa), May 19, 1860; *The Iowa Valley Democrat,* September 5, 1860; Pelzer, "The Disintegration and Organization of Political Parties in Iowa 1852–1860," 165; Pelzer, "History of Political Parties in Iowa 1857–1860," 223–24.

the Republicans undoubtedly stunned many of the Democratic faithful.[17]

In the meantime, the two major parties held conventions in Iowa's congressional districts to choose candidates for the House of Representatives. In the First District the Republicans nominated Curtis for a third term on a platform endorsing the principles of their national organization and noting the schism in the Democratic party. The latter met on July 11, three weeks after the Republican meeting, and picked C. C. Cole to oppose Curtis. Cole had been one of the unsuccessful aspirants for Iowa's high court in the 1859 elections. Cole's platform endorsed the Douglas wing of the party, approved the national platform, and supported a transcontinental railroad. Both candidates agreed to a joint tour of their district during August, September, and October.[18]

In the Second Congressional District the Democrats selected Samuels, of Dubuque, on a pro-Douglas platform, while the Republicans nominated Vandever for his second term. Samuels and Vandever also agreed to engage in a series of debates.[19]

To stimulate popular interest and attract the voters, the various parties formed political clubs throughout the state. These groups backed their local candidates, championed their national candidates, and were useful in sponsoring the debates of the touring congressional rivals, as well as the speeches of other political campaigners. Not only counties but also the larger cities boasted political clubs. Republican clubs functioned in Keokuk, Oskaloosa, Mount Pleasant, Davenport, Muscatine, and Knoxville, among other places. Democrats formed their Douglas club in Des Moines as early as December, 1859. Keokuk organized a

[17] William Penn Clarke to Fitz Henry Warren, July 24, 1860, in the Clarke Letterbook; *Weekly Iowa State Reporter* (Des Moines), July 25 and August 1, 1860.

[18] *South-Tier Democrat*, June 27 and July 18, 1860; *Montezuma* (Iowa) *Weekly Republican*, August 15, 1860.

[19] *Iowa Valley Democrat*, June 13 and July 25, 1860.

Douglas club to combat the Republican group there, while Muscatine had a Breckinridge club. As the campaign progressed, the Republicans also created semimilitary units called Wide-Awakes, which functioned primarily to drum up enthusiasm during political rallies. Often the Wide-Awakes staged parades before the campaign speeches of their candidates.[20]

Republicans strove to make the homestead question one of the major issues of the election. Earlier in the year the Iowa General Assembly had adopted a resolution asking Congress to enact the homestead legislation which Westerners had long desired. Congress did pass a homestead act, but President Buchanan vetoed the measure. The press scornfully criticized the administration for opposing homestead laws. The *Iowa State Reporter*, the zealous new convert to Republicanism, blamed the failure of Democrats to pass homestead legislation on the lack of a "disposition to befriend the poor white men who live by the work of their hands." The Republican organ in Montezuma excoriated the national administration for offering vast amounts of public land for public sale, thus benefiting speculators, while refusing to help the poor settlers with small grants from the huge public domain.[21] Democratic journals sought to parry Republican thrusts by accusing the latter of defeating Democratic homestead measures in order to secure the passage of Republican-sponsored bills. Nevertheless, one pro-Douglas Democratic paper was vituperative in its criticism of the President for his veto of the homestead act: "The Slave Propagandists demanded that the bill should be vetoed, and the pliant tool was swift to obey them. Let the pimps and hirelings of the old sinner defend this last act of his, if they dare."[22]

[20] Millsap, "The Election of 1860 in Iowa," 105–107ff.

[21] *Journal of the House of Representatives*, 8th General Assembly of Iowa, 1860, 98; Dubuque *Herald*, June 27, 1860, quoted in George M. Stephenson, *The Political History of the Public Lands*, 217; *Weekly Iowa State Reporter*, October 24, 1860; *Montezuma Weekly Republican*, August 15, 1860.

[22] Council Bluffs *Bugle* quoted in *Page County Herald*, June 22, 1860; Reinhard H. Luthin, *The First Lincoln Campaign*, 179.

In what had become a somewhat lackluster campaign, the Republican press endeavored to arouse popular indignation against the Democrats by accusing them of willful extravagance in Washington. Democrats, declared one paper, "have participated alike in the general plunder, bribery, and corruption." Other Republican journals sought to awaken "Bleeding Kansas" as a campaign issue. One partisan organ insisted that "the Democratic party, notwithstanding their former professions of love for freedom and free institutions, would, were it in their power, make Kansas a slave state."[23]

The dispirited Democratic press, thoroughly reflecting the disarray of its party, lamely responded by attacking one or another candidate, criticizing Republicans in general and Lincoln in particular, and raising anew the specter of race as an election issue. One paper belittled Lincoln as one whose talent was limited solely to rail-splitting. Another organ, commenting after election day, suggested that "the election of Lincoln may be of service to the body politic, which like the human body becomes occasionally disordered, and is restored to health and vigor by nauseating medicines."[24] A pro-Douglas journal predicted the dissolution of the Union as the inevitable result of a victory by Lincoln and indicated that the success of the Breckinridge ticket would also be fatal to the nation. Iowa voters, the editor warned, faced the following obvious alternatives as they pondered their choices: the election of Douglas would mean the success of self-government under the Constitution, but the triumph of Lincoln would really signal a victory of the Southern Negro and his friends who endeavored to elevate the black race to a level of equality with the white residents of Iowa. The Republican party, the paper insisted, masked its mismanagement of the state government by using appeals on behalf of the Negro as a cloak:

[23] *Montezuma Weekly Republican*, August 1 and 8, 1860.

[24] Dubuque *Herald*, November 8, 1860, quoted in Hubert H. Wubben, "Dennis Mahoney and the Dubuque *Herald* 1860–1863," *Iowa Journal of History*, Vol. LVI (1958), 291; *Iowa Valley Democrat*, May 13, 1860.

For four years, by the aid of the "irrepressible nigger," the Republican party have had complete control of your State government. Year after year, during this time, have your taxes been steadily increasing, and when you have attempted to remonstrate, your attention has been diverted therefrom by the never failing cry of "the nigger." While you were bewailing the fate of the "poor nigger in bondage," an unconstitutional and rapidly increasing State debt has been fastened upon you.[25]

Playing upon the anti-Negro race prejudices of native as well as foreign-born Iowans, Democratic papers repeatedly sought to focus public attention upon the often-used bogey of the Negro as a threat to the white man. In this vein the *South-Tier Democrat* of Corydon warned its readers that, since the Republicans had already desegregated the public schools, their victory in the coming elections would ensure the equality of the Negro and the white man.[26]

Republican editors not only vigorously denied that their party favored the equality of the races but also held a differing view of Lincoln and his qualifications for the presidency. To the party organ in Mount Pleasant, Lincoln was worthy of support because of his Western origins: "Honest, able and patriotic—reared in the west amidst its privations, he is a walking argument in favor of free labor and free institutions." A paper published on the Missouri slope characterized Lincoln as "a statesman of distinguished abilities, and a man of renowned honor, probity, and integrity." The Burlington *Hawk-Eye* simply declared, "Lincoln was not nominated because he split rails in 1830."[27]

[25] *Iowa Valley Democrat*, July 3, September 26, and October 31, 1860.

[26] *South-Tier Democrat*, January 18, 1860; David Rorer to Charles Mason, September 7, 1860, in the Mason Papers.

[27] Mount Pleasant (Iowa) *Home Journal*, May 26, 1860; Council Bluffs (Iowa) *Weekly Nonpareil*, May 26, 1860, quoted in Throne, "Iowa Newspapers Report the 1860 Nomination of Lincoln," 276–77; Boeck, "An Early Iowa Community," 403–404.

As the campaign drew to a close, Republican leaders were exuberant in their forecasts of success for their party in the state and national elections. They tended to minimize, if not entirely to ignore, the increasingly hostile mood which Southerners were displaying to the nation and discounted, at least publicly, the threats of secession current in the South. Republicans blandly dismissed talk about danger to the Union and insisted that the South would accept the verdict of the national electorate. The *Hawk-Eye*, for example, scoffed at the "old bugaboo of disunion" which was merely the time-worn "blatant threats of demagogues," repeatedly raised to intimidate the irresolute and the weak, but now become comic through persistent repetition.[28]

Republican State Chairman H. M. Hoxie predicted an easy victory for incumbent Congressman Curtis, provided the party could maintain its strength in the traditional Republican counties, Henry, Mahaska, and Washington. Apparently, however, signs of Republican overconfidence in the Second District somewhat troubled the Republican chairman. William Penn Clarke, also certain of his party's prospects, predicted that Lincoln would carry Iowa by at least ten thousand votes.[29]

The thoroughly demoralized Iowa Democratic party lacked the optimism expressed by its Republican rivals. Proadministration supporters were particularly gloomy. W. W. White, an anti-Douglas Democrat from Burlington, informed administration stalwart Charles M. Mason that he felt "considerable anxiety about the general result. I fear serious trouble with Lincoln's success." Another correspondent in Burlington, M. W. Robinson, told Mason that "the political horizon is rather dark for Democracy, and it is conceded that Lincoln will be elected. We had hopes of this state untill [*sic*] within ten days." However, he be-

---

28 Quoted in Boeck, "An Early Iowa Community," 404–405.
29 H. M. Hoxie to Samuel J. Kirkwood, September 21 and 26, 1860, in the Kirkwood Correspondence; William Penn Clarke to J. P. Sanderson, October 24, 1860, in the Clarke Letterbook.

lieved that Cole had a good chance of defeating Curtis in the congressional race in the First District.[30]

The appearance of Stephen A. Douglas for speeches at Dubuque, Cedar Rapids, and Iowa City climaxed, as well as added luster to, the Democratic campaign in Iowa. An estimated twenty thousand persons swarmed into the former state capital to hear Douglas speak on October 9. Sharing the speakers' platform with the "Little Giant" were various party leaders from Illinois and Iowa. During the course of his speech Douglas lashed out at the Republicans for opposing popular sovereignty, attacked Lincoln's pacifist position at the time of the Mexican War, and reminded his audience of his past efforts to secure passage of homestead legislation. He deprecated the appeals that were being made "to sectional passions and sectional ambitions." Sectional strife, he said, was a direct result of congressional attempts to interfere in the local affairs of states. Both the abolitionists of the North and the secessionists of the South merited public opprobrium, said Douglas, for arousing sectional partisanship. Indeed, both sides existed solely through their mutual antagonism. Douglas was particularly scornful of the disunionists of the South, interpreting the withdrawal of the Southern delegates from the Democratic convention as a maneuver to ensure his defeat. Moreover, he would attribute a Republican victory to the efforts of the administration men to defeat him.

After his critical remarks about his Republican and Democratic foes, Douglas struck a note of intent seriousness. "Whoever is elected President," he declared, "must be inaugurated, and after he is inaugurated he must be supported in the exercise of all his just powers." He ended his address with an appeal for the preservation of the Union:

We in the Northwest cannot permit the Union to be dissolved. We are emigrants from the East and from the South,

[30] W. W. White to Charles M. Mason, October 6, 1860, in the Mason Papers; M. W. Robinson to Charles M. Mason, October 22, 1860, *ibid.*

from the free states and from the slave states. . . . The Union cannot be dissolved without severing the ties that bind the heart of the daughter to the mother and the son to the father. This Union cannot be dissolved without separating us from the graves of our ancestors. We are bound to the South as well as to the East, by the ties of commerce, of business, and of interest. We must follow, with our produce in all time to come, the course of the Mississippi River into the broad ocean. Hence, we cannot permit this Union to be dissolved. It must be preserved. And how? Only by preserving inviolate the Constitution as our fathers made it.[31]

On November 6, Iowans went to the polls and administered a stinging defeat to the Democrats. Republicans carried the state offices by about a 13,500-vote margin. They recaptured both chambers of the Iowa General Assembly and swept the presidential and congressional elections. In the First Congressional District, Curtis won a third term, defeating C. C. Cole by a vote of 33,936 to 30,240. Curtis received 52.88 per cent of the ballots, the highest percentage a Republican candidate had thus far obtained in the First District. In the Second District the Republicans retained their control with ease. Vandever was reelected, defeating Samuels by a vote of 36,805 to 27,206. Vandever's 57.50 per cent of the total vote represented a gain of 4.68 percentage points over what he had received in 1858.[32]

The Republicans captured twelve counties which had voted Democratic in the 1858 congressional contests. Three—Allamakee, Jones, and Clinton—were in the northeast, and three others—Monroe, Van Buren, and Des Moines—were in the southeast. The remainder were in the western portion of the state. Of the latter, four counties—Woodbury, Monona, Harrison, and Mills—

[31] Pelzer, "History of Political Parties in Iowa 1857–1860," 226–28; Millsap, "The Election of 1860 in Iowa," 117–18; Charles A. Thodt, "Stephen A. Douglas Speaks at Iowa City, 1860," *Iowa Journal of History*, Vol. LIII (1955), 156–66.
[32] Election Records, 1848–1860.

adjoined the Missouri River. The remaining two counties which deserted the Democratic party in this area were Carroll and Guthrie. Democrats lured from their foes only three counties—Adair, Clay, and Ida—all in the western half of the state.

Lincoln carried Iowa for the Republicans, winning more votes than his three opponents combined. In Iowa, at least, his was not a minority victory. Lincoln received 70,316 votes; Douglas, 55,639; Bell, 1,763; and Breckinridge, 1,034. Lincoln received 54.61 per cent of the total ballots; Douglas, 43.21 per cent; Bell, 1.37 per cent; and Breckinridge, 0.80 per cent. Evidently, in Iowa Unionist sentiment was stronger than Southern sympathy.

Unionist support came chiefly from the southeastern counties —Cedar, Davis, Des Moines, Henry, Johnson, Lee, Linn, Muscatine, Scott, and Washington. In addition, the Union party obtained a considerable number of votes in Clinton and Dubuque counties in northeastern Iowa and in Fremont County in the southwestern tip of the state.

The Southern ticket had its strongest following in Clinton, Dubuque, Muscatine, Scott, and Van Buren counties in eastern Iowa, in Jasper County in central Iowa, and in Webster County in the north-central section of the state. Elsewhere in the state support for the Breckinridge slate was scattered.

Except for Dubuque and Lee counties, the Republicans carried the entire eastern half of Iowa. Democratic support in addition to Dubuque came largely from the southern tier and from the newer, sparsely populated western counties. Although the Democrats scored gains in most of the eastern counties in comparison to the totals they had obtained in 1856, the increases were not nearly enough to swing any county away from the Republicans. The latter took Jackson, Des Moines, and Van Buren counties in eastern Iowa from the Democrats. In western Iowa the Republicans lured five counties from the Democratic fold—Guthrie, Page, Pottawattamie, Taylor, and Monona. The split in the Democratic party undoubtedly cost Douglas Pottawattamie, Webster, and Woodbury counties, for Lincoln obtained slim pluralities there.

Several factors contributed to the Republican success in Iowa. An attitude of defeatism engulfed local Democrats throughout the campaign. By the time the results were known, their pessimism was transformed into bitterness and disillusionment. Thomas S. Wilson of Dubuque attributed the party's defeat to "New England Yankeeism . . . & its twin brother abolitionism." Editor Dennis A. Mahoney wrote that "the Democratic party is dismembered and demoralized." The split in the national organization, reflected in the schism in the state party, was a significant factor in the party's defeat in the state, for Douglas Democrats had to fight Breckinridge supporters as well as Bell and Lincoln men.[33]

The voters of Iowa evidently preferred the Republican platform to those of the other contenders. Cleverly drawn up to appeal to a broad spectrum of voters, the Republican statement of principles took a moderate stand on slavery, opposing only its extension into the territories. Most Iowans, normally against the spread of slavery, could accept such a plank. The difficulties in Kansas, recalled by the Republican press, helped discredit the doctrine of popular sovereignty as embodied in the Cincinnati platform and reiterated by the Northern Democrats in 1860. Even Democrats had begun to lose confidence in popular sovereignty.

President Buchanan's veto of the homestead measure played directly into the hands of Republicans. They had long sought to convince Iowans that, despite the favorable backing of the state Democratic party, the national Democratic leadership would never enact homestead legislation. Evidently voters in eastern Iowa agreed with the Republicans on this score. In western Iowa

---

[33] Thomas S. Wilson to Charles M. Mason, December 21, 1860, in the Mason Papers; D. A. Mahoney to Charles M. Mason, December 27, 1860, *ibid.*; W. W. White to Charles M. Mason, June 25, 1860, *ibid.*; H. M. Hoxie to Samuel J. Kirkwood, June 25, 1860, in the Kirkwood Correspondence.

the settlers were also vitally interested in federal-aid legislation in the form of homesteads, internal improvements, and land grants for railroad construction. Disappointment over the President's veto may have prompted Monona, Crawford, Guthrie, Harrison, and Shelby counties, which voted Democratic in 1859, to switch to the Republicans in 1860. The Democrats, nevertheless, received considerable support from the counties of northwestern Iowa. There the voters remained firmly behind the Democrats, apparently in the belief that the national party, led by Douglas, would not continue to ignore their homestead demands. Since most of the settlers of northwestern Iowa hailed originally from New England, the Middle Atlantic states, and Ohio, no other hypothesis seems to explain their endorsement of Douglas.

Altogether the Republicans received 13,900 more votes in 1860 than they had received in 1859. The Democrats managed to attract only 2,300 more voters to their banner. More than half the new Republican voters lived in the extreme eastern portion of Iowa. In nineteen counties, including Dubuque and Lee, the Republicans gained over 7,600 voters, while the Democrats increased their figures by only about 650. The increase in population between the 1859 state census and the 1860 federal census in sixteen of the counties may account, in part at least, for the Republican gains.[34] But in three counties—Lee, Louisa, and Wapello—where the population had declined by more than 2,900 persons, the Republicans increased their totals by almost 1,200. Apparently a sizable group of voters lost confidence in the Democrats and moved into the Republican column.

The role of the foreign-born voters, particularly the German-born element of the Old Northwest and adjacent areas, including Iowa and Minnesota, has long interested historians of the first Lincoln election. In recent years a number of younger scholars,

[34] John A. T. Hull (comp.), *Iowa Historical and Comparative Census, 1836–1880*, 196–99.

employing traditional as well as novel tools of scholarship, have reinvestigated and reevaluated the contributions, if any, of the German-born voters to Lincoln's victory. The results of this new research indicate that a thorough reexamination of the voting behavior in 1860 of the foreign-born element in particular, and of all the voters in general, would be worthwhile and instructive. Indeed, the use of computer techniques in such research makes this undertaking feasible.

An older generation of historians was convinced that the Germans gave their votes to Lincoln and thereby contributed significantly to his election. These historians accepted the boasts of various German editors and political leaders who claimed to influence and even control the voting patterns of their fellow countrymen.[35] A younger group of historians, however, has seriously challenged the notion that the real, as well as the self-appointed, leaders and formulators of opinion of the German-born rank and file could and did deliver the German vote to the Republican party. In recent studies they have advanced the thesis that the German vote in the Old Northwest and contiguous areas never left the Democratic column and that other explanations must be found for Lincoln's success at the polls in 1860.[36]

Students of the 1860 election in Iowa insist that the German vote was essential to Lincoln, that the significance of the German contribution to his triumph has probably been exaggerated, or that the Germans voted against Lincoln and for Douglas. Frank

[35] See, for example, William E. Dodd, "The Fight for the Northwest, 1860," *American Historical Review*, Vol. XVI (1910–1911), 774–88; and Donnal V. Smith, "The Influence of the Foreign-Born of the Northwest in the Election of 1860," *Mississippi Valley Historical Review*, Vol. XIX (1932), 192–204.

[36] Among these are George H. Daniels, "The Immigrant Vote in the 1860 Election: The Case of Iowa," *Mid-America*, Vol. XLIV (1962), 146–62; Robert P. Swierenga, "The Ethnic Voter and the First Lincoln Election," *Civil War History*, Vol. XI (1965), 27–43; and Thomas J. Kelso, "The German-American Vote in the Election of 1860: The Case of Indiana with Supporting Data from Ohio," unpublished Ph.D. dissertation, Ball State University, 1967. Earlier, the old contention was questioned by Joseph Schafer, "Who Elected Lincoln?" *American Historical Review*, Vol. XLVII (1941), 51–63.

I. Herriott was convinced that the Germans were important in securing Lincoln's nomination and election. Indeed, Herriott believed that the Germans were the major factor in the initial fusion victory in Iowa under Grimes and that they then transferred their allegiance to the Republican party largely because of the slavery and homestead issues.[37] Kenneth Millsap did not concern himself with the reasons for Lincoln's triumph but merely repeated the standard assertion of the older generation of historians about the Germans: "Despising slavery as reminiscent of the tyranny which they had left behind, the Germans held the balance of power in many communities and threw their influence to the antislavery forces."[38] Charles W. Emery agreed that most of the Germans were Republicans but was uncertain about the direction of their vote. He concluded that, "while the German vote was important in Iowa in 1860, it was not essential to a Republican victory."[39] George H. Daniels made a careful and detailed statistical analysis of the voting behavior of the immigrant groups in the state. To Daniels, "it seems that Iowa Germans were definitely inimical to Republican aspirations in the election of 1860," largely because of their disgust with prohibition and nativism, both of which they tended to associate closely with Republicanism.[40]

By way of comparison, Robert P. Swierenga, in his study of the voting record of the Dutch immigrants in the state, demonstrated that in 1860, as in 1858 and 1859, the Hollanders delivered their

[37] Herriott wrote several articles on the subject: "Republican Presidential Preliminaries in Iowa," cited earlier in this chapter; "Iowa and the First Nomination of Abraham Lincoln," *Annals of Iowa*, 3rd ser., Vol. VIII (1908); "A Neglected Factor in the Anti-Slavery Triumph in Iowa in 1854," *Deutsch-Amerikanische Geschichtsblätter: Jahrbuch der Deutsch-Amerikanischen Historischen Gesellschaft von Illinois*, Vols. XVIII–XIX (1918–1919), 174–355; and "The Germans in the Gubernatorial Campaign of Iowa in 1859," *ibid.*, Vol. XIV (1914), 451–622.

[38] Millsap, "The Election of 1860 in Iowa," 97.

[39] Emery, "The Iowa Germans in the Election of 1860," 450.

[40] Daniels, "The Immigrant Vote in the 1860 Election: The Case of Iowa," 155.

ballots to the Democratic column, in this instance to Douglas, by an overwhelming margin. Scholte, the generally acknowledged leader of the Dutch community, was a delegate to the Republican national convention and labored indefatigably for the party but failed to deliver the votes of the rank and file, who continued to abhor nativism and prohibition as they had done since the middle of the 1850's.[41] On the basis of the evidence, one can only conclude that the ethnic groups—which included the Irish, as well as the Germans and Dutch—did not desert the Douglas ticket as an earlier generation of historians supposed. Lincoln was victorious in Iowa because he gained the support of native-born citizens rather than the immigrant groups.

Lincoln's election to the presidency motivated a number of Southern states, led by South Carolina, to make good their threats to secede from the Union. Inexplicably, Republican newspapers continued to refuse to take seriously the activities of the Southern secessionists. One paper ridiculed the militancy of South Carolina before the state seceded. Later the same journal expressed the belief that South Carolina rued her ill-conceived, hasty action. The influential *Iowa State Gazette* of Burlington belittled the sincerity of the Southern extremists and assumed an obdurate posture: "Let the fire-eaters rave, to their heart's content. Their guns will be spiked at home. The Union sentiment at the South is strong enough to strangle the traitors who would plot for the destruction of the American government."[42] The Burlington *Hawk-Eye*, long scornful of the secessionists, also counseled against compromise: "The Republican party was a necessity of the times, to keep slavery from becoming national, and we will not abandon this ideal."[43]

In sharp contrast to the apparent naïveté of the Republican press, Democratic newspapers seemed to understand the gravity

[41] Swierenga, "The Ethnic Voter and the First Lincoln Election," 27–43.
[42] Quoted in Millsap, "The Election of 1860 in Iowa," 120.
[43] Quoted in Boeck, "An Early Iowa Community," 404–405.

of the rapidly deteriorating national political scene. Typifying the somber evaluation of the darkening clouds gathering on the nation's horizon were the comments of the Lyons City *Advocate*, which had supported the Breckinridge-Lane ticket:

> Already the disunion sentiment is assuming shape and form that it never before had, and while we hope for the best, we cannot but fear that the worst may occur, for what could be worse than a civil war in this country. Several of the southern states are already preparing for it, and that too in a manner that betokens honest intentions.[44]

The tragedy toward which the nation had been inexorably moving since the middle years of the 1850's would become sad reality within months after Lincoln's election. As previously, Iowans would influence and be influenced by the coming events.

[44] Quoted in Millsap, "The Election of 1860 in Iowa," 120.

Epilogue

Tнε 1850's were the significant years of the increasingly bitter sectional confrontation between the free North and the slave South. On the one hand, Northern leaders saw in the South an economy built upon the detestable foundation of slave labor retarding the development and growth of domestic industrial enterprise. More galling, perhaps, to Northern politicians was the prominent position of Southerners in the conduct of the national government. On the other hand, Southerners viewed slavery as necessary to their cherished way of life and to the maintenance of their political ascendancy in national affairs. Northern criticism alerted Southerners to the imminent danger which threatened them and united them against the North.

By 1850 the slavery controversy had reached a crisis. Moderates from both sides, however, sought to avert the tragedy of a divided nation. The Compromise of 1850, though not entirely satisfactory to everyone, considerably eased the anxiety and tensions in the country as the final pre–Civil War decade opened.

In Iowa the Democratic party had controlled the state's elective offices since her territorial period. Local party leaders hailed the enactment of the compromise measures, and Iowans generally welcomed them enthusiastically. Only the small Free-Soil and abolitionist elements remained dissatisfied. During the gubernatorial, congressional, and state elections in 1850 and the presidential, congressional, and state contests in 1852, the Democrats rallied Iowans to their standard by a plank unequivocably embracing the compromise. Because Iowa's congressional delegation, all Democrats, had supported the compromise bills, the state party claimed full credit for helping to save the Union from destruction.

With national catastrophe temporarily averted, Iowans bent their talents to attain objectives, which, as pioneers in a frontier state, they sought in common with other Westerners. They desired federal aid in the form of homestead legislation, internal improvements, and grants of land for railroad construction. In addition, the Whigs endeavored to convince Iowans of the importance of high tariffs and the need of revising the state constitution, while temperance forces labored to secure prohibition legislation. Free-Soilers and abolitionists sought to align Iowans behind the antislavery crusaders of the North.

Throughout the 1850's railroad mania possessed Iowans. Numerous conventions assembled at the county and state levels, and railroad promoters pressed the state legislature to petition Congress for a land grant to aid in the construction of railroads. During each session of Congress the state's Democratic delegation dutifully, but at first unsuccessfully, sponsored bills for land grants. Iowa Whigs, noting the fruitless efforts of the Democrats to secure grants of land, sought to convince Iowans that the Democratic party would not, or could not, satisfy their demands.

The national Democratic leadership, Whigs pointed out, continued to thwart the attempts of Iowa's Democrats to win land-grant legislation.

Railroad politics were responsible for the first defeat of the Iowa Democrats in 1852 in the Second District congressional race. There the regular party nominee, Lincoln Clark, generated animosity among Democrats in central Iowa, as well as in his home county of Dubuque. The leaders of the central counties, hoping for a railroad line from Davenport through Iowa City to the Missouri River, opposed Clark because he had identified himself too closely with the rival Dubuque and Keokuk road. Further opposition to Clark stemmed from an intraparty dispute in Dubuque, where George W. Jones squared off against Thomas S. Wilson. The Jones faction, intensely proadministration, suspected Clark of being a member of the Wilson circle. Although Clark placated Jones, he could not satisfy the Democrats in the central counties.

To capitalize on the split in the Democratic party in the Second District, the Whigs nominated a conservative, John P. Cook, known to possess "safe" opinions concerning railroad routes. Previously the Whigs had tried to arouse hostility toward the Democrats by accusing Senators Jones and Dodge of continually neglecting the central counties. Owing to the cleavage in the Democratic ranks, Cook became the first member of his party from Iowa to serve in the national House of Representatives.

Despite discord in northern Iowa because of the Jones-Wilson feud, the low state of the party in the central counties as a result of the railroad issue, and evidence of factional strife over internal improvements, the Iowa Democratic party remained the paramount political organization in the state. No other party offered an effective challenge. In 1854, Democrats hoped to enhance their popularity even more in Iowa.

Iowans had long displayed an interest in Nebraska, partly because they wanted more land, partly because they wanted a land grant, partly because businessmen were eager to outfit settlers crossing Iowa on their way to Nebraska, and partly because of the additional political patronage which such a territory would give to the Iowa delegation in Congress. Mercantile, railroad, and political considerations explain the substitution of Douglas' Kansas-Nebraska Bill for Dodge's original one-territory proposal.

The Kansas-Nebraska Act, however, provoked a storm of protest and criticism in Iowa. Resolutions from several counties, as well as petitions to the state legislature, had demonstrated that Iowans wanted the organization of Nebraska. Yet, when they learned of the provisions of the Nebraska Act, Iowans condemned the measure. The Democratic party in the state split over the question. The opposition of Iowans to the Kansas-Nebraska Act stemmed principally from three grievances: the specific repeal of the Missouri Compromise of 1820, which had prohibited slavery north of 36°30′ latitude in the Louisiana Territory; the reopening of the slavery controversy, which the Compromise of 1850 presumably had settled; and the possibility of the extension of slavery into the free territories.

Further complicating the turbulent political atmosphere stimulated by the outcry against the Nebraska bill was the temperance issue, which also had a corrosive effect upon the Iowa Democratic party. Heartened by Neal Dow's success in Maine, temperance supporters clamored for total prohibition in Iowa. Beginning in 1853, they threatened to form a separate political organization to secure their demands. Though most Democrats opposed prohibition, prominent individuals in the party endorsed the idea.

In 1854, Grimes rallied to his banner several splinter groups opposed to the Democrats. His fusion party included Free-Soilers, abolitionists, temperance supporters, opponents of the Kansas-Nebraska Act, and Whigs. Grimes was the first non-Democratic governor of Iowa, but his antislavery slogans alone did not bring him victory. Despite his strong denunciation of the Kansas-

233

Nebraska Bill, he would have lost the election had he not campaigned in support of internal improvements, constitutional revision, popular election of judges, and homesteads, as well as implying an endorsement of prohibition. Even his impressive though vain efforts to attract the foreign voters were directed to their inherent ethnic sensitivities rather than to their anti-slavery impulses. Other factors which helped Grimes were the question of the removal of the capital to Des Moines, the excessive overconfidence of the Democrats, and his personal popularity.

Although they had lost the gubernatorial election in 1854, the Democrats, campaigning on a strong pro-Nebraska platform, won the upper chamber of the General Assembly, the congressional seat in the First District, and all the state posts except the auditor's office. In the Second District the Whigs retained the congressman's office, which they had won in 1852.

Between 1854 and 1856 a series of changes occurred which hastened the alteration of the political complexion of Iowa. During this period a new wave of immigration flowed into the state. Originating largely in New England, the Middle Atlantic states, and Ohio, as well as from abroad, these newcomers differed from the earlier settlers in background, culture, and tradition. The new immigrants came from areas where slavery was regarded as a blot upon the national character. While not generally abolitionists, they were extreme in their opposition to the extension of slavery into the free territories. Moreover, New Englanders came from a region which, except for New Hampshire and Maine, had been politically hostile to the Democrats. Many of these newcomers, of course, had tarried in other states during their westward journey, some for many years. Nevertheless, they had lingered in places whose inhabitants held similar views concerning slavery.

Between 1854 and 1857 a new political organization, founded upon a platform of antagonism to foreigners and to Roman Catholics, mushroomed in Iowa. Entering candidates in the various state and national elections of 1855, 1856, and 1857, the Know-Nothing party attracted considerable support in eastern and southern Iowa. The dissolution of the Whig party during 1852–54 and the presence of several splinter groups unaffiliated with any political party encouraged the Know-Nothings to broaden their basis of appeal to the voters. They adopted an antislavery plank in an effort to secure the allegiance of Iowa's moral crusaders. The formation of another political party, however, shattered the plans of the nativists to provide the leadership for the various splinter elements.

Together with several former Whigs and Free-Soilers, including James Harlan and William Penn Clarke, Grimes perceived that a new political party had to be formed to institutionalize the fusion of the splinter groups which had rallied behind him in 1854 and to prevent the Democrats from recapturing the gubernatorial office and the legislature. Moreover, the evident dissension in the Whig ranks, manifested by the refusal of the conservatives to support Grimes in 1854 and by the difficulty of electing Harlan to the Senate in 1855, made imperative the formation of a new political party. Owing largely to Grimes's labors, the Republican party of Iowa emerged in 1856 to contend with the Democratic party for Iowa's political plums.

The passage of prohibition in 1855 and of the Iowa land grant in 1856 aided the infant Republican organization. Temperance supporters gravitated to the Republican fold because the Democratic party had generally fought the prohibition measure. Many individual Democrats who supported its adoption also bolted to the Republicans. Through their control of the state legislature the Republicans were able to obscure the role of the Democrats in winning the long-sought grant of land for the state. Republicans posed as the only group which would respond to Iowans' desires for land grants, homesteads, and internal improvements.

Aided also by the unrest in Kansas, the Republicans swept the Iowa elections in 1856. Obtaining decisive control of the assembly, they promptly redrew the boundaries of the congressional districts to their advantage by detaching Des Moines, Louisa, and Washington counties from the Second District and adding them to the First. Louisa and Washington counties were solid Republican strongholds, while Des Moines contained a powerful Republican minority.

The role of the foreign-born voters in contributing to the string of Republican successes in Iowa has, until recently, remained largely obscure and inconclusive. Several German-language newspaper editors, along with other self-styled leaders of the state's German-born community, began to attack the Democratic party because of the enactment of the Kansas-Nebraska Bill and the failure of homestead measures in the Congress. This criticism, together with the belief that these individuals wielded considerable influence among their fellow countrymen, motivated Grimes and his allies to seek the endorsement of these prominent figures for their fusion and Republican tickets.

The latest research, however, contravenes the thesis that the German-born voters accepted the platform of the Republican party and were especially significant in Lincoln's successful first campaign. Work by Daniels and Swierenga reveals that, in Iowa at least, the rank and file of the German- and Dutch-born voters ignored their own spokesmen, real or self-appointed, and remained steadfastly loyal to the Democratic party, to which they had been initially directed by these same, or earlier, leaders. Deep-seated anger provoked by nativism and temperance, both strongly identified with segments of the Republican organization, operated to keep these voters in the Democratic column. This strongly rooted antagonism, coupled with the specter of racial competition, cleverly suggested by Democrats as being the logical consequences of a Republican-oriented government, prevented these voters from faltering in their allegiance to the Democrats. Republican power was built upon a foundation of native-born voters.

Republicans controlled the constitutional convention which assembled in Iowa City in January, 1857, to create a new constitution. The delegates adopted articles which provided for the establishment of public banks, an increase in the state debt limit, new laws of incorporation, and the removal of the capital to Des Moines. In other articles the delegates permanently located the state university in Iowa City, created the office of lieutenant governor, and provided for the direct election of judges. Later in the year Iowans ratified their new constitution by a narrow margin.

At the April elections in 1857, Iowa Democrats exhibited signs of renewed strength by capturing two of the three state posts at stake. But in October the Republicans employed the new constitution to good advantage and edged past the Democrats to retain the gubernatorial office.

In 1858, Iowans suffered from severe economic hardship fostered by the decline in grain prices during the Panic of 1857, by the overextension in investments in real estate and railroad companies, and by recurring crop failures. The Democrats might have benefited from the Iowans' distress and returned to power, but the Republicans responded to the needs of the people with remedial legislation. They enacted relief measures to ease the financial burdens of the populace. At the same time they resisted the temptation to yield to the pressure of railroad entrepreneurs for state aid. Though Republican leaders were intimately associated with various railroad enterprises, they escaped popular identification with the railroad interests.

Iowa Republicans prospered from the controversy over the Lecompton constitution which divided the national and state Democratic parties in 1857–58. The old Jones-Wilson feud flared anew as the proadministration Jones faction assailed the Wilson-Clark group. The latter formed the nucleus of the pro-Douglas, antiadministration wing of the party. As a result of Republican

237

success at the polls, Grimes went to Washington to replace Jones in the Senate.

The following year, 1859, Dodge returned to Iowa after serving as minister to Spain. The two wings of the state Democratic party united to support his candidacy for the gubernatorial post. Absent during the crucial years of the recurrent Democratic strife, Dodge breathed new life into the organization as the party undertook its most energetic campaign of the 1850's. Dodge debated the issues with his Republican opponent, Kirkwood, in a series of arranged discussions throughout the state. They argued such questions as homesteads, government finances, slavery, and nativism. Despite the indefatigable efforts of a host of the state's Democrats, Kirkwood emerged the victor in an exceedingly closely contested race, and the Republicans remained in power in the state.

Democratic unity under Dodge, however, was short-lived. When the national Democratic party split at Charleston in 1860 over the slavery problem, the state party also divided. Many of the Jones proadministration faction supported the Southern presidential ticket of Breckinridge and Lane, but most of Iowa's Democrats backed Douglas for the presidency. The Jones group had never completely forgiven Douglas for his quarrel and subsequent break with Buchanan over the Lecompton constitution. In 1860 they sought to defeat him without reflecting upon the consequences of their action.

The Republicans, with Lincoln at their head, crushed a demoralized Democratic party by more than 14,500 votes. No victorious party had ever obtained such a resounding vote of confidence from Iowa's voters. And while loyal Democrats began to clamor for a thorough reorganization of their party, the Civil War not only blocked the plans of party leaders to regain political control of the state but also completed the Republicanization of the Iowa electorate.

Bibliography

Iowa Manuscripts

Le Grand Byington Letters, Microfilm, State Historical Society of
Iowa, Iowa City.
Cyrus C. Carpenter Letters, State Historical Society.
William Penn Clarke Correspondence, Iowa State Department of
History and Archives, Des Moines.
William Penn Clarke Letterbook, State Historical Society.
Samuel R. Curtis Papers, State Department of History.
Henry Clay Dean Collection, State Department of History.
Augustus C. Dodge Papers, State Historical Society.
Governors' Papers, State Department of History.
James Harlan Papers, State Historical Society.
George W. Jones Correspondence, State Department of History.
George W. Jones Papers, State Historical Society.
Samuel J. Kirkwood Correspondence, State Department of History.
Lucius H. Langworthy Papers, State Historical Society.
Ralph P. Lowe Papers, State Department of History.

239

Charles M. Mason Papers, State Department of History.
William Salter Collection, State Department of History.
Laurel Summers Correspondence, State Department of History.
James Thorington Collection, State Historical Society.
David S. Wilson Papers, State Department of History.

GOVERNMENT DOCUMENTS

Biographical Directory of the American Congress 1774–1949. Washington, 1950.
The Seventh Census of the United States: 1850. Washington, 1853.
The Eighth Census of the United States: 1860. Washington, 1866.
Census of Iowa by Counties as Returned to the Secretary of State for the Year 1854. Iowa City, 1854.
The Census Returns of the Different Counties of the State of Iowa for 1856. Iowa City, 1857.
The Census Returns of the Different Counties of the State of Iowa for 1859. Des Moines, 1859.
Congressional Globe, 31 Cong., 1 sess.–35 Cong., 2 sess. (December 3, 1849–March 3, 1859).
Election Records, 1848–1860. Ledger in office of the Secretary of State, Des Moines. Microfilm copy in Library, University of Iowa, Iowa City.
Journal of the House of Representatives, 3rd General Assembly of Iowa–8th General Assembly of Iowa. 1850–1860.
Journal of the Senate, 3rd General Assembly of Iowa–8th General Assembly of Iowa. 1850–1860.
The Statutes at Large and Treaties of the United States of America, Vols. IX, X. Boston, 1854–55.
Hull, John A. T., comp. *Iowa Historical and Comparative Census, 1836–1880.* Des Moines, 1883.
Shambaugh, Benjamin F., ed. *Documentary Material Relating to the History of Iowa,* State Historical Society of Iowa. 3 vols. Iowa City, n.d.
———, ed. *The Messages and Proclamations of the Governors of Iowa,* State Historical Society of Iowa. 7 vols. Iowa City, 1903.

Iowa Newspapers

Albia, *Weekly Republican.*
Anamosa Eureka.
Anamosa Gazette.
Bloomfield, *Iowa Flag.*
Bloomfield, *True Flag.*
Bloomfield, *Ward's Own.*
Bloomfield, *Western Gazette.*
Burlington, *Daily Hawk-Eye.*
Burlington, *Iowa State Gazette.*
Burlington Daily Telegraph.
Clarinda, *Page County Herald.*
Corydon, *South-Tier Democrat.*
Council Bluffs (formerly Kanesville), *The Frontier Guardian.*
The Davenport Gazette.
Davenport, *Democratic Banner.*
Des Moines, *Session Journal.*
Des Moines, *Iowa State Journal.*
Des Moines, *The Weekly Iowa State Reporter.*
Des Moines *Session Citizen.*
Dubuque, *Daily Miners' Express.*
Dubuque, *Weekly Times.*
Eddyville Free Press.
The Fairfield Ledger.
Fairfield, *Iowa Sentinel.*
Iowa City, *Daily Crescent.*
Iowa City, *Democratic State Press.*
Iowa City, *Iowa Capital Reporter.*
Iowa City, *Iowa Weekly Republican.*
Keokuk, *Des Moines Valley Whig.*
Keokuk, *Morning Glory.*
Lyons Weekly Mirror.
Marengo, *Iowa Valley Democrat.*
Montezuma Weekly Republican.
Mount Pleasant, *Weekly Observer.*

Mount Pleasant, *Home Journal.*
Muscatine, *Iowa Democratic Enquirer.*
New York Daily Times.
Sidney, *Fremont Herald.*
Sioux City Eagle.
Vinton Eagle.
Wapello Intelligencer.
Washington Press.
Webster City, *Hamilton Freeman.*
West Union, *Fayette County Public Review.*

DISSERTATIONS AND THESES

Agnew, Dwight L. "Beginnings of the Rock Island Lines, 1851–1870."
    Unpublished Ph.D. dissertation, State University of Iowa, 1947.
Boeck, George A. "An Early Iowa Community: Aspects of Economic,
    Social, and Political Development in Burlington, Iowa, 1833–
    1866." Unpublished Ph.D. dissertation, University of Iowa, 1961.
Harris, Faye E. "A Frontier Community: The Economic, Social, and
    Political Development of Keokuk, Iowa, 1820–1866." Unpub-
    lished Ph.D. dissertation, University of Iowa, 1965.
Kelso, Thomas J. "The German-American Vote in the Election of
    1860: The Case of Indiana with Supporting Data from Ohio."
    Unpublished Ph.D. dissertation, Ball State University, 1967.
Ralston, Leonard F. "Railroads and the Government of Iowa, 1850–
    1872." Unpublished Ph.D. dissertation, University of Iowa, 1960.
Sherman, Roy V. "Political Party Platforms in Iowa." Unpublished
    M.A. thesis, State University of Iowa, 1926.
Silbey, Joel H. "Pro-Slavery Sentiment in Iowa, 1838–1861." Unpub-
    lished M.A. thesis, State University of Iowa, 1956.
Sparks, David S. "The Birth of the Republican Party in Iowa, 1848 to
    1860." Unpublished Ph.D. dissertation, University of Chicago,
    1951.
Swierenga, Robert P. "Pioneers and Profits: Land Speculation on the
    Iowa Frontier." Unpublished Ph.D. dissertation, University of
    Iowa, 1965.
Toussaint, Willard I. "The Know-Nothing Party in Iowa." Unpub-
    lished M.A. thesis, State University of Iowa, 1956.

RECOLLECTIONS AND REMINISCENCES

Dey, Peter A. "Recollections of the Old Capitol and the New," *Annals of Iowa*, 3rd ser., Vol. VII (July, 1905), 81–105.

Garver, Frank H., ed. "Reminiscences of John H. Charles," *Annals of Iowa*, 3rd ser., Vol. VIII (July, 1908), 401–32.

Autobiography of Charles Clinton Nourse, Cedar Rapids, The Torch Press, 1911.

Stiles, Edward H. *Recollections and Sketches of Notable Lawyers and Public Men of Early Iowa*. Des Moines, The Homestead Publishing Co., 1916.

Todd, John. *Early Settlement and Growth of Western Iowa or Reminiscences*. Des Moines, The Iowa State Department of History and Archives, 1906.

COUNTY HISTORIES

Biographical and Historical Record of Ringgold and Decatur Counties Iowa. Chicago, The Lewis Publishing Co., 1887.

Biographical and Historical Record of Wayne and Appanoose Counties Iowa. Chicago, Inter-State Publishing Co., 1886.

History of Clayton County Iowa. Chicago, Inter-State Publishing Co., 1882.

History of Franklin and Cerro Gordo Counties Iowa. Springfield, Illinois, Union Publishing Co., 1883.

The History of Keokuk County Iowa. Des Moines, Union Historical Company, 1880.

The History of Madison County Iowa. Des Moines, Union Historical Company, 1879.

The History of Mahaska County Iowa. Des Moines, Union Historical Company, 1878.

The History of Warren County Iowa. Des Moines, Union Historical Company, 1879.

Alexander, W. E. *History of Chickasaw and Howard Counties Iowa*. Decorah, The Western Publishing Co., 1883.

Church, Harry, and Katharyn J. Chappell. *History of Buchanan County Iowa and Its People*. 2 vols. Chicago, S. J. Clarke Publishing Co., 1914.

243

Downer, Harry E., ed. *History of Davenport and Scott County Iowa.* 2 vols. Chicago, S. J. Clarke Publishing Co., 1910.

Fitch, George W. *Past and Present of Fayette County Iowa.* 2 vols. Indianapolis, B. F. Bowen and Co., 1910.

Fulton, Charles J. *History of Jefferson County Iowa.* 2 vols. Chicago, S. J. Clarke Publishing Co., 1914.

Howell, J. M., and Heman C. Smith, eds. *History of Decatur County Iowa and Its People.* 2 vols. Chicago, S. J. Clarke Publishing Co., 1915.

McCarty, Dwight G. *History of Palo Alto County Iowa.* Cedar Rapids, The Torch Press, 1910.

Oldt, Franklin T., ed. *History of Dubuque County Iowa.* Chicago, Goodspeed Historical Association, n.d.

Richman, Irving B., ed. *History of Muscatine County Iowa.* 2 vols. Chicago, S. J. Clarke Publishing Co., 1911.

Smith, R. A. *A History of Dickinson County Iowa.* Des Moines, The Kenyon Printing and Manufacturing Co., 1902.

Taylor, L. L., ed. *Past and Present of Appanoose County Iowa.* 2 vols. Chicago, S. J. Clarke Publishing Co., 1913.

BOOKS

Berwanger, Eugene H. *The Frontier Against Slavery: Western Anti-Negro Prejudice and the Slavery Extension Controversy.* Urbana, University of Illinois Press, 1967.

Brigham, Johnson. *James Harlan.* Iowa City, State Historical Society of Iowa, 1913.

Clark, Dan E. *History of Senatorial Elections in Iowa: A Study in American Politics.* Iowa City, State Historical Society of Iowa, 1912.

———. *Samuel Jordan Kirkwood.* Iowa City, State Historical Society of Iowa, 1917.

Cole, Cyrenus. *A History of the People of Iowa.* Cedar Rapids, The Torch Press, 1921.

———. *Iowa Through the Years.* Iowa City, State Historical Society of Iowa, 1940.

Eaton, Clement. *Henry Clay and the Art of American Politics*. Boston, Little, Brown and Company, 1957.

Fairall, Herbert S. *Manual of Iowa Politics*. Iowa City, Republican Publishing Co., 1884.

Gray, Wood. *The Hidden Civil War: The Story of the Copperheads*. New York, The Viking Press, 1942.

Gue, Benjamin F. *History of Iowa*. 4 vols. New York, The Century History Co., 1903.

Hamilton, Holman. *Prologue to Conflict: The Crisis and Compromise of 1850*. New York, W. W. Norton & Co., Inc., 1966.

Johannsen, Robert. *Frontier Politics and the Sectional Conflict: The Pacific Northwest on the Eve of the Civil War*. Seattle, University of Washington Press, 1955.

———, ed. *The Letters of Stephen A. Douglas*. Urbana, University of Illinois Press, 1961.

Litwack, Leon. *North of Slavery: The Negro in the Free States 1790–1860*. Chicago, University of Chicago Press, Phoenix Edition, 1965.

Luthin, Reinhard H. *The First Lincoln Campaign*. Gloucester, Mass., Peter Smith, 1964.

Malin, James C. *The Nebraska Question 1852–1854*. Lawrence, privately published, 1953.

Milton, George F. *The Eve of Conflict: Stephen A. Douglas and the Needless War*. New York, Houghton Mifflin Co., 1934.

Nevins, Allan. *Ordeal of the Union*. 2 vols. New York, Charles Scribner's Sons, 1947.

Nichols, Roy F. *The Democratic Machine 1850–1854*. Studies in History, Economics, and Public Law. New York, Columbia University Press, 1923.

———. *The Disruption of American Democracy*. New York, The MacMillan Co., 1948.

Overton, Richard C. *Burlington West: A Colonization History of the Burlington Railroad*. Cambridge, Harvard University Press, 1941.

Parish, John C. *George Wallace Jones*. Iowa City, State Historical Society of Iowa, 1912.

Parker, Nathan H. *Iowa as It Is in 1855*. Chicago, Keen and Lee, 1855.

———. *Iowa as It Is in 1856*. Chicago, Keen and Lee, 1856.

————. *Iowa as It Is in 1857.* Chicago, Keen and Lee, 1857.

Payne, Charles E. *Josiah Bushnell Grinnell.* Iowa City, State Historical Society of Iowa, 1938.

Pelzer, Louis. *Augustus Caesar Dodge.* Iowa City, State Historical Society of Iowa, 1908.

Porter, Kirk, comp. *National Party Platforms.* New York, The MacMillan Co., 1924.

Preston, Howard H. *History of Banking in Iowa.* Iowa City, State Historical Society of Iowa, 1922.

Rawley, James W. *Race and Politics: Bleeding Kansas and the Coming of the Civil War.* New York, J. B. Lippincott Company, 1969.

Ray, P. Orman. *The Repeal of the Missouri Compromise.* Cleveland, The Arthur H. Clark Co., 1909.

Sage, Leland L. *William Boyd Allison: A Study in Practical Politics.* Iowa City, State Historical Society of Iowa, 1956.

Salter, William. *The Life of James W. Grimes.* New York, D. Appleton and Co., 1876.

Sanborn, John B. *Congressional Grants of Land in Aid of Railways.* Bulletin of the University of Wisconsin. Economics, Political Science, and History Series. Vol. II. Madison, 1897–1899.

Shambaugh, Benjamin F. *The Constitutions of Iowa.* Iowa City, State Historical Society of Iowa, 1934.

Silbey, Joel H. *The Shrine of Party: Congressional Voting Behavior 1841–1852.* Pittsburgh, University of Pittsburgh Press, 1967.

Simms, Henry H. *A Decade of Sectional Controversy, 1851–1861.* Chapel Hill, University of North Carolina Press, 1942.

Smith, Theodore C. *The Liberty and Free Soil Parties in the Northwest.* New York, Longmans, Green and Co., 1897.

Stephenson, George M. *The Political History of the Public Lands.* Boston, Richard G. Badger, 1917.

Taylor, George R. *The Transportation Revolution, 1815–1860.* New York, Rinehart and Co., 1951.

Van Der Zee, Jacob. *The British in Iowa.* Iowa City, State Historical Society of Iowa, 1922.

————. *The Hollanders of Iowa.* Iowa City, State Historical Society of Iowa, 1912.

Van Vleck, George W. *The Panic of 1857.* New York, Columbia University Press, 1943.

Younger, Edward. *John A. Kasson: Politics and Diplomacy from Lincoln to McKinley.* Iowa City, State Historical Society of Iowa, 1955.

ARTICLES

Agnew, Dwight L. "Iowa's First Railroad," *Iowa Journal of History,* Vol. XLVIII (1950), 1–26.

———. "Jefferson Davis and the Rock Island Bridge," *Iowa Journal of History,* Vol. XLVII (1949), 3–14.

———. "The Mississippi and Missouri Railroad," *Iowa Journal of History,* Vol. LI (1953), 211–32.

Bergmann, Leola N. "The Negro in Iowa," *Iowa Journal of History and Politics,* Vol. XLVI (1948), 3–90.

Briggs, John E. "The Removal of the Capital from Iowa City to Des Moines," *Iowa Journal of History and Politics,* Vol. XIV (1916), 56–95.

Cain, Marvin R. "Edward Bates and the Decision of 1860," *Mid-America,* Vol. XLIV (1962), 109–24.

Clark, Dan E. "The History of Liquor Legislation in Iowa, 1846–1861," *Iowa Journal of History and Politics,* Vol. VI (1908), 55–87.

———. "Recent Liquor Legislation in Iowa," *Iowa Journal of History and Politics,* Vol. XV (1917), 42–69.

Daniels, George H. "The Immigrant Vote in the 1860 Election: The Case of Iowa," *Mid-America,* Vol. XLIV (1962), 146–62.

Dodd, William E. "The Fight for the Northwest, 1860," *American Historical Review,* Vol. XVI (1910–1911), 774–88.

Emery, Charles W. "The Iowa Germans in the Election of 1860," *Annals of Iowa,* 3rd ser., Vol. XXII (1940), 421–53.

Erbe, Carl H. "Constitutional Provisions for the Suffrage in Iowa," *Iowa Journal of History and Politics,* Vol. XXII (1924), 163–216.

Eriksson, Erik M. "The Framers of the Constitution of 1857," *Iowa Journal of History and Politics,* Vol. XXII (1924), 52–88.

———. "William Penn Clarke," *Iowa Journal of History and Politics,* Vol. XXV (1927), 3–61.

Flom, George T. "The Growth of the Scandinavian Factor in the Population of Iowa," *Iowa Journal of History and Politics*, Vol. IV (1906), 268–85.

Gallaher, Ruth A. "Money in Pioneer Iowa 1838–1865," *Iowa Journal of History and Politics*, Vol. XXXII (1934), 3–59.

Gannaway, John W. "The Development of Party Organization in Iowa," *Iowa Journal of History and Politics*, Vol. I (1903), 493–524.

Garver, Frank H. "History of the Establishments of Counties in Iowa," *Iowa Journal of History and Politics*, Vol. VI (1908), 375–440.

Gates, Paul W. "Land Policy and Tenancy in the Prairie States," *The Journal of Economic History*, Vol. I (1941), 60–82.

Goodwin, Cardinal. "The American Occupation of Iowa, 1833 to 1860," *Iowa Journal of History and Politics*, Vol. XVII (1919), 83–102.

Hamilton, Holman. "Democratic Senate Leadership and the Compromise of 1850," *The Mississippi Valley Historical Review*, Vol. XLI (1954), 403–18.

Hansen, Marcus L. "Official Encouragement of Immigration to Iowa," *Iowa Journal of History and Politics*, Vol. XIX (1921), 159–95.

Herriott, Frank I. "The Germans of Iowa and the 'Two Year' Amendment of Massachusetts," *Deutsch-Amerikanische Geschichtsblätter: Jahrbuch der Deutsch-Amerikanischen Historischen Gesellschaft von Illinois*, Vol. XIII (1913), 202–308.

———. "The Germans in the Gubernatorial Campaign of Iowa in 1859," *Deutsch-Amerikanische Geschichtsblätter: Jahrbuch der Deutsch-Amerikanischen Historischen Gesellschaft von Illinois*, Vol. XIV (1914), 451–622.

———. "James Grimes Versus the Southrons," *Annals of Iowa*, 3rd ser., Vol. XV (1925–1927), 323–57, 403–32.

———. "Iowa and the First Nomination of Abraham Lincoln," *Annals of Iowa*, 3rd ser., Vol. VIII (1908), 81–115, 186–220, 444–66.

———. "A Neglected Factor in the Anti-Slavery Triumph in Iowa in 1854," *Deutsch-Amerikanische Geschichtsblätter: Jahrbuch der Deutsch-Amerikanischen Historischen Gesellschaft von Illinois*, Vol. XVIII–XIX (1918–1919), 174–355.

——. "Republican Presidential Preliminaries in Iowa 1859–1860," *Annals of Iowa*, 3rd ser., Vol. IX (1910), 241–83.

——. "Whence Came the Pioneers of Iowa?" *Annals of Iowa*, 3rd ser., Vol. VII (1906), 446–65.

Hodder, Frank H. "Genesis of the Kansas-Nebraska Act," State Historical Society of Wisconsin *Proceedings* for October 24, 1912, 69–86.

——. "The Railroad Background of the Kansas-Nebraska Act," *The Mississippi Valley Historical Review*, Vol. XII (1925), 1–22.

Hubbart, Henry C. "Pro-Southern Influences in the Free West 1840–1865," *The Mississippi Valley Historical Review*, Vol. XX (1933), 45–62.

Johannsen, Robert W. "The Kansas-Nebraska Act and the Pacific Northwest Frontier," *Pacific Historical Review*, Vol. XXII (1953), 129–41.

——. "The Kansas-Nebraska Act and Territorial Government in the United States," *Territorial Kansas: Studies Commemorating the Centennial*, 17–32. Lawrence, University of Kansas Publications, 1954.

Langworthy, L. H. "Dubuque: Its History, Mines, Indian Legends, etc.," *Iowa Journal of History and Politics*, Vol. VIII (1910), 366–422.

Lee, Robert E. "Politics and Society in Sioux City, 1859," *Iowa Journal of History*, Vol. LIV (1956), 117–30.

"Letters of James W. Grimes." *Annals of Iowa*, 3rd ser., Vol. XXII (1940), 469–504, 556–88.

Millsap, Kenneth F. "The Election of 1860 in Iowa," *Iowa Journal of History*, Vol. XLVIII (1950), 97–120.

Nichols, Roy F. "The Kansas-Nebraska Act: A Century of Historiography," *The Mississippi Valley Historical Review*, Vol. XLII (1956), 187–212.

Pelzer, Louis. "The Disintegration and Organization of Political Parties in Iowa 1852–1860," Mississippi Valley Historical Association *Proceedings* for 1911–1912, 158–66.

——. "History of Political Parties in Iowa 1857–1860," *Iowa Journal of History and Politics*, Vol. VII (1909), 179–229.

————. "The History and Principles of the Democratic Party of Iowa, 1846–1857," *Iowa Journal of History and Politics*, Vol. VI (1908), 163–246.

————. "The Negro and Slavery in Early Iowa," *Iowa Journal of History and Politics*, Vol. II (1904), 471–84.

————. "The Origin and Organization of the Republican Party in Iowa," *Iowa Journal of History and Politics*, Vol. IV (1906), 487–525.

Petersen, William J. "Population Advance to the Upper Mississippi Valley 1830–1860," *Iowa Journal of History and Politics*, Vol. XXXII (1934), 312–53.

Pierce, Paul S. "Congressional Districting in Iowa," *Iowa Journal of History and Politics*, Vol. I (1903), 334–61.

Ralston, Leonard F. "Governor Ralph P. Lowe and State Aid to Railroads: Iowa Politics in 1859," *Iowa Journal of History*, Vol. LVIII (1960), 207–18.

Roll, Charles. "Political Trends in Iowa History," *Iowa Journal of History and Politics*, Vol. XXVI (1928), 499–519.

Ross, Russell M. "The Development of the Iowa Constitution of 1857," *Iowa Journal of History*, Vol. LV (1957), 97–114.

Russel, Robert R. "What was the Compromise of 1850?" *The Journal of Southern History*, Vol. XXII (1956), 292–309.

Sage, Leland L. "The Early Life of William Boyd Allison," *Iowa Journal of History*, Vol. XLVIII (1950), 299–334.

Salter, William, ed. "Correspondence of A. C. Dodge and Thomas H. Benton on the Public Lands, the Homestead Bill, and the Pacific Railroad," *Annals of Iowa*, 3rd ser., Vol. VIII (1908), 296–98.

————. "Old Letters," *Annals of Iowa*, 3rd ser., Vol. VIII (1908), 500–16.

Schafer, Joseph. "Who Elected Lincoln?" *American Historical Review*, Vol. XLVII (1941), 51–63.

Schmidt, Louis B. "The Miller-Thompson Election Contest," *Iowa Journal of History and Politics*, Vol. XII (1914), 34–127.

Smith, Donnal V. "The Influence of the Foreign-Born of the Northwest in the Election of 1860," *The Mississippi Valley Historical Review*, Vol. XIX (1932), 192–204.

Snyder, Charles E. "Curtis Bates," *Iowa Journal of History and Politics*, Vol. XLIV (1946), 291–313.

Sparks, David S. "The Birth of the Republican Party in Iowa, 1854–1856," *Iowa Journal of History*, Vol. LIV (1956), 1–34.

———. "The Decline of the Democratic Party in Iowa, 1850–1860," *Iowa Journal of History*, Vol. LIII (1955), 1–30.

———. "Iowa Republicans and the Railroads 1856–1860," *Iowa Journal of History*, Vol. LIII (1955), 273–86.

Stiles, Edward H. "Prominent Men of Early Iowa," *Annals of Iowa*, 3rd ser., Vol. X (1911–1913), 250–64.

Swierenga, Robert P. "The Ethnic Voter and the First Lincoln Election," *Civil War History*, Vol. XI (1965), 27–43.

Teakle, Thomas. "The Defalcation of Superintendent James D. Eads," *Iowa Journal of History and Politics*, Vol. XII (1914), 205–44.

Thodt, Charles A. "Stephen A. Douglas Speaks at Iowa City, 1860," *Iowa Journal of History*, Vol. LIII (1955), 153–66.

Throne, Mildred. "C. C. Carpenter in the 1858 Iowa Legislature," *Iowa Journal of History*, Vol. LII (1954), 31–60.

———. "Contemporary Editorial Opinion of the 1857 Constitution," *Iowa Journal of History*, Vol. LV (1957), 115–46.

———, ed. "Iowa Newspapers Report the 1860 Nomination of Lincoln," *Iowa Journal of History*, Vol. LVIII (1960), 228–80.

Van Der Zee, Jacob. "The Mormon Trails in Iowa," *Iowa Journal of History and Politics*, Vol. XII (1914), 3–16.

Wubben, Hubert H. "Dennis Mahony and the Dubuque *Herald* 1860–1863," *Iowa Journal of History*, Vol. LVI (1958), 289–320.

Younger, Edward. "The Rise of John A. Kasson in Iowa Politics 1857–1859," *Iowa Journal of History*, Vol. L (1952), 289–314.

Index